MALFORMATION

When Bad Things Happen to the Right Kind of People

PAUL MCMONAGLE

WESTBOW
PRESS®
A DIVISION OF THOMAS NELSON
& ZONDERVAN

WestBow Press books may be ordered through booksellers or by contacting:

WestBow Press
A Division of Thomas Nelson & Zondervan
1663 Liberty Drive
Bloomington, IN 47403
www.westbowpress.com
844-714-3454

ISBN: 978-1-6642-2263-2 (sc)
ISBN: 978-1-6642-2264-9 (hc)
ISBN: 978-1-6642-2262-5 (e)

Library of Congress Control Number: 2021902259

Print information available on the last page.

WestBow Press rev. date: 02/26/2021

CONTENTS

CONTENTS

PROLOGUE

Good day! My name is Paul McMonagle (pronounced like "monocle" with a "Mc" in front of it). For Harry Potter fans, it is almost like Professor McGonagall just an "M" instead of a "G" and you've just about got it. You and I, at best, will be conversing together for the period of two-hundred-plus pages for the purpose of coping with a tragedy, specifically, a malady, thus "malformation." For whatever duration of time it takes you to traverse this swamp of information, let me say from the outset, it will not be an easy jaunt. We are going to visit the swelling tidewaters of the academic community; the battling waves push and pull back the grains of sanity as they are slowly drawn out into the deep swell of the horizon. We are going to see the prospect of scientific treatment after scientific treatment of success change from ivory to ashes as the former ideologies and treatment plans fail to stop the proverbial cranial bleeding. But the glimmer of hope in this anthology is not found in this author's survival nor your own. Death, unfortunately, has an extremely high success rate for acquired brain injury and traumatic brain injury survivors. Considering this, I implore you, if I may, I challenge you to consider the sheer weight of your life and the lives of those you love in the scope of eternity. This is not intended to frighten you or turn you away. It is intended to encourage you to view your life as a gift, your relationship with others as vital, and every moment of the present a blessing that God has given.

Follow me if you will to a less connected time, namely the year 2000. In southeast Alabama, the internet was in a lot of homes but not all of them. The weekend frolic for much of the youth was your local football team Friday night and then Saturday sleep-in. In this context, there we find the dreams of many a freshman, namely a freshman at Auburn University. Chasing that promise of a six-figure salary as a software developer in

"Hotlanta," the dreams of a cushy job and far too much caffeine came crashing down. The catalog of this journey is varied, and as such, I can only offer my experiences. Yours differs, to be sure. It is to this end that all persons regardless of their birth are destined to meet Jesus. As the Westminster Catechism says, "Man's chief end is to glorify God, and to enjoy him forever."1 More recently, John Piper revised this slightly in stating: "The chief end of man is to glorify God *by* enjoying Him forever" (Piper, 2005). This is true as well, yet both statements capture what should be our aim: the glory of God by the enjoyment of Him forever.

This process is not all semantics though, as to enjoy God one must follow Christ. To follow Jesus means to be willing to lay down everything to pick up the cross. Lest you fear this will be a sermon, please understand, this is a narrative of survival. Yet within this narrative are threads of grace, mercy, and hopefully encouragement to a larger segment of the population. You may be a survivor, and to you may He bring healing. To the caregiver, may He bring hope. To a friend, may this encouragement bring understanding. And finally, to the general population of readership, may this serve as an introduction or reintroduction of those out there who need your help, your word of encouragement, and moreover, your active belief that there is Someone greater.[1]

Generally, this will be the flow of the manuscript. Though we have already seen a brief section intro, now the reintroduction and postintroduction, if you will, to the topic will take place through the eyes of the brain-injured mind. This is intentional as it represents the dualistic approach to life this author has unwillingly undertaken. Previously, I saw the world one-way; post-TBI, I see and approach it differently. Nothing stated previously was incorrect by my knowledge. But with the new information gained through each chapter, the reader should be able to see a bit clearer the end aims of this author much like a brain-injury survivor. This is calculated for me and reader alike as it helps the readership to see both how it was assumed to be and what it truly *could* be. For instance, and as a primary test candidate, consider the patient, Paul (this author). I was a successful student, a successful interscholastic competitor, successful business owner at the age of fifteen to seventeen, and a scholarship winner to go to Auburn University (War Eagle!). Now with

---

[1] https://en.wikipedia.org/wiki/Westminster_Shorter_Catechism.

this list of accomplishments and promising future ahead, nothing could have prepared me as a student to be forced to relearn how to walk, talk, read, and write again if I wished to continue with my academic journey. I write this not as one who can say this was easy or preferred, but I did have to choose, many times over, to "press on toward the goal for the prize of the upward call of God in Christ Jesus."[2]

Fast-forward eighteen years to the time of this writing, and you will have seen residence in three different states, marriage to the most exquisite specimen of beauty in the form of my beloved glass menagerie, Leslie. Coupled with the additional bountiful blessing of two beautiful daughters, let's recount my story, to add to your story, and hopefully travel together to a new vantage point. This will be a bumpy ride. This road is not well-traveled. Moreover, it is largely through high jungle, meaning pitfalls, dangerous organisms, and treacherous persons exist along the path. But where's the fun in an easy stride? Thanks be to Christ, however, as it is my belief that it is for such a time as this that He intends for you to read this catalog of treatments.

For the volume, each chapter is spelled out with the theme demarcating the section of my journey experienced prior to the bleed, then by the succeeding chapter immediately following with lessons learned, paths tried and failed, and then finally summed up. Thus, if looking for, say, my proposed solution to rehab difficulties, you may wish to look at chapter 4.5: Re-Rehabilitation. If you are looking for the means to live with your new circumstances, read the preceding chapter 4: Habilitation. I have cited most of the scripture references from the New American Standard Bible. Yet I want you to know, whether it be ESV, NASB, KJV, or others, the Bible is the Word of God in the original Hebrew, Aramaic, and Greek translations. The nuances of language and shifting of meaning within a language are all arguments fit for small talk with a linguist over coffee. For our purposes, scripture is reading for discovery of Truth from God's Word. Specifically, from 2 Timothy 2:16–17: "All scripture is inspired by God and profitable for teaching, for reproof, for correction, for training in righteousness; so that the man of God may be adequate, equipped for every good work." With this in mind and with your curiosity hopefully piqued, let's start the journey at the beginning, introducing the players

---

[2] Philippians 3:14.

ACKNOWLEDGMENTS

A special thank you to my Lord and Savior Jesus Christ "For since in the wisdom of God the world through its wisdom did not *come to* know God, God was well-pleased through the foolishness of the message preached to save those who believe" (1 Cor. 1:21)" I cannot unless you do, but thank you so much for using me for your good pleasure. I love you, my Lord, Savior, and friend.

Second, a thank you to my wife and my second love, who has stood by me and shown me countless times over what a Proverbs 31 woman truly is to be. I love you, my wife and cherished love.

Third, to my children, may whatever befalls you and whatever uplifts you solely be by and from the hand of Jesus as He reminds you how great a love He has for His own. I love you and pledged from the beginning to give you the best support I was able. You made your daddy a very blessed and oh so pleased father. I love you, my darlings.

All scripture is from the New American Standard Bible (NASB) unless otherwise noted.

CHAPTER 1

Introduction?

<hr/>

As we have yet to be properly introduced, my name is Paul McMonagle. (Like a monocle, then pop a "Mc" in front of it.) I'm a thirty-something, husband to Leslie, father of two, son of Ron and Earnie, son-in-law to Rick and Sharon, left-handed, five-feet-eleven-inch, brown-haired, blue-eyed, Caucasian male. I'm blood type A positive, if you need to know. Any other information you need of me, Google® it.

Now if that doesn't grab your attention, great! The point of this introduction was simply to make with the niceties. To point out on the exterior, I'm basically a very average male. I can remember the trusty World Book Encyclopedia for writing my grade-school book reports, not Wikipedia. I was born in 1981, before the World Wide Web. I remember what it was to be mystified digging through the set, looking in the World Book Encyclopedia for the letter of "pneumonia." (It was not in the "Ns," much to my chagrin.)

I remember *before* the internet using Print Shop Deluxe on our Commodore 64 computer. I remember the joyful screech of dial-up to the local BBS—Bulletin Board System before internet was in our area. I'm not particularly tall, not particularly dashing, nothing noteworthy on the outside. It is my belief that God intended this, as He tends to use ordinary people to do extraordinary things.

You likely are no different. Jesus wants to save you and show you His plans for your life. As we walk down these pages, you may find items of identification as well. If you do, fantastic! This is an unintended blessing. You may find points of disagreement. This book never was intended to be the end of your searching. It is merely a guidepost along the way, hopefully to point you to the answer, or at the very least the proper way of phrasing the questions you may have. Effectively, we are going to lay out a new order of operations. Picking up this term from my own daughter's homework, "Order of operations—The whole point is to have one way to *interpret* a mathematical statement." (Khan Academy, 2018). The purpose of having an order of operations for the brain injured is to *interpret* an injury in the correct manner.

As we travel down this road a ways, you will hopefully find pieces and instances of yourself in these pages. There may be circumstances or occurrences when you would say, "Yeah, I remember when I did that," or, "Wow, I wouldn't have gone about it that way." Moreover, you likely will see something that maybe you *haven't* experienced. Let this book be a warning; you are facing a challenging road ahead, and all this is well and good. This is not written to give you advice on all or any part of your life. This is meant to detail how one survivor dealt with his challenges.

As I've counseled some and parented to my own children many times over, mistakes are memories. Those memories can become a legacy of God's faithfulness to us. The point of leaving a legacy of learning is to use these memories to better the world around us, ourselves individually, and others. Furthermore, our concern is with the recovery of those memories.

What you do with the results of those mistakes is the difference between a victim and a victorious mentality. What I've learned, what I've failed at, and how my wife and I thus far have dealt with this terrible malady of brain injury—this becomes our story. When we are long gone, our legacy will be all that remains. Thus, what legacy will you leave for the world that remains?

As we dive in, first the happy part of the story. I was born in Pensacola, Florida, moved with my parents to New Brockton, Alabama, and graduated high school from NBHS in 1999, with all the promise of the new millennium beckoning me to try it out. I was successful in school, had an academic scholarship to Auburn University, and I was a successful business partner in my high school job. I looked forward to making big money in the metropolis of Atlanta, Georgia.

As a matter of fact, starting out as a student at Auburn in 1999 on into the spring of 2000, it looked like a valid hypothesis. Yet about two weeks before finals, I remember being up in the dorm watching a movie with my girlfriend. Suddenly I experienced an excruciating headache, stood up, threw up from the pressure, and passed out. From then on, I only remember snapshots of the next one to two years of my life. The paramedics from the local hospital in Opelika, Alabama, transported me to East Alabama Medical Center because they determined I had suffered a traumatic brain injury from a rupture of a genetic anomaly called an arteriovenous malformation or AVM.

Now if you've never been in the ER, it's a chaotic place. Not because of the management or personnel working there. My family and I have met so many unknown faces and persons who will never be known personally. But nevertheless, they are thanked so much because they have saved so many lives, of which I am one of them! Nurse Bill, I'm looking at you! After it was determined that an intracranial bleed was what had taken place, it was medically decided that to properly treat the ICP, or intracranial pressure, I needed to be transported to the University of Alabama at Birmingham, which was roughly two hours away. Per my mother's recollection, I was driven by ambulance to UAB and began my medical roller-coaster ride that has not stopped, even to this day.

That only serves as a brief introduction to what would appear to be a "fairly normal" concussion, contusion, or some other cranial accident. Instead, it was determined that I had suffered a rupture of an AVM. What had appeared to be simple head trauma instead was found to be life-or-death treatment of a potentially hereditary cerebral disorder, which worldwide affects a miniscule amount of people. "The annual risk of hemorrhage from a cerebral arteriovenous malformation is approximately 3%" (Solomon, 2017).

This was news to the family at the time. And because it was prior to the mobile device propagation of today, cordoned each member in the waiting room to the confines of their own past medical experience. One face, whose first name only I recall, is Nurse Bill. Nurse Bill was everything a patient would hope for in a nurse, and nothing you would expect from a medical caregiver. I recall his willing disobedience to granular regulations if it meant bringing some comfort to the patient. As an example, he brought me ice chips when, at the time, I was ordered no fluids or solids for surgery. Nurse Bill, I don't know your last name, or if you are even still practicing, but your deeds and your attitude will never be forgotten—in a good way!

So that you will not be subject to the same arbitrary restrictions, I think we need to define what an AVM is. First, a description of regular blood flow in the brain is provided by the neurosurgical team of Harvard University: "Normally in brain tissue the blood enters through major cerebral arteries but then passes through smaller arterioles and subsequently into the capillary bed. Capillaries are tiny vessels in the brain tissue, as elsewhere in the body, that allow the blood to deliver necessary oxygen and glucose to the brain and remove the end products of brain metabolism from the brain. After passing through the capillaries, the blood enters the venous system of the brain. In the veins, blood is usually blue because the oxygen has been delivered to the tissue and therefore the oxygen content of the blood is lowered. Conversely, in arteries there is a high content of oxygen as the blood enters the brain after passing through the lungs and being replenished with oxygen; therefore, arterial blood is red" (Christopher S. Ogilvy, 2018).

Per the Mayo Clinic: "An arteriovenous malformation (AVM) is an abnormal tangle of blood vessels connecting arteries and veins, which disrupts normal blood flow and oxygen circulation" (Mayo Clinic, *Mayo Clinic Family Health Book*, 5th ed., 2020). To put the definition in layman's terms, as that is what I posses, an AVM is a tangle of blood vessels that is created by design in your brain or other location in your body from birth. It is a design anomaly.

Honestly, it initially seemed as though it was a mistake, but more on that later. Admittedly, you probably don't need an anatomy lesson, but the definition of this disorder needs to be made more public. It needs further propagation to more than just the medical community. As I recall a recent cultural quip, awareness breeds kindness. Perhaps that was used by a local humane society sign, and it still rings true. If you're not aware of your neighbor's plight, you may never know what they are dealing with in the dark and lonely hours of the year. So back to the layman's definition, this tangle of vessels is the matter at hand. Let us seek to briefly set our minds on the unknown misery of the moment and peer into the mind of the brain injured.

MALFORMATION

For this author, the beginning of year 2000 offered all the promises of a new year, with the bonus of a new millennium just around the corner. It was in this new era that a series of seemingly random events were so tightly woven together that the belief of one survivor turned from horror to hope. This is my story. Further, it may very well be like your story. This book was written from the perspective that I believe there are no such things as chance and coincidence. Even the book of Proverbs says, "The lot is cast into the lap, but its every decision is from the LORD" (Prov. 16:33 NIV). Rather, a series of intentional divinely directed occurrences in each individual life offer the opportunity to reform the personality into something altogether different.

Malformation is precisely this. It is a recounting of the series of events that have placed one southern simpleton into the ocean swell of life-everlasting. The plain truth is that none of these events happened by chance. No happy set of circumstances placed me in this spot. It was the divine hand of God. The decision that should present itself is this: "How should I both act and react to this event?"

This is the question that should be asked more often, rather than feelings *about* something (which is tantamount in many cases as to leveeing judgment in many lives). This is also the option that should be selected rather than carnal reaction. This question separates the mind of humankind from the nature of beast. So, the question, "how *should* I react to this event?" is officially the most important question for human behavior since the insidious question asked of humanity by the serpent: "Did God really say you may not eat of this fruit?" Imagine if Adam and Eve, in response to the question of the serpent instead *together* retorted, "God said we are not to eat the fruit of this tree" (Gen. 3:3 NASB, Baker, ed. 1995). The possibilities are beyond imagination, but alas, Adam and Eve ate, as would you or I, so we are left in the mess that we are in!

If the reader at this point is confused, welcome to the world of the neurologically injured! The purpose of this book is not to help you to understand how one with a brain injury thinks. Instead, it is to let all who read this volume see how a common thread of grace ties every life to the other and simply waits for you to tug to call on Him! Hopefully by the end of the volume, you will gain the ability to tie the two worldviews together yourself. First you have the realm of the secular. Your job, your hobbies, your friends, and the like. Then on the flip side of the coin, you have the sacred. In this you have the church, the Bible, the things you were perhaps raised in but have long been forgotten as you are too busy for that side of life. That would be impossible due to the variety of injuries. The purpose of the book is to refer you to the One who allowed the injury. If I may be so bold, the One who planned and caused the injury. You see, Jeremiah the prophet of yesteryear who presided as prophet of Israel while the entire Jewish nation watched Babylon ransack Jerusalem, penned the prophetic utterance from God: "'For I know the plans I have for you,' declares the LORD, 'plans to prosper you and not to harm you, plans to give you hope and a future'" (Jer. 29:11). The question circles back to you then. Will *you* believe that God *does* have plans to prosper you and not to harm you? It is my belief that God has something extraordinary planned for the lives of all who are willing to believe in and walk by faith in Christ! Please note, however, that I did *not* say easy, fun, or financially prosperous.

Akin to the captured people of God during the days of Esther, oftentimes the Lord's use of people as you and I see it does not mesh with logic as we see it. King Xerxes was not a Jehovah-follower as best as we can ascertain. But even pagan kings learn after their deaths that Jehovah God is holy, set apart, and to be worshipped alone! Further, in His sovereign wisdom, God has set in the structure of time *all* persons and events in such a way as to draw *all* who would come to Him through their own volition. The history of this drawing is beyond the breadth of this volume. However, just as Esther in her marriage to the pagan King Xerxes allowed for the deliverance of the people of God for that time, this author believes there are effective deliverers for this day for the people who suffer from brain injury. However, through the narrowed scope of brain injury, the treatment of the disorder will briefly be traced in light of His amazing grace.

Traumatic brain injury as a distinct condition was called by various names. For the World War II generation, the term "Shell-Shock" was given to soldiers who had experienced traumatic brain events and as such, were often mentally forced into a state of partial paralysis. The alarming truth being brought to light now is that through the researchers of PTSD or post-traumatic stress disorder, there may have been some permanent cognitive altering of the brain. Coupled now with the discovery of traumatic brain injury blasts on the battlefield, and we begin to understand what has happened to many of our soldiers and servicemen. Therefore, Congress signed into law the "TBI Act of 1996". This bill "authorized funding for prevention, surveillance, research and State grant programs to improve service delivery and access for individuals with traumatic brain injury" (National Association of State Head Injury Administrators, 2018).

Following the initial passage in 1996, the bill has gone through several revisions, with the latest being in 2014, which saw then President Barack Obama sign S.2539 into law. This provided funding to the TBI Act of 2014 through 2019. For more information, please consult the National Association of State Head Injury Administrators in Alabaster, Alabama. Their address is below:

National Association of State Head Injury Administrators
(NASHIA)
PO Box 1878
Alabaster, AL 35007

For the law to continue, it had to be reauthorized and as such in house bill HR 1098, or more specifically H.R. 1098 (113th): Traumatic Brain Injury Reauthorization Act of 2014.

Second, you can contact the national Brain Injury Association of America at

Brain Injury Association of America

PO Box 7416 Merrifield, VA 22116-7416

Phone: 703-761-0750

Fax: 703-761-0755

For Brain Injury Information Only **1-800-444-6443**.

For the action points scattered throughout this volume, you will find them given as a guideline, merely as a point where you can interact you can see the initial funding, as well as ongoing funding for research of this problem. The dilemma exists when the patients are quickly running out of resolve. I make mention of this as you have an action point already! If you are in the United States, contact your representative and request that he or she support brain injury awareness. You can contact the Brain Injury Association of America as a quick instance to stave off suicide; the National Suicide Prevention Lifeline can be reached twenty-four hours a day at 1-800-273-TALK. Further information can be found in the appendix: "Redemptive Workers" section.

In this recounting, it would behoove us to stop alongside a parallel point of reference, the Christian scriptures, to which this author will refer throughout the work. The Bible has been, is, and will be the chief and only source of lasting Truth for this survivor. As such, many times I will refer to its pages. If you don't believe in its provability, consider that even scripture says, "Now faith is the assurance of things hoped for, the conviction of things not seen" (Heb. 11:1).[3] So there is a bit of trouble right at the outset; much of what can be experienced is only done so through faith in Christ. If you have not trusted in Christ, I encourage you to consider talking with a believer. I suggest https://www.ptl.org/, the Pocket Testament League. It is an interdenominational organization committed to sharing the good news of Jesus across the world. They are not aligned with one church or another. They are committed to getting the good news of the Bible in your hands so that you can read the good news for yourself and decide for yourself whether Christ is the answer for the questions of this life. As Trinity (the character, not the Holy Trinity) said to Neo in the Matrix, "It is the question that drives us, Neo. It is the question that brought you here. You know the question, just as I did" (Brothers, 1999). For Trinity it was effectively, What is real? For the individual seeking Truth, the answer is Jesus Christ. The question then should be, what do I do with this Jesus? After all Jesus Himself said, "Jesus said to him, 'I am the way, and the truth, and the life; no one comes to the Father but through Me'" (John 14:6).

Having introduced you to myself and the Rock on which I stand, let me give you a glimpse of what would be helpful and where this volume

---

[3] Hebrews 11:1.

is going. Let us take a brief stop at our first destination, the land of Uz.[4] Uz is the home of one of the earliest known entrepreneurs, Job. For those unfamiliar with Job, he certainly was a successful businessman. In fact, Job 1:3 says, "His possessions also were 7,000 sheep, 3,000 camels, 500 yokes of oxen, 500 female donkeys, and very many servants; and that man was the greatest of all the men of the east" (Job 1:3). From the temporal situation, Job had "it" in spades. This was precisely when the house of cards fell. In the very same book, just a few verses later you read of tragedy that killed his kids, loss of his homestead, and loss of his livestock. When we read of Job's reaction: "He said, 'Naked I came from my mother's womb, and naked I shall return there. The LORD gave, and the LORD has taken away. Blessed be the name of the LORD" (Job 1:21). Did the sting of the loss touch Job? Of course! Yet in this loss, he remained resolute and dependent on the God he served. The book goes on to describe the worthless advice of his friends: Eliphaz the Temanite, Bildad the Shuhite, and Zophar the Naamathite. The striking truth of these friends is that when they were silent, they provided support, love, and care for Job. As you can read in Job 2:11–13:

> Now when Job's three friends heard of all this adversity that had come upon him, they came each one from his own place, Eliphaz the Temanite, Bildad the Shuhite and Zophar the Naamathite; and they made an appointment together to come to sympathize with him and comfort him. When they lifted their eyes at a distance and did not recognize him, they raised their voices and wept. And each of them tore his robe and they threw dust over their heads toward the sky. Then they sat down on the ground with him for seven days and seven nights with no one

---

[4] Uz is also connected with Edom in Lamentations 4:21. The most plausible location, then, would be east of Israel and northeast of Edom, in what is now North Arabia. The LXX has "on the borders of Edom and Arabia." An early Christian tradition placed his home in an area about forty miles south of Damascus, in Baashan at the southeast foot of Hermon. https://bible.org/download/netbible/ondemand/bybook/job.pdf.

speaking a word to him, for they saw that his pain was very great.

Interestingly, this highlights the first truth of aiding a brain-injured individual as well. It is not what is said but what is felt in your presence. In the hospital, there is so much always going on from the beeping monitors to the painful blood checks. As troublesome as this is, there is seldom a time when the patient is left alone. Yet, persons always are available. This is intentional and necessary for the brain-injury survivor as well. Considering this, you and I need to reconsider what the implications of introduction are. I realize this seems humorous or possibly trivial. Let's refocus on the problem at hand. The person you once were will not return. That person has effectively passed away. As several studies have shown, your old self is gone. One such study shows that among veterans returning from the Iraq/Afghanistan conflicts, "Despite representing only 8% of the population, veterans account for 23% of the homeless population" (Charles Antoni & COL Michael A. Silverman, 2012). Can you see the challenge brewing for the returning veteran? For a brain-injury survivor, he or she is effectively reintroduced to a world being seen through a new set of eyes for the first time.

The problem may be like that of Job's friends—your prejudices and life experiences do not equate to the truth of the life of one who has experienced the injury. This does not preclude you from helping. It should give you pause to recommend advice. Regarding this, in the 1970s scientists developed the Galveston Orientation and Amnesia Test (GOAT) to evaluate cognition serially during the subacute stage of recovery from closed head injury" (Ph.D., O'Donnell, & Grossman, 1979). The GOAT, developed for assessing the person's ability to interact with others specifically, "is a 0-100-point scale to assess memory and orientation after a brain injury, specifically to determine if an individual has recovered from posttraumatic amnesia" (Deborah Caruso, 2010). Posttraumatic amnesia simply means that after a traumatic event, your mind, in coping with the trauma, inserts a blank spot. For those who were alive when the World Trade Center was attacked in 2001, some remember everything. Others have a blank spot of the day because their mind blocked it out. What the GOAT gives us is a truth that often is overlooked by many family and friends; namely though the patient wishes to interact, he or she cannot because the person cannot pin down reality.

Admittingly, I have been at the receiving end of failing the GOAT criteria. In both 2000 and 2010, I have periods of lucidity and periods where I imagined that alien spacecraft were hurdling to earth at breakneck speed. Perhaps it was my love of sci-fi movies and literature, but being a fan of sci-fi and having a brain injury is not a safe combination! Understanding what is real, what's a dream, and what's true is exceedingly difficult for a brain injury survivor. The author can attest, the term "get a grip on reality" has never been more present than after a brain injury!

Promulgated by a number of organizations, let us adopt the mission of the TBI Act of 2008 as our initial aim in using their six tenants for public awareness.

- **Improve Identification:** strengthen the identification of military-service-related TBI among current military SMS and veterans, including those who do not seek care from the military or VA health-care systems. Emphasis will be given to improving data-collection initiatives and data sources to obtain a more comprehensive picture of the problem and impacts of TBI in this population. All four participating agencies should continue to foster and strengthen collaboration to this aim.
- **Standardize Definitions:** use standard clinical and surveillance definitions and severity classification of TBI among US military and civilian health-care providers and researchers to improve reporting. Update these definitions periodically as more precise, sensitive, and valid terms and definitions are available.
- **Standardize Classification:** improve the coding and classification of TBI by working across agencies. All four participating agencies should continue to meet with professional, academic, health-care, and coding organizations to discuss improvements in ICD-10-CM and TBI severity measures that can allow comparison of cases and outcomes.
- **Enhance Dissemination:** promote dissemination of information to non-VA facilities regarding TBI services available through the

VA health-care system since 2007, including baseline screening and follow-up assessment and evaluation.

- **Strengthen Research:** continue research into the consequences of deployment-related TBI, including prospective investigation of the impact of single or multiple insults to the brain and risk for cognitive decline or other health conditions later in life, which might occur among SMS and veterans. Share findings with civilian health-care providers.
- **Follow Evidence-Based Prevention Strategies:** continue reducing risk factors, improving quality of protective equipment, and ensuring adherence to evidence-based strategies and guidelines. (Thomas R. Frieden, June 2013, https://dvbic.dcoe.mil/dod-worldwide-numbers-tbi)

Granted these are for military veterans with brain injury, they are useful for the general public as well. Now these targets are commendable, to say the least, but there is a means of accomplishing these functions within a stratum of another established agency that predates both modern medicine and even the American citizenship: the church! It would be my aim to take the generalized aims of this organization to outline the specific aims of this volume.

With this piece of knowledge, let me now attempt to reintroduce you with the scope and understanding of the brain-injured person. One word of caution, however; findings from one among many like-minded studies suggest: "The author concluded that in patients with AVM of the deep brain structures selective retrograde amnesia was found after severe intraventricular hemorrhage on the background of combined dysfunction of medio-basal regions (preferentially, right hemisphere) and diencephalon region" (SB, January 2002, 32–36). What this means is some of those who suffered from a brain bleed also suffered amnesia for the time during their bleed. Others experienced blocks of blanked time in their long-term memory. Again, I have experienced this recently. While driving home from the grocery store a few years ago, I was 1.4 miles from home. Suddenly, I "lost my map." When I say this I mean, it is like my mind is wiped of the map to get home. I had to call my wife, who was home and get directions.

Strange though it may seem, the information you are acting upon

MALFORMATION

may or may not be accurate if delivered by the patient. The first order of business, then, is to accurately define the problem. All the way back in 1943, we have an early mention of the arteriovenous aneurysms by Dr. R. Wyburn-Mason: "very few cases of arteriovenous aneurysms of the mid-brain have been recorded" (Wyburn-Mason, September 1943). As it was in 1943, so it is today; one must consult with doctors, patient-care records, and family members in tandem with the patients themselves for the most advisable means of ascertaining the truth of the situation. For the medical professionals, this phenomenon is probably illogical. For the brain-injury survivor, it is, unfortunately, increasingly commonplace.

CHAPTER 1.5

Reintroduction

We just highlighted the premise we are dealing with: brain injury is a disorderly, disruptive, and sometimes deadly business. Let me say right here, if you need help, please get help. As a former pastor, there is not simply just a need to find Christ, but an urgent need to repent. The injury you have sustained likely was not caused by your open rebellion against God. Likely it was more insidious. Christ is not malevolent and wanting to see His creation suffer so that He can rejoice. Rather, Jesus Christ is a redeeming Savior. He redeems the time, redeems the interests, redeems the relationships that you have. Redeeming, in this context means, "a. to buy back, repurchase or b. to get or win back" (Merriam-Webster, 2018). With Christ being the Chief Redeemer, let me pause briefly and encourage you to find a Bible, find a church, and most importantly, find Christ. Now for the purposes of definition of the more temporal issue, we will adopt that of the Centers for Disease Control and Prevention's for TBI. That specific CDC guidance says "CDC defines a traumatic brain injury (TBI) as a disruption in the normal function of the brain that can be caused by a bump, blow, or jolt to the head, or penetrating head injury" (US Department of Health & Human Services, 2018.) Additionally, however, let us define the other, more nefarious problem: a brain injury that is not caused by impact at all, but by hereditary factors, genetics, or birth. For a more precise definition, let us review information from the Brain Injury Association of America: First, "a traumatic brain injury (TBI) is defined as an alteration in brain function, or other evidence of brain pathology, caused by an external force. Traumatic impact injuries can be defined as closed (or nonpenetrating) or open (penetrating) (www.biausa.org/). Now the url may change, but the Brian Injury Association of America has a number of resources and will be a great contact!

Before we get too entangled in the phraseology of the problem, it would best behoove the reader to understand that the moments that affect the individual with a ruptured AVM are minutes not hours. Often in the ER, the moments spent in triage merely trying to figure out why the person was brought in are often when tragedy can strike the most pronounced. Though I have been in the ER now a number of times at a number of facilities, I can say with limited experience that a more precise method of triage at the ER admittance level could alleviate some of the waiting and wonder that treks through family members as the medical personnel are diligently treating. Ruling out that it is not a heart attack or an epileptic seizure *could* move treatment persons to properly triage the case to a resident neurologist and neurosurgeon, thereby saving time on the patient's part of valuable brain decay, time on the triage team in trying to treat for mere headache, and time on the family's part of wondering what has suddenly happened! Even more so, creating a category of classification for AVM rupture in the triage training manual per hospital would have in my case prevented hours of waiting and wondering Though the criteria seem very fluid and thorough, there is no specifically defined category for an arteriovenous malformation, which is a type of acquired brain injury present from birth. What is more, the precise origin of an arteriovenous malformation is a traumatic impact or TBI though it was not caused by impact to the cranium in many cases. I would surmise that the team of professionals needed for head trauma is in some cases different than general ER. When dealing with decisions on a minute-by-minute basis that could mean life or death, proper triage is of critical importance!

The reason for bringing to light the confusion is not to "muddy the waters," but rather to bring to focus the exact issue where this volume's tertiary focus lies. To reintroduce a problem sometimes requires a redefinition. As the AVM is, by the strictest classification, an acquired brain injury with allegedly nontraumatic consequence, the classification needs to be refined, the diagnosis, further fastidious, and the proper care of such persons brought into the light. Traumatic brain injury is a horrible consequence of a number of occasions. From car accidents to sporting events to merely a slip on the rug at home, the reasons are many. For those who have done none of such things but instead are terrorized by a ruptured AVM, it can be a horror which, if not properly treated and patiently prepared for in the future, can be fatal.

Without being too forward, the sense of urgency you detect in the author's voice is not of worry but concern. I was a pastor for a short time before my third brain bleed. I saw life and death and wrestled with the consequences of those choosing to walk apart from the Lord. I can say from that perspective that a life lived without the hope of Christ is a life eternally wasted. That is not to say that the individual may not contribute and give to others. The progeny that is produced or the worldly wisdom that is shared may even be remembered. Yet to live without Christ and to then face an eternity of punishment merely because the choice was made to live apart from the very One Who made you is fallacy! Turn to Christ! With that pastoral persuasion out of the way, now we begin our walk down the road of the injured together. I am but one out of millions around the world who have experienced brain injury. For some this occurs from some job or industrial accident. It is estimated that it would be helpful if we understand the impact of the brain-injured community of the world. For instance, in the world, the United States holds an abnormally high level of gun-related penetrating head trauma. "Gunshot wounds are the major cause and account for 40% of all head injury deaths (World Health Organization: Neurological Disorders, public health challenges, 2006, 180.) This is not cited to enter into debate as to gun violence or Second Amendment arguments. Rather it is used as a point that the facts that need to be addressed are hiding right under our noses.

To further highlight this issue, the impact on the public is further guised. As one views the recent age-adjusted rates of fatal injury, the United States has a relatively high death rate as compared to other industrialized nations. What is not shared, however, is how many of those deaths are AVM related. This is currently unknown due to there being such a relatively small global populace of malformed brains. Yet in 2020, are we ready to state that someone born with an AVM is doomed to death because of the culture's unwillingness to take relatively simple precautions to detect? Would you be willing to spend a few extra dollars to your health care to detect the lesion that is 50 percent fatal in the year 2020?[5] In the United States, per a recent UNICEF report, scientists found: "Early childhood is important precisely because approximately 80 percent of the brain's capacity develops before the age of 3 and because the period between birth and primary school provides opportunities to tailor developmental education to the child's needs. Studies suggest that the children who are at greatest disadvantage stand to benefit the most" (The State of The World's Children, 2013.) With this fact already presenting itself, it stands to reason that the children of the world need to be treated. It goes without saying that the children have a distinctive medical advantage in the recovery of disorder as their growth and development is at its highest level. Yet those in countries with less than ideal living conditions need not have but another factor of an AVM to deal with. The detection and treatment need to be brought to light and dealt with in the medical community.

What would you say to a mother or father if their child was gone because of a genetic disorder that was unforeseen, as the occurrence

> Definition of Brain Injury
>
> "In 1997, the Brain Injury Association of America, Inc. adopted the following definition: an acquired brain injury is an injury to the brain that has occurred after birth. The injury commonly results in a change in neuronal activities that effects the physical integrity, the metabolic activity, or the functional ability of the cell. Causes of acquired brain injury include external forces applied to the head and/or neck (e.g., traumatic brain injury with or without skull fracture), anoxic/ hypoxic injury (e.g., cardiopulmonary arrest, carbon monoxide poisoning, airway obstruction, hemorrhage), intracranial surgery, vascular disruption (e.g., arteriovenous malformation (AVM), thromboembolic events, fat emboli), infectious diseases, intracranial neoplasms, metabolic disorders (e.g., hypo/hyperglycemia, hepatic encephalopathy, uremic encephalopathy), seizure disorders and toxic exposure (e.g., substance abuse, ingestion of lead and inhalation of volatile agents.) The term does not refer to brain injuries that are congenital or brain injuries induced by birth trauma." —Brain Injury Services of Southwest Virginia

---

[5] "Hemorrhage Rates and Risk Factors in the Natural History Course of Brain Arteriovenous Malformations,"
W. Caleb Rutledge,1 Nerissa U. Ko, 2 Michael T. Lawton,1 and Helen Kim3, *Transl Stroke Res.* 2014 Oct; 5 (5): 538–42.

of AVM is so rare it is not typically tested? Of course, suggesting that children be tested for all disorders is neither practical nor cost effective. But if it were seen that to test for this type of arteriovenous malformation required a simple swab of saliva from the child, would it be worth it then? For checking for HHT, a type of genetic disorder that causes most AVMs in the body, a simple swab of saliva is all that is needed!

If anything is made abundantly clear in recent days, to treat the disease, you must first assemble the appropriate team to best bring about a resolution of the disorder. In the case of an arteriovenous malformation, the classification alone can be a challenge. Though the disorder typically occurs within the brain, the actual disease is a been discovered in a variety of portions of the human body. Though there are more than a few genetic and hereditary maladies that can occur in the brain, it seems somewhat misleading to lump an arteriovenous malformation into the same category as an object striking one's cranium! For the patient whose skull is struck, no damage occurs prior to the object hitting him or her. As such, the bleeding and trauma will occur in a generally predictable fashion. But when one's brain bleeds in an unexpected fashion triggered by exercise, or straining in the restroom, something abnormal has occurred. Beyond exercise and physical exertion, "Ischemic strokes (blocking during pathway of blood vessel) occur as a result of an obstruction within a blood vessel supplying blood to the brain. The underlying condition for this type of obstruction is the development of fatty deposits lining the vessel walls. This condition is called atherosclerosis" (American Heart Association/ American Stroke Association, 2017). After recognition of this subject as being significant and significantly missed, what needs to be changed within the current practice of medicine and patient care to be aware of the condition's existence? Further delineation from a typical traumatic brain injury coupled with further separation from typical emergency room acquired brain injury would seem to be a start.

The first test that I would like to suggest being included in emergency room admissions procedures for brain trauma is a simple swab of the mouth. Per the aforementioned HHT organization, "The Surgeon General launched a national initiative to encourage all American families to learn more about their family health histories" (CDC.gov, 2020). Per the Center for Disease Control of the United States you could: "Enter your family health history. Learn about your risk for conditions that can run in families. Print your family health history to share with family or your health care provider. Save your family health history so you can update it over time" (CDC.gov, 2020). For further directing specific genetic anomalies, the RASA1 gene has been found to be the cause of many instances of AVM occurrence though not all. Per the gene map below, a difference in the gene has been shown to be the marker of the malformation. This discovery conveys the exciting prospect of being able to correctly identify, before the bleed, persons with AVM in their genetic code! How many persons could have staved off a crippling and potentially fatal bleed by swabbing the mouth? If you have a family history of AVM or "brain bleeds," discuss the prospect of testing with a simple swab to possibly avert tragedy!

As of 2014, "Intracerebral hemorrhage (ICH) accounts for 10% to 15% of all strokes representing ≤2 million cases annually worldwide" (Nickalus R. Khan et al., 2014). Per a study for AVM HHT, for instance, another cerebral chromosomal disorder containing AVM diagnosis, "A new locus for hereditary hemorrhagic telangiectasia (HHT3) maps to chromosome 5" (Cole SG, 2005). This again is a common diagnosis type of AVM that occurs for testing by a simple swab of the mouth can detect some cerebral defects. Imagine for a moment if the nurse initially swabs the mouth of your affected family member when he or she is admitted into the ER for extreme headaches. That is not particularly intrusive, not particularly pain-inducing, and frankly, not particularly expensive. This has little effect on anyone other than potentially saving the life of the one brought to the ER! Further, it provides a helpful initial diagnostic which could potentially move the patient from a basic triage into a more time-imperative treatment based on the time constraints within the typical triage of AVM and cerebral contusions. However, HHT is but one type of the AVM disorder. To fully understand, please consult your doctor for more information.

Having broached the topic of genetics, triage, and AVM diagnosis, the question that you may have is "How prevalent is this disorder?" The good news is that it is rare. Please refer to your neurologist and/or neurosurgical team for specific medical inquiries. As one survivor to potentially another, my intention is to bring awareness to the disorder. You may review the websites referenced in the chapter for the latest numbers, as they are frequently updated. Moreover, for those that do have it, it can be tested for prior to rupture. Third, the test does not even require a blood sample for HHT but rather a simple swab of the mouth. Please understand, this is not a necessary test to include in normative triage, but for those who enter the ER unconscious or in great head pain, it would be a cost-effective test.

At this point you may be saying, "So what actually is this AVM?" Well, I'm glad you asked! As I have only been on the receiving end of the knife both gamma and traditional, let us look at what this malformation of veins within the body of an individual who suffers from this infirmity is. Basically, from a nonmedical professional, an AVM or arteriovenous malformation is a tangle of blood vessels comprised of veins and arteries (hence *arterio* and *venous*) *mal* (Latin for bad) formation. When you break the word down, you may begin to see what it means. It is a misformed or poorly formed pocket of veins or arteries in the body that compromises the general integrity of the membrane walls. It then creates a weakened pocket or wall of tissue that during times of increased blood flow could rupture. The pocket of blood often bursts, filling the vessel with blood that commonly would be contained within the artery or vein not outside the vein or artery. This blood, when contained within the artery or vein, is perfectly fine. The blood contained on the outside of the vessel wall is dangerously and critically damaging. I liken it to a drainage ditch. When rainfall happens in a normal city the waters are contained within the sewers and runoff areas such that no land, home, or businesses are affected. When the runoff comes in such a terrifically powerful way in such a short amount of time, it can cause localized flooding. When a membrane wall collapses or a vein or artery experiences such a sudden unexpected flow of blood, the membrane ruptures, thereby causing a "flash flood" of sorts in the individual's brain. As one might imagine, with the human brain being a sealed and closed blood-flow system, this causes the person to experience an excruciating and often fatal brain phenomenon of encephalitis, increased ICP, or intracranial pressure, and sometimes death.

Continuing, when outside the capillary, the blood is actually toxic to the external membrane of the veins and arteries, leading to damage that could be life-threatening. If such a rupture occurs, it is imperative that the patient is transported to the nearest medical facility in order that the patient's life may be spared from the tragedy of death. Typically, when blood incenses brain tissue, the resultant outcome varies from disability, paralysis, and sometimes even death. The plague of brain AVM awareness must be promoted lest another person is tragically and suddenly removed from this earth, all because he or she never knew about a ticking timebomb in his or her head waiting to explode!

Regarding the development of AVM in a person's brain, the formation of an AVM occurs simultaneously with the formation of the remainder of the brain. As such, medically suggesting for an alternative formation is out of the question. The normal arterial and venial formation processes are unencumbered by any outside action on their creation. Thus, the map or pathways for the creation of these malformations must be hereditary or related to the genetic makeup of the individual. As research for this disorder is still in its infancy, through my years of living, I have had the medical professionals from several hospitals corroborate that AVM research, although certainly advancing beyond where it was twenty years ago, certainly has a long way to go. I was directed through my research to an organization specifically dedicated to the research and cure of one type of the recurrence of AVM. You can find out more at www.curehht.org. That organization is currently engaged in researching for the recurrence and origination of HHT (hereditary hemorrhagic telangiectasia) AVM. While this is a test of one type of AVM, nevertheless it is advocating discovery of AVM in the populace. As the incidence of AVM is relatively small, one of the aims of the CureHHT organization is to bring about societal awareness. "HHT affects 1.4 million people across the world, but 90% of those people are undiagnosed. Raising awareness for this disease is key to increasing diagnosis and treatment for all" (CureHHT, 2018). There will be more on this organization in the pages that follow. However, the test itself to discover if you have it is relatively minor. With a simple swab of the inside of the mouth, you are done. From there, genetic testing can be run on the patient's saliva to test for AVM/HHT existence. While not a test for every instance of AVM (including mine) it is a start for triage to analyze saliva for the detection of AVM.

In the HHT AVM instance above, you may notice that the mention of HHT AVM is an even smaller subsection of AVM existence. Per one study: "The population prevalence of brain AVM is estimated to be 10–18 per 100,000 adults, with a new detection rate (i.e., incidence) of approximately

1 per 100,000 person-years. Overall mortality rates in AVM patients range from 0.7%–2.9% per year" (W. C. Rutledge, N. U. Ko, M. T. Lawton, and H. Kim, 2014). (Hemorrhage rates and risk factors in the natural history course of brain arteriovenous malformations: Translational stroke research 5, no. 5: 538–42. https://doi.org/10.1007/s12975-014-0351-0).

When you figure that even the AVM collective is such a small percentage of the population, the question that occurs in my mind, frankly, would be: "Who cares?" But I would wager that for the lives that it saves, the addition of a saliva test would not overburden the medical community too much. The cause for the incorrect growth is suspected to be genetic, and further research is being done along these lines. For the screening for those who have this disorder, the test is relatively simple. A swab of the mouth allows for initial testing in a person to see if he or she may possess the gene mapping for this disorder. If so, then a cerebral angiogram can be conducted on the patient to screen for AVM presence. If detected, then the doctor can plan with the patient appropriate treatment of the AVM in the person's body. Please note, this is the optimal means of finding the AVM because the other way of discovering it is by rupture. Personally, having endured such a calamity of AVM rupture three or four times, depending on the doctor you communicate with, this is not pleasant. For a cerebral hemorrhage, the survivability is nominal; without valid study data, it is difficult to ascertain the precise number. As the clinicians in the ARUBA (A Randomized Trial of Unruptured Brain Arteriovenous Malformations) study affirmed: "This theoretical sketch of what needs to be done recognizes that some clinicians and patients may still opt out. We contend that obtaining these results would be extremely improbable; for this reason, and contrary to what Elhammady and Heros wrote, the trial we propose also includes a registry of treated and observed patients" (Mohamed Samy Elhammady, Feb. 2017). Along these ARUBA guidelines, further investigation is due. Now the initial discovery venue of the ARUBA study is completed; it stands as a baseline for further interpretation by the medical community for treatment options.

Within AVM formation, there are a variety of instances and circumstances into which AVM can occur. Surely more will be discovered. Yet for now, the two primary medical designations are hereditary hemorrhagic telangiectasia and the Osler-Weber-Rendu syndrome. Of note, neither condition comprises the totality of AVM instance. Per the Brain Aneurysm Foundation: "Each year 30,000 people will suffer a ruptured arteriovenous malformation (Brain Aneurysm Foundation, 2020 Advocacy Newsletter)." This comprises only those in the United States! There is little research funding going to general AVM much less for the even more granular HHT or OWR offshoots. The point being, and that coming from a nonmedical professional but affected survivor, we need to make the culture around us aware of our unique needs only to develop proper treatment of the disorder before we perish in our young adult years from a disorder that could have been dealt with with no long-term deficits.

General AVM

From the National Organization for Rare Disorders (NORD):

> As the name suggests, vascular malformation of the brain is an umbrella term for at least six conditions in which blood vessels of the brain are affected. Such malformations are classified into several types in which the symptoms, severity, and causes vary. These types of VMB are: (1) arteriovenous malformations (AVM), abnormal arteries and veins; (2) cavernous malformations (CM), enlarged blood-filled spaces; (3) venous angiomas (VA), abnormal veins; (4) telangiectasias (TA), enlarged capillary-sized vessels; (5) vein of Galen malformations (VGM); and (6) mixed malformations (MM.) (National Organization for Rare Disorders (NORD), 2017).

Specifically, "The capillary bed is where the blood exchanges oxygen and nutrients with the body tissues and picks up waste" (Mario Zuccarello & Andrew Ringer, 2018). While this listing is generally inclusive, it is advisable that with all medical determinations to consult your doctor for precise diagnosis and treatment options.

MALFORMATION

Hereditary Hemorrhagic Telangiectasia (HHT AVM)

Though there are many medical advances regarding many studies and angles of research, of the cerebral malformations, one of the more illustrious advances of AVM treatment is the discovery of Hereditary Hemorrhage Telangiectasia or HHT. Denoted by the persistent nosebleeds many patients often experience, HHT is a condition of some AVM incidence in which the patient is given a minor warning regarding his or her condition. Please note, this does not include all AVM manifestations. It does, however, include some. While initially bothersome, if noted by the treatment facility as a possible marker for further cranial disorder, the patient may alleviate further medical complications and stave off any catastrophic disaster. Again, the symptoms are using frequent nosebleeds as a marker. While a nosebleed is certainly a nuisance, it is by no means disastrous. Yet if recognized as an intimation of something greater, it could be leveraged to stave off future calamity on the part of the patient! If you or a loved one is experiencing nosebleeds, and you suspect it may be related to this condition, the organization, CureHHT has a website www.curehht. org. Again, mere awareness of this condition is the first step in combating this illness.

First, for those who have been diagnosed with this condition, please register at https://curehhtresearchnetwork.org/. You will be prompted to fill out a short questionnaire to investigate the probability of HHT occurrence. You will see the form in appendix: Revisited. Second, register your family medical history at https://phgkb.cdc.gov/FHH/html/index. html. It is here, a site owned and managed by the United States Centers for Disease Control, that the medical community can examine both the specific disorder of HHT as well as correlate these conditions with others in your family. Again, HHT is only one type of AVM. But of the occurrences of AVM, the HHT variety presents itself 10.4% of the time (Brinjikji W1, 2017).

Osler-Weber-Rendu Syndrome (OWR)

Like the HHT disorder, the other cerebral condition specifically related to AVM formation is deemed the Osler-Weber-Rendu syndrome or OWR. Defined by Klaus-Dieter Lessnau, MD, FCCP, "Osler-Weber-Rendu disease (OWRD) is a rare autosomal dominant disorder that affects blood vessels throughout the body (causing vascular dysplasia) and results in a tendency for bleeding" (Klaus-Dieter Lessnau, 2018). Specifically, in OWR, the blood vessels contract, or narrow. If one has this condition, when blood flow is increased, the artery walls tend to tear. Per this condition designation, the medical professionals as always will be your first correspondence of survival. However, you must recognize that upon discovery of this disorder, like any other, you then must decide for yourself what the next step will be for you. The OWR "is an uncommon autosomal dominant disease that occurs in approximately one in 5,000 to 8,000 persons" (Olitsky SE). Hereditary hemorrhagic telangiectasia: diagnosis and management. *Am Fam Physician*. 2010; 82 (7) :785-90). Therefore, affecting only a handful of persons, your decisions to address this malady is nevertheless known and treatable, but you must be your own advocate to get the medical treatment needed.

Based on the conditions' above genetic pairing, both HHT and the Osler-Weber-Rendu syndrome are genetic, possibly hereditary, and as such pending further investigations in distinctive populations. Both specific conditions only concentrate on a fraction of the population. Further, the overall segment of persons with an AVM is miniscule in the scope of a global population of some 7 billion people. Yet for the one who has this disease, it can mean life or death. Though looking at this disorder through the lens of a simple return on investment or cost-benefit analysis may preclude specific research and treatment, nevertheless it is a known and identified condition. We are not dealing with merchandise but individuals. I believe we are dealing with the magnificent creation of the King of kings! As the Hippocratic oath states, "So long as I maintain this oath faithfully and without corruption, may it be granted to me to partake of life fully and the practice of my art, gaining the respect of all men for all time. However, should I transgress this oath and violate it, may the opposite be my fate" (North, US National Library of Medicine, https://www.nlm.nih.gov/hmd/greek/greek_oath.html).

In summation for testing for AVM, HHT, Osler-Weber-Rendu, and other genetic malformities referenced in this book, it is of utmost importance to recognize that these are not predominantly externally noticeable or traceable conditions. With HHT, nosebleeds are frequent, which may give the doctors a clue as to what is taking place. Yet most children will at some point of play in school experience a nosebleed. Likewise, everyone at some point will have a headache; we all exist in a world of sin! Nevertheless, we must be careful to pay attention to the frequency and severity of such occurrences. If the nosebleeds are frequent and not precipitated by any physical contact, what then is the cause? If the headaches are not triggered by anything such as allergies, congestion, or hay fever, then what is the cause for the individual to have headache? If anything needs to be modified in our thinking of health, perhaps merely an expanding of the breadth of infection to which we are susceptible.1 To further complicate, apart from nosebleed, there is little outside criteria for AVM!

> "The clinical features of headache in children with CVD are variable and may have specific characteristics related to increased intracranial pressure and intracranial bleeding or non-specific features mimicking primary headaches such as migraine- and tension-type headache.
>
> With the advances of neuroimaging, the diagnosis of CVD is made relatively easy and many lesions are detected before producing symptoms".

https://link.springer.com/chapter/10.1007/978-3-319-54726-8_15

(Abu-Arafeh I., 2015) (2017) Headache: Comorbidity with Vascular Disorders. In: Guidetti V., Arruda M., Ozge A. (eds) Headache and Comorbidities in Childhood and Adolescence.

Headache. Springer, Cham. https://doi.org/10.1007/978-3-319-54726-8_15

Anoxic brain damage

Another brief final entry to the brain damage categorization for this volume is that of anoxic brain damage. Although rare, "Anoxic brain damage is injury to the brain due to a lack of oxygen. Hypoxia is the term to describe low oxygen. Brain cells without enough oxygen will begin to die after about 4 minutes" (Public Health Agency of Canada, 2018). Anoxic brain damage is caused by a variety of means, but not typically caused by malformed arteries or veins. Typical causes are those of "blood clot, stroke, shock, and heart problems, like heart attack (Mount Sinai Hospital, 2018). Brain damage attributed to this condition is rarely genetic, hereditary, or congenital. Although the substantive cause of damage may vary, the concern is with the outcome of care. As such, let us briefly consider the diagnosis that may need to be updated to specify and quantify care of patients more clearly. Please also consider that any information provided here is given with the understanding that this is one survivor talking to you. The author received no medical training whatsoever. Therefore, please consult with your doctor to determine what would be the best plan of attack for your specific situation.

Screening criteria

When reviewing medical examinations or screenings, you should have them interpreted by your general practitioner at the very least, with a possible further referral to a medical specialist. As with many medical conditions, the chances for carrying this disorder of AVM are slim. Yet the risk of having this disorder and allowing it to go untreated could be catastrophic. As proof, a recently concluded trial deemed the ARUBA study, or A Randomized Trial of Unruptured Brain Arteriovenous Malformations, found that in the option to treat those found to harbor an AVM lesion, the choice was given to treat the malformation or not. For the study, 223 patients participated in the trial. Of the 223, 114 were assigned to medical treatment either by gamma knife, embolization, or other interventions. The rest were given therapeutic treatment such as blood pressure medication or other noninvasive medication. After six years, the study was stopped because of superiority in the medicinal management rather than surgical intervention. While this is good to know for those who can continue taking pills to manage their blood pressure, those of us who discovered the disorder by a rupture possibly might seek further medical intervention. To insure that the patients receive the informed and reliable diagnosis, it would be best to consult both your general practitioner and a neurologist if you suspect you have any symptoms or have a family history of stroke.

Further, after gleaning from the National Organization for Rare Disorders (NORD), recessive genetic disorders happen when the recessive gene is inherited from both parents. If you receive the malformed gene from one parent, that demarcates you as a carrier of the disease but not necessarily a person infected with it. The risk for two carrier parents to both pass the defective gene and, therefore, have an affected child is 25 percent. Yet following this, the parents then create a 50 percent chance that their offspring will havel the disease. While I in no way ever will support eugenics or abortion in any form, I do want parents to be aware that if you have a malformation in your history, the pronounced malady may be prevalent. As a rule to be prepared rather than blindsided by the discovery, you or your family members might consider it worthwhile to perform the testing. Further, it is recommended to conduct the testing for peace of mind if a family member has one of these conditions. It can produce both ease of mind and aid the medical staff to be aware of possible future conditions in your family.

The final screening mechanism to be mentioned is that of difference of patient value. What is meant by this understanding is simply this: as a Christian, my belief and conviction is that all humanity is created in the image of God. This shared conviction is likely felt by many even outside the Christian circles. Regardless of your view of eternal rest, few patients wish to end their life prematurely. And as such, what steps or changes need to be taken to ensure that the best care is given to patients today to extend their stay on earth? Further, as a parent, it is my belief that my children are created in the image of God. If you think you were created in the image of distant monkey relatives, that is your prerogative. But if we are created in the image of God, then it would stand to reason that the creation of anyone or anything by accident or chance is out of the question. This should further gain credulity in the view of any new parent or proud grandparent seeing their offspring blossom. Therefore, do everything in your power to best provide for those you have charge over for a brief time that they might further the knowledge of Christ and the awareness of His goodness to the greater community of the world!

At the close of this chapter, one item remains that would be beneficial to the brief discussion—the Hippocratic oath taken by many medical doctors today:

> I will use those dietary regimens which will benefit my patients according to my greatest ability and judgement, and I will do no harm or injustice to them.
>
> I will not give a lethal drug to anyone if I am asked, nor will I advise such a plan; and similarly, I will not give a woman a pessary to cause an abortion.
>
> In purity and according to divine law will I carry out my life and my art.
>
> I will not use the knife, even upon those suffering from stones, but I will leave this to those who are trained in this craft.
>
> Into whatever homes I go, I will enter them for the benefit of the sick, avoiding any voluntary act of impropriety or corruption, including the seduction of women or men, whether they are free men or slaves.
>
> Whatever I see or hear in the lives of my patients, whether in connection with my professional practice or not, which ought not to be spoken of outside, I will keep secret, as considering all such things to be private.
>
> So long as I maintain this oath faithfully and without corruption, may it be granted to me to partake of life fully and the practice of my art, gaining the respect of all men for all time. However, should I transgress this oath and violate it, may the opposite be my fate. (National Institute of Mental Health, Translated by Michael North, National Library of Medicine, 2002.)

MALFORMATION

The restatement of the oath is meant to serve this purpose. As a reminder to the medical professionals, staff, families, and patients alike, the doctor rooted in this oath has pledged to be bound by this oath that "in purity and according to divine law will I carry out my life and my art" (North, the Hippocratic Oath, 2018). Surely the world has seen by and large the genuine care and concern many medical professionals have with the eradication of any disease that would detract from the general wellbeing of the individual. This would include for the doctor an obedience in the case of a Christian medical practitioner. Their attempt all the more to adhere to the living Savior, to the Divine law of His Word and the Divine will that "For God so loved the world that he gave his one and only Son, that whoever believes in him shall not perish but have eternal life" (John 3:16). If you are being treated for any disease, understand that the disease was for the purpose of drawing you to Himself. If you and the treating professionals approach treatment from this vantage, then you recognize just how precious your life is to Christ. As you recognize this, perhaps it is best now to consider what He has in store for you in lieu of this illness.

CHAPTER 2
Cognition?

———— ❦ ————

According the to the American Psychological Association, cognition refers to the "processes of knowing, including attending, remembering, and reasoning; also, the content of the processes, such as concepts and memories".[6] Using this accepted medical definition to lay the groundwork of our concept of reality, we now need to define what causes knowing, elucidates the processes, and determines what we do with said ideas. This defining a medical and psychological term is difficult in such a volume and frankly was never the author's intention. It is rather a new mind-set to which you are encouraged to adopt—namely, that this issue of brain aneurysms exists. More and more there are examples in the news of individuals who will struggle with their malady for the rest of their lives on this earth. What is more, this volume is by no means intended to define terms of which the author has had no vocational training. One such resource that does hold some answers is the organization Answers in Genesis. Led by Dr. Kenneth Ham, the group is comprised of hundreds of workers, scientists, researchers, and volunteers who seek to reconcile the wayward scientific misgivings with the truths of the Christian scriptures. Though not expressly supporting this volume, the author and his family subscribe to many of the beliefs of this group, as they are founded and grounded in the Word of God. You may check out www.answersingenesis. org if you are interested in finding out more. Their creation museum in Petersburg, Kentucky, is a fantastic Biblical and scientific account of

———————

[6] American Psychological Association. APA Dictionary of Psychology, https://dictionary.apa.org/cognition.

creation, the flood referenced in Genesis, and a synthesis of the Bible and the world as we live.

Though not 100 % accurate because the museum was created by humans after the Fall, it gives a biblical and scientific account of creation. Moreover, it gives a scientific reason for the thousands of years advocated by the Christian scriptures as antithesis of the millions, billions, or trillions of years, whatever amount the scientific community of ardent evolutionists believe. This book is not the end-all for brain injury. But just as the chapter says, it is the "cognition" that the community of brain-injured persons needs to be sought out and sought after in order that even they would be cared for rather than sitting and suffering in silence!

To pivot to a current struggle with this disorder, as a fan of Third Day in the 1990s and 2000s, the lead singer Mac Powell was a regular staple of audio bliss in our household. However, Mac's wife, Aimee, suffered a life-changing brain rupture in 2019 that forced her and Mac to begin to deal with this struggle. As of 2020, they are still dealing with this disease, with Mac and Aimee undoubtedly facing new challenges at home, difficulties on the road, and difficulties with life in general. However, better understanding the notion that humanity is created in the image of God, this author, properly trained, believes the Word of God to give us a far greater outlook from the outset. Let the reader suppose that the subject we are dealing with is a divinely created being. If you consider that you and I are crafted in an image of the Divine, Jesus Christ, we begin to see a different future on the horizon. Then we already begin from a greater starting point than being a descendant to some long-lost amoeba in years long forgotten. By the way, this author does not wish to disrespect the scientific community by saying such a statement. Many in the medical community are legitimately God-fearing, hardworking caregivers. For that matter, many in the medical profession may have little to no regard for God but nevertheless treat their patients with the care, concern, and aid that provide an example that other humans should mimic! Yet the fact remains that there are many questions that secular science grapples with only by faith that Christian medical minds have both logically and scientifically dealt with ad-nauseum.

For one such example, consider Dr. Kenneth Ham with his Answers in Genesis project, the Creation Museum. (https://answersingenesis.org/, https://creationmuseum.org/about/) Their museum deals specifically with the struggle between faith and science in a logical and scientific manner. Stemming the foundation of this process of thought millions of years ago through evolution creates a problem. If you believe that you originated from the gradual evolution from single-celled organisms to the complexity of cells of today, a host of evidential difficulties still are fiercely disagreed with from a scientific perspective. For more information, consult the organization Answers in Genesis at www.answersingenesis.org. This is evidence based on the truth of the Christian scriptures as opposed to the ever-evolving theories of modern science. This author cannot accept by faith the big bang with all its holes and problems when the Bible so clearly teaches by faith and evidence the truths of life, existence, and the universe itself. If the Bible so clearly and reliably teaches creation in a matter of days, we then are faced with a decision.

Since neither you nor I were there at the beginning, spoken Word, big bang, or otherwise, let us examine the evidence. Before you shut this book here, consider this: Your brain was created at the time of conception and began its marvelous and miraculous formation. This is not a treatise or an apologetic discourse. There is no time for that. If then you, like me, were forced to find out you had a brain AVM by rupture, you were already one person of the 1 percent of persons who had a cerebral aneurysm.[7] Moreover, "An estimated 6 million people in the United States have an unruptured brain aneurysm, or 1 in 50 people. The annual rate of rupture is approximately 8 – 10 per 100,000 people or about 30,000 people in the United States suffer a brain aneurysm rupture. There is a brain aneurysm rupturing every 18 minutes".[8] From the Toronto Brain Vascular Malformation Study group, "The risk of bleeding over one's lifetime may be high especially if the AVM is discovered in a young person. Ruptured brain aneurysms are fatal in about 40% of cases. Of those who survive, about 66% suffer some permanent neurological deficit" ("Brain Aneurysm

---

[7] An arteriovenous malformation can develop anywhere in your body but occurs most often in the brain or spine. Even so, brain AVMs are rare and affect less than 1 percent of the population. https://www.mayoclinic.org/diseases-conditions/brain-avm/symptoms-causes/syc-20350260.

[8] https://bafound.org/about-brain-aneurysms/brain-aneurysm-basics/brain-aneurysm-statistics-and-facts/. Brain Aneurysm Foundation

Statistics and Facts," 2018)[19]. The author and the reader alike must come to a quicker and more thorough alleviation of this unfortunate malformation to the immediate purpose of longevity of life.

To bring this closer to home, one study from www.stroke.org says that annually there is a 2 to 4 percent risk of rupture of an AVM. This data given back in 1996 is largely unchanged even today because the risk of bleed from an AVM has no preventative or often physical warning signs except for patients with HHT, which we will discuss more at length later![10] Further, having gone through three bleeds, I can as best describe the feeling of the worst headache in your life. Twice now I have passed out from the pain. The first bleed, I stood up, passed out, vomited, and then lay there motionless on the floor while paramedics came rushing in. This is not typically a survivable anomaly. Further, the mortality rate per this study of number of AVM ruptures ranges from 12 to 66 percent per the NIMH (W. Caleb Rutledge, 2014, pp. 45-66). Yet of those who survive, decreased vision, slower reaction to stimuli, and disability are often the outliers awaiting a survivor.

The preceding sets of stats should show what a rather shocking rarity an AVM can be. Moreover, if you are an unfortunate possessor of an AVM and still breathing, the good news is you're alive! You and I have been afforded an opportunity to get down to an appropriate treatment of this disorder not only for us but for those to come. The cognition of this condition should prompt a reevaluation of your surroundings. Tragically, around the time of the writing of this book, "the federal government only spends approximately $0.83 per year on brain aneurysm research for each person afflicted" ("Brain Aneurysm Statistics and Facts," 2018). If you consider that "hospitalization costs for endovascular and surgical treatment of unruptured cerebral aneurysms in the United States are substantially higher than Medicare payments" there is trouble ahead

---

9

[10] Findings listed in: https://www.ahajournals.org/doi/full/10.1161/01. str.27.1.1#:~:text=Untreated%20AVMs%20have%20a%20widely,of%202%25%20 to%204%25.&text=The%20cumulative%20lifetime%20bleeding%20risk,only%20 should%20be%20recommended%20rarely. The annual rate and risk of bleed is largely unchanged since the discovery of AVM.

(Brinjikji W, 2012). Therefore, you may have noticed at this point that there is a distinctive issue with the cost of treatment of patients who have this disorder. For pediatric patients, for instance, "the clinical features of headache in children with CVD (cerebrovascular disorder) are variable and may have specific characteristics related to increased intracranial pressure and intracranial bleeding or nonspecific features mimicking primary headaches such as migraine- and tension-type headache. With the advances of neuroimaging, the diagnosis of CVD is made relatively easy and many lesions are detected before producing symptoms" (Abu-Arafek & Mack, 2017, 163-71). How does one informally diagnose a brain bleed from a headache in a child? How does a patient with migraines discern between that and a microhemorrhage? Is there any solution to this problem? It would seem in the 2020s there would be someone more than hospice to call.

As you have heard a brief introduction to AVM, what are the symptoms of it? Although a symptom like a migraine *may* be the cause: for the author, a headache so excruciating it forced me to the floor, then vomiting because of the immense pressure was the only somber notification. Again, according to the Mayfield Clinic, the following symptoms are signs of a ruptured cerebral AVM:

1. Sudden onset of a severe headache, vomiting, stiff neck (described as "worst headache of my life")
2. Seizures
3. Migraine-like headaches
4. Bruit: an abnormal swishing or ringing sound in the ear caused by blood pulsing through the AVM (Mayfield Brain & Spine, 2018, https://mayfieldclinic.com/pe-aneurrupt.htm).

One marker of the possible irregular brain activity is the presence of absence seizures. Formerly known as grand mal seizures, these seizures may lend the victim to brief periods of spacing out or seeming unconsciousness. Per the website epilepsy.org, "An absence seizure is a generalized onset seizure, which means it begins in both sides of the brain at the same time. An older term is petit mal seizures. Absence seizures usually affect only a person's awareness of what is going on at that time, with immediate recovery" (MD & Patricia O. Shafer RN, 2018). If you or a loved one is experiencing these symptoms of seeming unconsciousness, lethargy, or inability to form cohesive thoughts or language, it would be prudent to consult your doctor for a possible further check. Although it likely is simply a spaced-out period (everyone's mind wanders from time to time), it also may be a means for your body to communicate to you that there is something nefarious going on with your cognitive processes.[11]

At this juncture the recognition of the problem should bring about effective treatment as so many prior medical conditions have as well. In the author's own state, the bylaws of the Virginia Brain Injury Council state: "The vision of the Virginia Brain Injury Council is that Virginians and their families who experience disability due to brain injury will build a quality of life of their choosing" (Virginia Brain Injury Council, 2016). Dating this problem of effectual brain aneurysm mitigation back to an earlier physician's treatment in 1863, German physician Rudolf Virchow's treatment suggested "three components to thrombosis [clotting of the blood], stasis [a stoppage or slowdown in the flow of blood], endothelial or vessel wall injury [such as an aneurysm], and hypercoagulability [abnormal tendency for blood to clot].[12] More precisely, with this information you can see the complexity of medical diagnosis! A better public awareness is needed to both understand the existence of aneurysms and to treat the disorders with more careful diagnosis and treatment at the ER level.

To review, we have at this juncture two questions that need answering. First, how do we deal with matter at hand—namely, treatment of an aneurysm? This is a subject that cannot be fully answered by this volume as it is a deeply personal decision between you and your health-care provider. As one who has gone through five cranial procedures, two gamma knife surgeries, one shuntectomy, one craniotomy, and one shunt revision, I can tell you *some* of the procedures are a "breeze" such as the gamma

---

[11] An arteriovenous malformation can develop anywhere in your body but occurs most often in the brain or spine. Even so, brain AVMs are rare and affect less than 1 percent of the population. https://www.mayoclinic.org/diseases-conditions/brain-avm/symptoms-causes/syc-20350260.
[12] Medical author: William C. Shiel Jr., MD, FACP, FACR. https://www.medicinenet.com/script/main/art.asp?articlekey=9245.

knife. Others will require all the strength, fortitude, and sedation you can muster. Here we will pause to review the typical treatment options for a cerebral AVM.

The second question that must be dealt with, however, is whether those who are found to have AVM should be operated on at all, as multiple studies suggest. Brain aneurism surgery is a risky endeavor no matter which method you choose. More will be discussed in this chapter, but all treatment options introduce their inherent risks to the patient of cranial bleeding, stroke, aneurism rupture, mild radiation risks, and other medical complications. Therefore, surgery in any capacity presents the family and in particular the individual with a weighty list of options to consider. Before dissuading you from surgical intervention, let the author state from his own opinion that this was a bad choice for my context. First in 2000, I experienced a rupture while sitting in a dorm room with a friend. Second, in the hospital in the summer of that same year, I had another rupture. Third, while preparing a sermon to deliver, I had a third bleed. It is my nonprofessional but very genuine opinion that waiting is not an option. Also, a study of unruptured AVM was completed in recent years that further encouraged surgical interpolation rather than simply waiting for something to pop.[13]

Regarding the risks listed in the ARUBA (A Randomized trial of Unruptured Brain Arteriovenous malformations) study, "There were several reasons why complete obliteration was not achieved in all cases: inadequate nidus definition in four patients, changes in the size and location of the nidus in five patients due to recanalization after embolization or re- expansion after hematoma reabsorption, a large AVM volume in five patients, a suboptimal radiation dose to the thalamic and basal ganglia in eight patients, and radio resistance in three patients with an intranidal fistula" (Kwon Y, December 2000). Further, "An excellent recovery (mRS 0–1) could be found in 28/41 (68%.) All 7 patients who remained in unfavorable state (mRS ≥ 3, n = 6) or death (mRS 6, n = 1) were initially admitted in comatose or poor clinical condition without exception" (Klaus-Peter et al., 2018). Opting to wait to see if the AVM is innocuous is akin to waiting to see if the hungry shark will bite when swimming

---

[13] The stop the pop campaign is currently in effect as of this writing. More is available at www.stopthepopnow.org.

the shallows at the beach! When you are swimming in his waters, you must take precautions to make sure you are safe. Leveraging your better judgment and the doctor's professional opinion will yield a much better rate of literal return from surgical intervention!

Two organizations that have been created to drive awareness and fund-raising are the Joe Neikro foundation created by the late Joe Neikro's daughter, Natalie. First, the Joe Neikro organization is created in memory of former Houston Astros player Joe Neikro, who passed away from a ruptured aneurysm. The Joe Neikro foundation, based in Houston, Texas, is a nationwide private organization dedicated to the research and hopeful eradication of the disorder of AVM. Currently their Facebook group https://www.facebook.com/JoeNiekroFoundation/ hosts the annual Joe Neikro Knuckle Ball, which hosts donors to donate to the research and discovery of novel treatment of AVM.

Second, the Brain Aneurysm Foundation of America is the United States' premiere foundation of medical research for brain aneurysm awareness. The current "Stop the Pop" campaign created by the national Brain Aneurysm Foundation is driving awareness among the masses. For the national Brain Aneurysm Foundation's Stop the Pop campaign, the website https://www.stopthepopnow.org offers state by state contacts and resources to drive awareness and advocacy for AVM. Having overviewed two of the largest brain aneurysm awareness groups, let us view briefly four of the more commonly employed means of alleviation used by doctors.

Treatment Option 1: Embolization

In 1960 the first medically documented use of the embolization procedure in the brain was recorded in literature. Without giving the details of the procedure, the role of embolization is stated: "Embolization may be used as an independent curative therapy or more commonly in an adjuvant fashion prior to either micro- or radiosurgery" (Jason A. Ellis & Sean D. Lavine, Role of Embolization for Cerebral Arteriovenous Malformations, 2014 Oct.-Dec.) While embolization is useful as a means of rerouting blood to alternate flows inside the brain, it is suggested to consult with your surgical team to determine the depth of the lesion, the most surgically viable option, and the longest lasting procedure for your specific instance.

Also, as was found in one study for embolization, factors precluded those from participating in the embolization process. Essentially, among those patients referenced in the study, some bled during the procedure, some experienced only partial mitigation of the malformation, and some did not survive the procedure. Again, it is best to talk to your doctors prior to making any surgical decisions if possible.

Of further note, "ischemic injury alters the integrity of the cerebral microvasculature by initiating processes that degrade matrix content, decrease endothelial cell and astrocyte matrix receptor expression, and increase permeability of the blood-brain barrier" (Zoppo, 2008). That is, if you have surgery, the functional cell walls are compromised. Thus, if the doctors need to further operate, there may be a higher risk of bleed because the cell walls have already been breached. Again, to this I would add, when not given an option due to rupture, for me personally I would say please proceed! Though treatment by embolization is often an efficacious option, it is recorded in multiple journals and studies to be a means of mitigation with risk. Approximately 7 percent of patients in one study undergoing embolization suffered a fatal bleed. Whereas the risk of bleed was stated from the outset, nevertheless let the reader understand that the risks are there! (Jason A. Ellis & Sean D. Lavine, Role of Embolization for Cerebral Arteriovenous Malformations, 2014 Oct–Dec). Further, "before radiosurgery, the goals of embolization are to shrink the size of the AVM, particularly at the periphery; address feeding vessel aneurysms and other high-risk features; and, ultimately, to reduce the size of the radiation field required for treatment" (Tamargo and Huang, 2012).

The use of embolization for vascular and neurovascular lesions is an effective and welcome addition to the surgeon's tool set of treatment. Yet for the deep-seated lesions, a possibly more effectual and less intrusive option exists.

Treatment Option 2: Gamma Knife

Developed and used first in 1975, Professors Borje Larsson of the Gustaf Werner Institute, University of Uppsala, and Lars Leksell at the Karolinska Institute in Stockholm, Sweden, "...began to investigate combining proton beams with stereotactic (guiding) devices capable of pinpointing targets within the brain" (Rector and Board of Visitors, 2018). It was then utilized for development in other countries, with the United States building multiple locations with the gamma knife equipment. For this author, the gamma knife setup at the University of Alabama at Birmingham was sufficient to treat the cranial AVMs. For more on the procedure, you may visit the UAB website direct at www.uab.edu search for "gamma knife." For the details of the procedure, a brief walkthrough is given: "The instrument delivers 201 tightly focused cobalt radiation beams to one point in the brain. The radiation beams and dose are so precise that they affect only the targeted tissue while relatively sparing the surrounding healthy tissue.

First, the doctor/procedural staff will fit the patient's head with a head frame that will hold the cranium upright and in place. Local anesthetic will be used to affix the metal frame to the individual's skull. Second, the person will be allowed to lie down in a comfortable position while the medical treatment team adjusts the gamma knife delivery device to the person's height, weight, and location of the AVM. Third and finally, the delivery system of 201 gamma knife beams will be used to painlessly eradicate the affected portions of leakage. Although many studies have been conducted as to the value of the gamma knife treatment, one example should suffice to give the overall results. In one study, a total of fifty-one patients were treated with Gamma Knife. Of them, fifty patients experienced successful treatment with one patient having the novel instance of regrowth. To best understand your risks and benefits, please consult your treatment team. Having been through the treatment procedure twice personally, this author can attest that aside from the loud "banging" of the machine itself, these are by far the easiest and most painless surgeries this author has ever endured!

Notwithstanding a handful of failed attempts to eradicate the lesion, an inability to clearly see the location of the nidus or malformed lesion, a large portion to treat, an underestimate of the amount of gamma knife radiation, and re-formation of the affected area were the causes for ineffective treatment. In layman's terms, the causes for failure in gamma knife surgery are vague AVM definition, a large segment of occupied space in the brain, not enough radiation at treatment time, an AVM that went deeper than previously calculated, or organic material that had a resistance to radiation treatment. In another study, a survey of elderly patients was taken postsurgery. Of note, among the elderly, the positive results of gamma knife, provided you are eligible, to have gamma knife or cyberknife surgery, I personally would recommend the procedure as it is very minimal in pain and highly effective! There have been a rare number of AVM regrowths postsurgery, but these cases are by far exceptions to the norm.

One more item of note is that among the few risks, there is a risk of bleeding not from the cranium but the groin from the angiogram. Per a summation study: "The causes of failed GKS (Gamma Knife Surgery) for treatment of AVMs seen on 3-year follow-up angiograms include inadequate nidus definition, large nidus volume, suboptimal radiation dose, recanalization/re-expansion, and radio resistance associated with an intranidal fistula" (Kwon Y1, 2000, pp. 104–106). This means that in the cases in which gamma knife failed to eliminate the leaky aneurysm, the scientists were forced to tell the patient that the treatment was ineffective. In other words, the patient who has already been leveled with a diagnosis that he or she has a defective active blood transport system in his or her head, now has a failed treatment in attempting to deal with the problem!

In a study released in 2000: "One hundred twenty-three of these 415 patients underwent follow-up angiography after GKS. After 3 years the nidus was totally obliterated in 98 patients (80%) and partial obliteration was noted in the remaining 25" (Yang Kwon, "Analysis of the causes of treatment failure in gamma knife radiosurgery for intracranial arteriovenous malformations," December 2000). In another case as well, "It is believed that an ill-defined margin, laminar flow, and effects of previous surgery might add to difficulties in a proper visualization and delineation of an AVM. Further, a small remaining shunt may be overlooked if the angiogram is not carefully analyzed or if the angiogram is of inferior quality. It should be stressed that partial or almost total obliteration of an AVM is no protection against re-bleeding" (W. Y. Guo, Even the Smallest Remnant of an AVM Constitutes a Risk, 1993, pp. 21–15). In yet another study, "AVM obliteration was achieved in 222 (74%) patients after the first round of radiosurgery and in 47 (69%) after the second. The overall chance of cure was 92% (269 patients)," which yields an extremely high success ratio for brain surgery (Roman Liščák, June 2007)!

The aforementioned is a survivor talking to you. As always, please consult with your doctor regarding the risk and benefits of this surgical procedure. Generally, you can expect to go through these steps during the procedure:

- **head frame placement**

  The patient will be fitted with a metal frame affixed to the cranium using local anesthetic and screws. The worst pain I felt during the procedure was a very minor prick from the needle to numb the skin where the frame would be affixed.

- **AVM location imaging**

  The treatment team will next take pictures of your head with the frame affixed to determine. Please remember the gamma knife operators will be firing painless lasers into your skull. You want to be sure they get the measurements exactly right!

- **radiation dose planning**

  With the completion of the imaging, the treatment team will determine the dosage amount of radiation to treat the disorder. Though not the same as chemotherapy, the effective amount of gamma knife to be given to the lesion is determined at this step. The great news is that it is only to the lesion and not to any other portion of the brain or body.

- **radiation treatment**

  If using the gamma knife created by Leksell, the gamma knife radiation consists of 201 focused beams of radiation that pinpoint only the area of malformed lesion on your person. Unlike traditional surgery, which requires contamination of the affected area by outside objects, in gamma knife only the radiation specifically targeting the lesion is used.

Treatment Option 3: Craniotomy

The third treatment option is something more invasive but nevertheless effective in certain instances of treatment. Dubbed the craniotomy for the opening of the cranium, this procedure involves cutting through the skin, into the cranium itself to remove a section of the skull and manually remove the affected AVM. For this procedure, your doctor will overview the process. Usually, you will be placed under anesthetic during the operation. Having been through this procedure as well, the skull will have a bone flap section cut out using a craniotome. Following this, the surgeon will remove the affected portion of brain tissue. General anesthetic is used although determining your mental state will be decided by your doctor and treatment team. For further questions, please consult the physician or care team responsible for the procedure.

Treatment Option 4: Novel Treatments

Offered only in conjunction with other treatments, for the rehabilitative side of therapy, researchers are finding novel treatment options such as art therapy advanced by promoting the arts as well as the creative nature of persons. With the author being married to an artist, the prospect of the value of calming visual depictions can be helpful. Advanced by the nourishment hypothesis, the American Art Therapy Association in 2015 was introduced to the in-depth fiber- based narrative art therapy intervention (F-NAT.) (King, 2016, 218). Bear in mind, this recovery method does not deal with the initial bleed but rather the follow-up of the bleed. This is not to be missed, however, as the road to recovery is long and arduous. Surviving the bleed merely means you often become a blank canvas. The wonderful news yet is that in becoming this canvas, a wonderful new creation for display to the world can be painted if yielded to the appropriate Painter's hands. From the American Art Therapy Association, "Art Therapy is an integrative mental health and human services profession that enriches the lives of individuals, families, and communities through active art-making, creative process, applied psychological theory, and human experience within a psychotherapeutic relationship" (American Art Therapy Association, 2018). More information on the Art Therapy Association can be found in the "Redemptive Workers" section of the appendix.

Treatment Option 5: Do Nothing

After reviewing the options, you may be saying to yourself, "What if I just continue like before?" Now I would be criminal to give medical advice, as I was not trained nor will I ever be medically proficient. Again, this author is not a medical doctor. I never intended to be, nor intended to be involved with, this tangle of confusion known as AVM. Yet, I was given this malformation, which possibly you or your family member was as well, and so here we are. It was advised by a doctor that my brain had one or two more spots of possible rupture after the successful gamma knife treatment in 2009. As such, I was discharged from the hospital to be scheduled for the final AVM to be removed soon afterward. Instead of getting it treated in time to surgically remove the AVM, however, it bled on February 10, 2010. That is why perhaps I am so zealous to encourage you to have the lesion treated rather than simply wait it out. Further, if the ARUBA study is to be taken into consideration, simply doing nothing can have fatal consequences. Please consult with your doctor if you have questions regarding any medical content discussed. Please consult with your family and friends if you need veracity to indicate you should live. Finally, consult the Christian scriptures if you are doubting that He has plans for your life beyond the AVM!

What I am not telling you is to get the procedures done as soon as possible because it is a ticking time bomb, though from my view, they are. What I am advising is to have the treatment done as soon as medically advisable rather than delaying because the medical officials are not immediately familiar with your specific case. Along those lines, do you remember ever playing "telephone?" Basically, one child would start with a somewhat off-the-wall message to relay to the other child some six or seven people down the line. By the time it got to the last kid on the other end, it was a mess compared to the original message. Instead, I'm coming to you as a fellow brain injury survivor and, if you like, a friend! Do something! If you do not feel your instance of treatment is progressing quickly enough, get a second opinion! Any treatment by gamma knife, cyber knife, embolization, or craniotomy is much more efficient and survivable as opposed to rupture, in my view.

To back up my urgency, in yet another study, the doctors found that thirty-five, or 13.31 percent of their testing group had another bleed after the first bleed. This effectively happens repeatedly. Study after study shows that though the medical professionals can both diagnose and in some cases treat the disorder, there is still a gaping hole of those who had AVM and now have passed away. My wife and I recall watching *Mythbusters* when we had our first child. I saw on the news that one of their team members died suddenly at a relatively young age. A few moments and a couple of searches later, I found that he died from an AVM, ruptured brain aneurysm.[14] He didn't know he had it, and as such it was too late when it ruptured. I was blessed during my third incident to only have the AVM bleed enough to expose itself just enough to highlight the path of the faulty membrane. Typically, this would have been a catastrophic and likely fatal event. Please do not consider, in my view, doing nothing as a valid option.

Cost of care

There is power in facts. The first fact that would benefit the community at large is the cost of care for the brain injured as compared to the average hospital admission. Per a 2005 study: "In 2005, estimates of the cost of TBI ranged from $25,572 to $30,730 per mild case and from $252,251 to $383,221 per moderate or severe case" (AANS, 2016) (Terra C. Holdeman, 2008). That number is not a typo. I can attest that by the grace of God and the faithful servants of His, He has provided everything we could need. Nevertheless, the dismal possibility that you could face such lifelong debt and little to no career, and the prospect of brain injury is terrifying! The

---

[14] Brain aneurysm foundation. Mythbusters Host Grant Imahara Dies From Brain Aneurysm
https://bafound.org/news/mythbusters-host-grant-imahara-dies-from-brain-aneurysm/.

cost jumps from $25,000 to 30,000 for a mild case to $250 to $380,000 for a severe case of TBI. This is for the individual admitted from typical traumatic brain injury—*typical* caused by such as a fall, an object falling on the person, gunshot, or other malady.

Now with this, consider that the brain injury survivor has experienced no traumatic event outside of the cranium precipitating the injury. The psychological scars left from the injury can often be just as lasting as the surgical scars left on the cranium! To gain some sense of perspective, according to a study conducted in 2012: "In 2010, the average cost per hospital stay was $9,700 and the aggregate cost for all hospital stays totaled $375.9 billion" (Agency for Healthcare Research and Quality, 2013). Certainly, no one suspects an emergency hospitalization. That is why most hospitals name their emergency rooms as such! Moreover, a catastrophic brain bleed is not even on most people's "radar."

My wife and I can validate that the cost of a joyful hospitalization for birth is met with great celebration! Yet the months after wrestling with the hospital bills brings a somber tone to the festivities. For my brain bleeds, we spent many dollars paying off the health-care system, which does not regularly expect such a calamity to happen. While the United States is now allocating some funds to brain aneurysm research, currently it is woefully underfunded. Preventing aneurysm development, in my limited experience, is likely much more cost effective that treating a person in their twenties or thirties for full-time hospice care until death. You should be aware that the United States certainly is allocating some of the funds yet needs more targeted research and allocation to properly mitigate the problem. Per the ARUBA study, of the 977 patients studied, 94.2 to 98.1 percent of the patients who had an unruptured AVM had the lesion successfully dealt with prior to rupture! The bad news is that of 977 patients, 5.9 percent of the persons died. This comes out to fifty-seven patients who did not make it through the ARUBA study.

The preceding numbers highlight a modicum of urgent changes that need to be made. First, considering that the cost of care should never in my opinion be the deciding factor as to whether a human life is elected to continue or not, the question should then be changed to how can the medical community, counseling community, rehabilitation community, and general environment of support personnel be changed to accommodate the inclusion of the brain-injured person? If it is presupposed that these persons will cost more for general life, what sacrifices need to be expected by their caregivers and family? Sadly, they must be expected to live a shorter life span.

Generally, there have been few quantitative studies overarching all the brain injury community. However, one such study completed in 2009 shows a thirty-six-year-old survivor with traumatic brain injury to have a life expectancy of forty-five-plus more years. While this is significant and generally encouraging, the question now turns to recognizing what quality of care and life could be expected with those who have had a brain injury. The preceding is the TBIMS Life Expectancy Calculator, which can answer some TBI-related life expectancy questions. Yet, there is no national or international registry of those who have suffered TBI, ABI, or diseases related to these, just as there is largely no national data set as well to poll.

Although there is no all-encompassing TBI mortality data, some troubling data returns have been given. Per the CDC's 2015 data:

Data for United States in 2015

- Number of deaths: 2,712,630
- Death rate: 844.0 deaths per 100,000 population
- Life expectancy: 78.8 years
- Infant mortality rate: 5.90 deaths per 1,000 live births (National Center for Health Statistics, 2018)

That data is for the general public. But now the matter at hand, for the AVM survivor we find this piece of data: "the cumulative risk of hemorrhage from an asymptomatic AVM is 44%" (Kevin M. Cockroft, 2007) (stroke.org/10.1161/STROKEAHA.107.504613). That number is correct. For those who have an AVM but do not have symptoms or any other issues related to that AVM manifest, there is a 44 percent chance of rupture over the course of their lifetime! I am not a medical professional, but I am a survivor who has had three bleeds; doing nothing is not an option in my view!

Please bear in mind that the heading "Data for the United States in 2015" is for the general populace of the United States, not AVM. Now let us take the data that we have been given regarding traumatic brain injury and circumfuse this into the data we have per the CDC and ARUBA studies. The burden of cost for this brain-injured family soon will be discovered. Yet with the burden of care for these persons, what could be done to curb the cost early on? As one who has endured some of this with employer health benefits and some without, in my opinion it would be wise to move to applying for disability as soon as the prognosis from the doctor comes back that the person has a brain injury. Wrangling about the cost-benefit analysis can be done after the fact. More pressing for today is a mobilization and awareness in our culture of the disease and its effect on the populace. The motivation is akin to the recent COVID-19 crisis. Though highly politicized, the point remained that there was an illness that did not have a cure or a vaccine. What was the reaction? Motivation from many persons to mitigate by developing a vaccine. Now the reason for the quick application for disability is no different! It is to allow for the medical system to both identify and work through its normal processes, unfortunately including an appeal in some cases. Otherwise, the patient could be trapped in the uncomfortable position of determining the eligibility for Social Security while leaving the working community at large not knowing precisely how to proceed. Further data shows that only a small sampling of three persons with multiple brain anomalies were studied for life expectancy within the ARUBA grouping.

From this data, a few items of note need be highlighted. First, "Hemorrhagic stroke accounts for approximately half of stroke in childhood. Unlike arterial ischemic stroke, there are no consensus guidelines to assist in the evaluation and treatment of these children. These rare vascular lesions are considered to be already present at birth" (Klaus-Peter Steina, August 2017). Due to the discovery of the lesion, there surely must be a more modern means of healing. In my experience, detection of a single aneurysm should present the medical personnel with the warning that the individual may have others. As I can attest, the first discovery of AVM was from a near-fatal rupture in 2000. After rehab, I proceeded for ten years with no further issues. But once I went for another scan per doctor's orders, other AVMs were discovered. I am not suggesting that the treatment team did anything wrong. Unfortunately, the lesion of AVM in another part of my brain did bleed prior to surgery. It was not dealt with fast enough. I do not fault anyone in missing the speed at which the lesion ruptured. I do caution all who have been told to "watch and wait" to consider a different opinion.

In another study among sixty-three AVM patients, correlative data was found. This one concluded in 2011: "Sixty-three patients with a mean follow-up time of 11.0 years (range, 1 month to 39.6 years) were identified. Twenty-three patients (37%) experienced a subsequent rupture. The average annual rate of rupture was 3.3%" (Aki Laakso, 2011). Further, it was found: "One year after the first subsequent rupture, 6 patients (26%) had died, and 9 (39%) had moderate or severe disability" (ibid.).

A brain-injured person has three items of support that need to be pursued as soon as the diagnosis is given. First, the survivor needs to apply for Social Security at www.ssa.gov. This process is long and arduous, but nevertheless must be applied; the cost of care will undoubtedly go up soon as medical complications invariably compound as procedures began to compound. Yet it is also worth noting to date there has only been one instance recorded in literature of double recurrent AVM; therefore, the risk of AVM recurring is relatively nominal. For the lifetime of medical complications the patient will have, I strongly advise early application for Social Security.

Second, it is strongly advisable that the survivor have an advocate who will detail his or her medical records, receipts, and the like both for Social Security and for doctors. This is a long process, with the general application for Social Security taking some time—anywhere from six to twelve months. Of note, section 11.18 of the Social Security Blue Book is the location for the Social Security application that needs to be noted. The contents of the section are below:

"**11.18 <u>Traumatic brain injury</u>**, characterized by A or B:

A. Disorganization of motor function in two extremities (see 11.00D1), resulting in an extreme limitation (see 11.00D2) in the ability to stand up from a seated position, balance while standing or walking, or use the upper extremities, persisting for at least 3 consecutive months after the injury.

OR

B. Marked limitation (see 11.00G2) in physical functioning (see 11.00G3a), and in one of the following areas of mental functioning, persisting for at least 3 consecutive months after the injury:

1. Understanding, remembering, or applying information (see 11.00G3b(i)); or
2. Interacting with others (see 11.00G3b(ii)); or
3. Concentrating, persisting, or maintaining pace (see 11.00G3b(iii)); or
4. Adapting or managing oneself (see 11.00G3b(iv).)" (Social Security Administration, 2018) (Social Security Administration, 2020)

The United States triage results should serve to illustrate the point as follows. "The study population included 104 patients (41 admitted to the ICU and 63 admitted to the SU.) After controlling for differences in baseline characteristics, there were no differences in poor functional outcome at discharge (93% vs 85%, P = .26) or in mean mRS (2.9 vs 3.0, P = .73.)" (Department of Neurology, 2018) What the researcher surmises this to mean is this. Although there is diligent work being done both to save the lives of those admitted and to treat those who undergo this malady, the resultant outcome is life largely up to the patient's own genetic makeup and biological fortitude. That means that the surgical outcome of your surviving this occurrence is left up to your genes and gentry not the skill or precision of the doctor alone. Proportionately in the ARUBA study, "The ARUBA trial showed that medical management alone is superior to medical management with interventional therapy for the prevention of death or stroke in patients with unruptured brain arteriovenous malformations followed up for 33 months" (A Stefani, MD And, 2014). The current strata of acceptability are nowhere proportionate to the American dream or even American nightmare.

The results of one study from Canada illustrate the difficult felt worldwide: "Of 1507 patients diagnosed with SAH, 5.4% (95% CI, 4.3 to 6.6) had a missed diagnosis. The risk was significantly higher among patients triaged as low acuity (odds ratio 2.65; 95% CI, 1.46 to 4.80), as well as in nonteaching hospitals (adjusted odds ratio 2.12; 95% CI, 1.02, 4.44.) Neither ED SAH volume nor on-site CT availability explained the effect of teaching status" (Marian J. Vermeulen, Missed Diagnosis of Subarachnoid Hemorrhage in the Emergency Department, 2007). What this data tells the reader is that although the facility into which the patient is admitted is a teaching hospital, meaning they are actively involved in research, or nonteaching hospitals servicing the community into which they are built, the hospital should be prepared to treat or refer all who come in their doors. Further, "about 1 in 20 SAH patients are missed during an ED visit" (ibid.).

If you are suffering from a debilitating traumatic brain injury, it is recommended that you apply for benefits early and as soon as you are found to be unable to work. This does not preclude you from working. However, as is the case with many brain-injury survivors, the cost of care and the need for urgent medical attention necessitates advanced planning before further costly medical conditions prohibit you from making the necessary changes prior to being found medically untenable. For those interested, the listing of currently financing institutions of the Traumatic Brain Injury Model Systems or TBIMS are located below in appendix: Redemptive Workers.

For continual evidence, "rare instances of AVM recurrence despite negative finding on postoperative angiography have been reported in both children and adults. In this paper, the authors present the case of a 33-year-old woman with 2 AVM recurrences" (Patrick J. Codd, "Recurrent cerebral arteriovenous malformation in an adult," September 2008). To belabor the point, the medical technology and processes are not established enough in this author's opinion to with certainty offer a consolatory and comforting word if a patient has multiple active cranial AVMs.

Data for Canada and Japan

It is telling to note further studies from different portions of the world as well. For this study, it is worth noting that the data is some eleven years old. As such, the data may not be reflective of the current life expectancy or results of brain injury triage within a Canadian Japanese emergency ward of today. Continuing on the subject of life expectancy, we come to the diagnosis in the Ontario hospital system over a three-year period as well from April 2002 to March 2005. "Of 1507 patients diagnosed with SAH, 5.4% (95% CI, 4.3 to 6.6) had a missed diagnosis" (Marian J. Vermeulen, "Missed Diagnosis of Subarachnoid Hemorrhage in the Emergency Department," 2007).

In Japan, "Most initial misdiagnoses occurred in nonteaching hospitals (72%). Of those presenting with headache, 55% did not undergo a computed tomography (CT) scan. In addition, SAH was missed in the patients who underwent CT scans. The clinically diagnosed re-rupture rate was 27%. Mortality among all cases was 11%" (Yasushi Takagi, MD, 2017). Interestingly, similar results were found in one Japanese study as well. In the Japanese study, "Most initial misdiagnoses occurred in nonteaching hospitals (72%.) Of those presenting with headache, 55% did not undergo a computed tomography (CT) scan." Therefore, as an initial remedy to just this one study, it would be advisable to perform a CT scan to rule out rupture aneurysm. While the patient may argue against such expensive action, the risk of death justifies the cost of treatment in this researcher's mind. Also, "the presence of recurrent cerebral AVMs after complete extirpation by modern microsurgical techniques indicates that cerebral angiography in the early postoperative stage, the golden standard to assess the disappearance of cerebral AVMs, is not sufficient to eliminate the risk of hemorrhage, and careful long-term follow-up studies should be planned (Department of Neurosurgery, Kyoto University School of Medicine, 1999; 9 (3)." Furthermore, for an AVM to recur, typically requires the patient typically to be of an age in which brain vessels are still being formed, which is typically between the ages 0-18.

Paying off an expensive hospital bill certainly outweighs the cost and lifetime grief of a loss of life. Thus far the triage and treatments prescribed have only served to compound the problem. Perhaps it is at this crucial point that a notice needs to be served to the emergency room and ER nursing and doctoral care team as to the importance of quick and veridic triage to the top of the emergency care team's list as the patient brought in facing a brain bleed has hours or minutes to live.

MALFORMATION

The real cost of care

The true burden of care and cost of concern is the detriment to society both as to the individual and to society. It is tragic anytime anyone loses a loved one. But for an extra burden of care, when the loved one loses his or her life unexpectedly or prior to the typical cycle of aging causes extreme loss. As observed by Kristi Kanel: "Counselors do not have to be perfect models of cultural sensitivity, but they do need to be aware of cultural, ethnic, religious, and gender issues that may affect the crisis intervention process" (Kanel, 2007, 39). As with any cost of loss, there is by the author's estimation, no price too high to pay for a patient against the scope of eternity. As such, while an unlimited budget is impossible, an increased budget for the scanning for AVM existence would be a worthwhile venture in many AVM cases as a starting point, especially when the check would simply be a swabbing of the patient's mouth!

For more information regarding this genetic testing, "Telangiectasias are commonly detected on the buccal mucosa, tongue, lips, face, fingers, and chest, while AVMs are often found in the lung, liver, or brain. Diagnostic criteria, called the Curacao criteria, have been established for HHT. Diagnosis requires the presence of at least three of the following: epistaxis, telangiectasias, a visceral lesion, and family history of HHT in a first degree relative" (Opko Health, 2018). If we consider that the solution to something as insidious as AVM could be as simple as swabbing the mouth and then sampling the blood from a person to detect AVM triggers, it is this author's befuddlement that this has not already been included in the typical battery of testing imposed in every ER when a patient is admitted. However, recurrence is miniscule, as in the case of one patient who experienced cerebral AVM regrowth. If you suspect this to be your condition, please consult with your doctor. Yet be aware: "Surgical excision of 'operable' cerebral AVMs, preceded by embolization in selected cases, is highly cost-effective when compared to observation alone or to a policy of surgery for large- and medium-sized lesions and radiosurgery for small (< 3 cm) lesions. This conclusion assumes that an experienced team performs the surgery and embolization, as well as the selection of patients for surgery with or without embolization" (Nussbaum ES, Jan. 1995). The option of doing nothing, such as treatment option 5 showed earlier in this chapter, unfortunately in my opinion is not a legitimate choice.

Genetics or Classification to Blame?

With the recent devotion to study of capillary malformations—the classification of AVM and genetic basis for classification—it would be this author's suggestion to begin a new addition to the classification of arteriovenous malformations. Again, as further classification becomes possible, further individual study then becomes possible as well. Per the National Institute of Neurological Disorders and Stroke, "Most often AVMs are congenital, but they can appear sporadically. In some cases, the AVM may be inherited, but it is more likely that other inherited conditions increase the risk of having an AVM. The malformations tend to be discovered only incidentally, usually during treatment for an unrelated disorder or at autopsy" (National Institute of Neurological Disorders and Stroke, 2018). What this means to the common working individual is oblivious that an AVM even exists! What is more for AVM patients, the criteria to even identify the AVM and subsequently deal with the disease in still needing further classification.

Coupled with the classification dilemma, widespread treatment of the disturbance is still a concern as well. From a study released in February 2018, "Ninety-seven patients satisfied inclusion criteria for our study. Mean age was 34.9 ± 16.4 years, with 50.5% male. Thirty-one (32.0%) presented with hemorrhage, and 32 (33.0%) presented with visual disturbance. Average AVM size was 4.0 ± 2.5 cm. Twenty-five (25.8%) were conservatively managed, 13 (13.4%) underwent surgery, and the rest were managed by radiosurgery (52.6%) or embolization (8.2%), with an obliteration rate of 38.9% in treated patients. During average follow-up of 5.4 years, 6 patients (6.7%) hemorrhaged yielding an annual hemorrhage rate of 1.2% for all patients, and 0.0% for surgically treated patients" (Yang W, 2018). Per the study's admission of the individuals surgically treated, the annual rate of rupture was 1.2 percent for those untreated. Yet for the same study, those had surgically treated, had a 0.0% risk of rebleed! Again, I am no medical professional. I am a survivor of two or three ruptured AVMs—the first out of the blue and the second rupture while waiting on surgery to be scheduled. The initial truth that can be gleaned is that while the extenuation of the blame may be the first reaction, the mitigation of the problem should be the reaction after review.

Beyond the average rate of occurrence and outcome, what starts or begins an AVM formation? In 2018, research was published revealing that "Preliminary findings show that RNA expression from circulating neutrophils carries an IA-associated associated signature. These findings highlight a potential to use predictive biomarkers from peripheral blood samples to identify patients with IAs" (Tutino VM, 2018). This was published in 2018, so as you might imagine, the predictive value of testing the blood for AVM prior to rupturing instance is extremely new. Yet, with this new testing strata, the disease of AVM can be detected, thwarted, and treated often before any horrendous rupture or disability besets the candidate. Further information from the Brain Aneurysm Foundation implores, "Our recommendation is for any individual who has two or more relatives (e.g., mother, father, brother, sister, aunt, uncle, grandparent, cousins) with a brain aneurysm be screened for aneurysms starting in their twenties and then every 5 to 10 years thereafter" (BA Foundation, 2018). Per another study concluded in 2017, "In our consecutive series of 46 paediatric patients, there were 18 (39%) male and 28 (61%) female patients (mean age 11.6 years (SD 4.3), range 2–17 years). The vast majority of patients suffered from symptomatic lesions (n = 45.) 35 patients (76%) sustained rupture of their AVM. Molded by the high number of hemorrhagic events in our cohort we consider an invasive approach to paediatric AVMs to be justified" (Steina et al., 2017). In yet another study, "The best estimates for new detection of an AVM are 1 per 100,000 population per year (about 3000 new cases detected per year in the U.S.) The population prevalence is about 10 per 100,000, for example, there are probably about 30,000 individuals in the U.S. who harbor an AVM or have had an AVM that was treated. They occur throughout life, but the peak onset of symptoms is 35-40 years of age" (Gunel and Machuk, 2013). The statistics could be further justified by other studies; suffice to say, perhaps the frequency of medical treatment techniques needs to be escalated.

As the determination and routing of the problem has been established as one of the primary points of concern, what needs to be done to correct this issue? First, the proper diagnosis from the triage level needs to be done. This means the nurses and triage professionals need to correctly be aware of the critical importance of timeliness in the instance of AVM rupture. For recent evidence of the contrary, "These findings indicate that delaying intervention for at least 4 weeks after the initial hemorrhage subjects the patient to a low (< 1%) risk of hemorrhage" (Beecher JS, 2017). In yet another study done, "One hundred ninety-six initial hemorrhages occurred in 10,348 patient-years for an annual initial bleed rate of 1.89%; 44 of these 196 patients had a repeat bleed in 591 patient-years for an annual rebleed rate of 7.45%" (Bruce E. Pollock, 1996). However, though the findings state that the patient is within a less than 1 percent chance of bleed twice over, as a victim of the <1%, could there be a better way of determining the risk?

The point the author is trying to make is that genetic malformations are just entering the scope and reach of current medical technology. This should be acceptable although unfortunate to anyone with any genetic misfortune imaginable from loss of hair, short stature, weak eyes, or bad teeth. This is an unavoidable consequence of genes. "Preliminary findings show that RNA expression from circulating neutrophils carries an IA-associated signature. These findings highlight a potential to use predictive biomarkers from peripheral blood samples to identify patients with IAs" (Vincent M. Tutino, Jan. 17, 2018). What this essentially means—and this to the AVM survivor should be exciting—is that screening for AVM, its occurrence, and its hereditary value could be checked and dealt with prior to rupture.

Moreover, there is further reason for treating this disease sooner than later. "Particularly young children seem to bear a higher risk for haemorrhage from their AVM. Treatment of pediatric AVMs can be achieved safely in experienced hands with a high rate of complete elimination and good clinical outcome" (Stein et al., 2018). As observed also in a study from 2017, "Excellent outcome was seen in 90% of patients with modified RBAS score <1, 66% of patients with score 1–1.5, 50% patients with score 1.5–2, and 43% of patients with score >2" (Marks et al., March 2017). The risk for children is elevated due to the formation of the vessels. Yet the formation of these veins must occur for the child to grow to an adult.

What the readership should be hopeful for, however, is a day and age soon when genetic maladies such as an AVM become a treatable condition rather than a quick death sentence. For this author, having to hope for on the next morning all the while silently dreading the thought of possible recurrence of rupture can be unnerving. Having been told now twice that it wouldn't rupture and having it rupture nonetheless weakens the author's reliance on what the doctors assure. Yet, understanding that this life, regardless of ailment, is only temporary gives hope. A hope set in understanding that this frame that I am currently in is only my tent, if you were, while my mansion is being prepared. And with that understanding, let us turn to a more fruitful discussion of what recognizing my true hope should be in and introduce you to the same.

CHAPTER 2.5

Recognition

—————————◦◦◦◦◦—————————

With medical funding reaching out to further swaths of the hospitals to reach a broader sample of society, patients who are roughly seventy years of age and older used to be treated with penicillin and sent home. Now with medical advances, patients are afforded targeted care for many maladies and diseases. Just as the black plague was the invisible scourge of the Middle Ages, today a parallel is drawn to an unruptured AVM. It is recorded that "in a Europe coping with the results of the Black Death and against the background of the Hundred Years War Pope Innocent VI spent most of his ten-year pontificate trying to revive it (dependence on the Catholic Church)" (Riley-Smith, 1987). Turning the page to today, the legacies of recent presidents is yet to be judged by a similar issue—namely, disease for the brain injured. The state is unintentionally forcing all persons left with a debilitating brain injury altogether dependent on the state for their well-being. In just the author's lifetime, President Ronald Reagan, President George H. W. Bush, President Bill Clinton, President George W. Bush, President Barack Obama, on up to President Donald Trump, there is a distinct failure to properly deal on the neurocognitive level with the soldiers and military servicemembers returning from combat other than just to monetarily provide for them by way of the Veterans Administration and Social Security, then push them aside. Was the repetitive brain injury and permanent disabling of the servicemen and servicewomen worth the victory in the Afghanistan/Iraq conflicts? Will the legacy of the COVID-19 epidemic leave a path of neurocognitive disability that is left largely undetected and thus untouched by the greater community after its initial waves are stilled? One of the largest variances with the conflicts being the general ignorance, whether willful or casual, of the permanent impact a brain injury will have on the household. With the heart of the COVID-19 still waiting to be fully dealt with as the scourge continues, the medical community still needs to allocate increased funding for the neurological portion of patient assessment.

Perhaps closer to home, "The rates of ED (emergency department)-treated SRR-TBIs (Sports- and recreation-related traumatic brain injuries) increased during 2001-2012, affecting mainly persons aged 0 to 19 years and males in all age groups. Increases began to appear in 2004 for females and 2006 for males. Activities associated with the largest number of TBIs varied by sex and age. Reasons for the reported increases in ED visits are unknown but may be associated with increased awareness of TBI through increased media exposure and from campaigns such as the Centers for Disease Control and Prevention's Heads Up" (Coronado et al., 2015). As a reminder:

To carefully classify TBI/ABI/HBI let us use the classification from the Alzheimer's Association:

- o **Mild traumatic brain injury,** also known as a concussion, either doesn't knock you out or knocks you out for 30 minutes or less. Symptoms often appear at the time of the injury or soon after, but sometimes may not develop for days or weeks. Mild traumatic brain injury symptoms are usually temporary and clear up within hours, days or weeks, but they can last months or longer.
- o **Moderate traumatic brain injury** causes unconsciousness lasting more than 30 minutes. Symptoms of moderate traumatic brain injury are similar to those of mild traumatic brain injury but more serious and longer-lasting.
- o **Severe traumatic brain injury knocks** you out for more than 24 hours. Symptoms of severe traumatic brain injury are also similar to those of mild traumatic brain injury but more serious and longer-lasting (Alzheimer's Association, 2018).

The distinction of brain injury being further clarified, the aim of this volume is not to advocate one political persuasion over another. Further, it is not the purpose of this book to avoid banter about what could or should have been done. Rather, it is to awaken the reader to the problems of this present era as you are drawing breath at this age to enact, act, and react in this day and time regarding brain injury and mitigation thereof. Another study among 561 patients with cerebral AVM states: "Therapeutic effects and outcomes of SRS (stereotactic radiosurgery) are similar in elderly and nonelderly patients. Treatment-related neurologic deficits are rare, and longer EFS (event-free survival) can be expected" (Hirotaka Hasegawa, January 2018, pp. e715-e723 October 21, 2017). Therefore, cerebral AVM can be treated, but it must be found in time to be treated.

When your era is reviewed one hundred years from now, you will be gone from this earth. The only lasting value to your legacy will be the impact on your culture in your context. In the brief time that you spent on this earth, what did you do with the time you were given? It conjures to the forefront for this author a narrative found in the New Testament record by Jesus. To further delve into the separation between modern culture and the brain-injured populace, let us parallel between the story of the rich man and Lazarus found in Luke 16.

The normal individual (the rich man)

LUKE 16: 19-31 THE RICH MAN AND LAZARUS

"Now there was a rich man, and he habitually dressed in purple and fine linen, joyously living in splendor every day. 'And a poor man named Lazarus was laid at his gate, covered with sores, and longing to be fed with the crumbs which were falling from the rich man's table; besides, even the dogs were coming and licking his sores.' 'Now the poor man died and was carried away by the angels to Abraham's bosom: and the rich man also died and was buried. 'In Hades he lifted up his eyes, being in torment, and saw Abraham far away and Lazarus in his bosom.' "And he cried out and said, 'Father Abraham, have mercy on me, and send Lazarus so that he may dip the tip of his finger in water and cool off my tongue, for I am in agony in this flame.'" But Abraham said, 'Child, remember that during your life you received your good things, and likewise Lazarus bad things; but now he is being comforted here, and you are in agony. 'And besides all this, between us and you there is a great chasm fixed, so that those who wish to come over from here to you will not be able, and that none may cross over from there to us.' "And he said, 'Then I beg you, father, that you send him to my father's house— for I have five brothers—in order that he may warn them, so that they will not also come to this place of torment.' But Abraham said, 'They have Moses and the Prophets; let them hear them.' "But he said, 'No, father Abraham, but if someone goes to them from the dead, they will repent!' "But he said to him, 'If they do not listen to Moses and the Prophets, they will not be persuaded even if someone rises from the dead.'"

There was no separation between the two ideas of a secular and a sacred society, as this social arrangement had no separation of the secular and sacred. Much like some portions of the American populace wish for today, there was no delineation between the church and state. Now the polar converse of this one position is that of a secular society much akin to the Marxist or Communist China, which wishes to elevate the accomplishments of man apart from any intervention by a higher power. It was said by C. S. Lewis, a previous atheistic evangelist upholding the guise of mankind's reason over the things of God: "It is quite true that if we took Christ's advice we should soon be living in a happier world. You need not even go as far as Christ. If we did all that Plato or Aristotle or Confucius told us, we should get on a great deal better than we do" (Lewis, 1952, 86). Yet later in his converted life to Christianity, Clive Lewis stated: "Thus in the very act of trying to prove that God did not exist—in other words, that the whole of reality was senseless—I found I was forced to assume that one part of reality—namely, my idea of justice—was full of sense. Consequently, atheism turns out to be too simple. If the whole universe has no meaning, we should never have found out that it has no meaning. (*Mere Christianity*, 45–46) Suffice to say, Christ deals with this at length in the gospels as well. The meaning is Jesus, and until you find Him, you will be left searching!

For the story, Jesus proceeds to explain how this poor man Lazarus and the rich man both pass away. Now the rich man, expecting prosperity, is instead met with torment, horror, and despair as his life everlasting is bereft of any comfort. Why is this? A clue is given in the text, "But he [Abraham] said to him, 'If they do not listen to Moses and the Prophets, they will not be persuaded even if someone rises from the dead'" (ibid, Luke 16:30.) What is Christ asking the learned religious experts of His day to recognize? Simply a truth they have missed for the entirety of their lives. Beyond all the education, beyond all the conversations, beyond all the teachings they have received and teachings they have given, they have missed the one truth that should have imbued them with power and enlightened them to a world otherwise obscured by their own pride. This life is not your own. Someone else paid for it, and to Him allegiance is due.

Now let us bring the parable of the rich man and Lazarus to the current subject. A Bible lesson is not intended here. This volume is written to make the general population aware of the condition and plight of AVM. Furthermore, it is typed to make those who are treating the condition aware of possible points of research and intervention that may have yet to be investigated. The rich man was "habitually dressed in purple and fine linen" (Luke 16:19). You can see that not only was this person wealthy, but he was lavishly and noticeably wealthy. His habit was to dress in the fine linens and purple-dyed fabric, which would draw attention to his social standing. His upper garment was of purple wool, his underclothing of Egyptian byssus (white cotton), which among the Hebrews was frequently used for delicate and luxurious materials (Meyer, 1829). If you assume the rich man was one who normally concerned himself with his own business, his own matters, and his own life, it seems sensible that he would have little concern if any knowledge of Lazarus. In fact, based on the New Testament record, no account of external information regarding Lazarus is given. What parallels to this person listed in the story and the person who happens upon this story today? Perhaps that the existence of persons beyond our vantage should at the very least cause a notion of charity to rise within.

Thankfully, in the United States this charitable organization was already built into society. For those who become unable to have a steady income due to disability, the Social Security Administration has been given domain. Expressly, section 11.18 in the Social Security Blue Book states:

The brain injured individual (*the poor man*)

    A. Disorganization of motor function in two extremities (see 11.00D1), resulting in an extreme limitation (see 11.00D2) in the ability to stand up from a seated position, balance while standing or walking, or use the upper extremities, persisting for at least 3 consecutive months after the injury.

    OR

    B. Marked limitation (see 11.00G2) in physical functioning (see 11.00G3a), and in one of the following areas of mental functioning, persisting for at least 3 consecutive months after the injury:

1. Understanding, remembering, or applying information (see 11.00G3b(i)); or
2. Interacting with others (see 11.00G3b(ii)); or
3. Concentrating, persisting, or maintaining pace (see 11.00G3b(iii)); or
4. Adapting or managing oneself (see 11.00G3b(iv).) (United States Social Security Administration, January 2019)

To draw the correlation, for the rich man in the story, the view was that his sustenance and life were comprised within him alone. That there were those beyond themselves that could not survive without the help and aid of others, based on this section of the text of scripture, for the rich man this was never a thought. Without pressing the scriptures beyond their intent, consider what is being intimated. As a Christ follower, if you or I are in a position in life to support others, then perhaps it would behoove us to ask to what extent is our responsibility to fellow humans? A brief political treatise will follow but only to illustrate the imperfection of our current political situation in highlighting the situation to come. Moreover, lest you read this as a political commentary, all political systems fail save One in Whom all rulers, kingdoms, and authorities will bow to worship the Savior Jesus Christ.

MALFORMATION

The book of Acts speaks of the apostle Paul's sermon on the Areopagus in Athens:

> So Paul stood in the midst of the Areopagus and said, "Men of Athens, I observe that you are very religious in all respects. For while I was passing through and examining the objects of your worship, I also found an altar with this inscription, 'TO AN UNKNOWN GOD.' Therefore, what you worship in ignorance, this I proclaim to you." (Acts 17:22b-23).

The apostle was speaking as a Christian to learned and upper-class persons. As he spoke, he sought to drive a mental wedge in their thinking as to what was effectively missing in their line of reason. As a politically active citizen, the author does not wish to identify with any political party. The American (specifically the United States) political system is the only system of which he has ever been a part. The right to vote, the right to protest, the right to worship all are personal political rights that are often not afforded in other parts of the world. Yet having had friends hailing from France, Nigeria, Mexico, Albania, and other places, it would be beyond this author's scope to assert if one form of government is better than another!

Having the conviction that the best form of government is a dictatorship run by a benevolent dictator (which does not exist save One person, namely Jesus) echoes today as you can read:

> Come then, tell me, dear friend, how tyranny arises. That it is an outgrowth of democracy is fairly plain. Yes, plain. Is it, then, in a sense, in the same way in which democracy arises out of oligarchy that tyranny arises from democracy? How is that? The good that they proposed to themselves and that was the cause of the establishment of oligarchy— it was wealth, was it not? Yes. Well, then, the insatiate lust for wealth and the neglect of everything else for the sake of money-making were the cause of its undoing. True, he said. (Plato, *Republic*, Rep. 8, 2011).

67

The point is that the rich man in the story about Lazarus, corrupted by sin and the love of wealth, has neglected the sight and plight of his fellow man. The King of kings never will cast out a "rich man" for being rich but rather will cast out any man or woman who does not bow the knee to Jesus Christ!

To synthesize further though on a lesser plane, as Plato highlights, the tyranny of democracy is not from the White House down but your front door out. We as Christians have an admonition to charity and benevolence. If we neglect this responsibility, then the failing of personal responsibility transfers the burden to the government's shoulders. Once leveed with this task, then charity becomes institutionalized such that it is equaled out among the citizens. The United States has long sought to provide its citizens with ample opportunity for such actions on their own since its conception. Betterment and protection of her citizenry have been understood since the nation's birth. Lest forced to recall a civics lesson, simply recall the preamble to our constitution:

> *We the people of the United States, in order to form a more perfect union, establish justice, insure domestic tranquility, provide for the common defense, promote the general welfare, and secure the blessings of liberty to ourselves and our posterity, do ordain and establish this Constitution for the United States of America.* (Jefferson, 1776, italics added).

The founding fathers held in their hearts the general aim at the well-being, tranquility, and health of the populace insofar as the family unit was able. Nevertheless, this preamble was not government mandate but arbitrium gratis! This notion of gratitude and giving should be led off by the people of the body of Christ, by this author's estimation.

Again, even the ancient Jewish mind held this notion of functional grace recorded to be in the Jewish mind by Josephus in The Wars of the Jews:

> O Varus, the great folly I was guilty for I provoked those sons of mine to act against me, and cut off their just expectations for the sake of Antipater; and indeed, what kindness did I do them; that could equal what I have

done to Antipater? I have, in a manner, yielded up my
royal while I am alive, and whom I have openly named
for the successor to my dominions in my testament, and
given him a yearly revenue of his own of fifty talents, and
supplied him with money to an extravagant degree out of
my own revenue. (Josephus, Antiquities of the Jews, Book
17, CXXXII, August 3, 2013)

In short, the principle of kindness to the disadvantaged, the disabled, and the downtrodden had been instituted long before the IDEA act of 2004! We will discuss the continuing fight for recognition and inclusion in public education in the pages to come, but for now, recognition is what is most needed in culture, by this author's estimation. In summation for the healthy, the notion of charity and general welfare ought not just be compelled only by law, but the innate love of the common citizenry.

It is this point at which the distinction can be made between the rich man and the beggar in the biblical text. The rich man has the monies within his possession to alleviate the financial suffering of the beggar. Yet the ability to remove suffering does not preclude the rich man from the duty to do so. The rich man perhaps became wealthy because of his hard work and diligence to his craft, and as such he should be able to enjoy the fruits of his labors. Perhaps he should be unencumbered by the trappings of higher taxation for the rest. It is this delicate line of juxtaposition between peaceful prosperity and obnoxious opulence that should call to the church to consider what, if any, welfare is his responsibility to the masses for care. To further illustrate this point to modern day, a brief example will be given; from Maxwell Air Force Base in 1997 a patient was admitted initially with headache. Following the medical record, the patient was misdiagnosed with a migraine. Instead, the patient was having an AVM rupture. By the time the rupture was discovered, the patient was left disabled due to the doctor's misdiagnosis.

Now, I am not suggesting that the United States should shoulder the burden of the entirety of the world's brain-injured persons. Yet the medical billing arena can offer an introduction to the cost of care of this ailment. Left untreated, the disorder of AVM in a person is unsustainable, irresponsible on the part of the medical treatment team per studies such as the ARUBA study, and, by my opinion, untenable. The tools to treat the disorder and persons with the maladies are present in the medical community. Prior notice of this ailment of this portion of the populace unfortunately is largely not. Organizations such as the Christian Institute on Disability, started by Ms. Joni Tada, show both a need and an option for service. From their website www.joniandfriends.org please note the following action items the Joni and Friends organization is doing:

1. Evangelize people affected by disabilities and their families
2. Train, disciple, and mentor people affected by disabilities
3. Multiply disability effective churches
4. Promote a biblical worldview on disability through education and policy

Now if one were to take this generalized Christian modus and layer this on top of the proposed mitigation strategy of the US government, we are met with a mixture that at the very least better informs our treatment of the disabled.

FIGURE 16 – NIDILRR MODUS

As the federal government's primary disability research agency, NIDILRR achieves this mission by:

- providing for research, demonstration, training, technical assistance and related activities to maximize the full inclusion and integration into society, employment, independent living, family support, and economic and social self-sufficiency of individuals with disabilities of all ages;
- promoting the transfer of, use and adoption of rehabilitation technology for individuals with disabilities in a timely manner; and
- ensuring the widespread distribution, in usable formats, of practical scientific and technological information.

National Institute on Disability, Independent Living, and Rehabilitation Research

MALFORMATION

Recognizing the responsibility the United States wishes to play in treatment of its citizenry, consider now the Christian organization Joni and Friends, which specifically aims to help those who are disabled achieve wholeness in life and well-being. Therefore, if one were to postulate from a Christian perspective that the best outcome for the persons with brain injury would benefit from a relationship with Him, what would that look like? Perhaps a life united with Christ, found in Him and seeking to be used by Him for His good purposes. Perhaps the synthesis of Joni and Friends with the NIDILRR akin to the chart below would be helpful. Thus, the aim of the Christian worker in the government position of influence should be one who seeks to:

- provide for research, demonstration, training, technical assistance and related activities to maximize the full inclusion and integration into society, employment, independent living, family support, and economic and social self-sufficiency of individuals with disabilities of all ages;

    o   This is accomplished by:
    o   Evangelizing people affected by disabilities and their families, then training, discipling, and mentoring people affected by disabilities

- promoting the transfer of, use and adoption of rehabilitation technology for individuals with disabilities in a timely manner;

    o   This is accomplished by:
    o   Train, disciple, and mentor people affected by disabilities

- ensuring the widespread distribution, in usable formats, of practical scientific and technological information.

    o   This is accomplished by:
    o   Multiply disability effective churches

Though it may seem artificial, the point remains that there is a disconnect between the patient and the organizations meant to help the patient. As both my wife and I, transplants from Texas and Florida,

Alabama then residences in Alabama, Texas, and Virginia, this author can attest there is a wildly different purview of expertise and general knowledge of assistance for the brain-injured individual. In conjunction with the NIDILRR and Joni and Friends categorization, the classification of the person is tantamount. To properly classify the patient, the medical community also developed the Rankin Scale for Neurologic Disability. This scale determines the patient's response to external stimuli to diagnose neurological urgency in the emergency room situation. The scale showcases the medical worker's diagnosis of interaction with the individual.

The question that arises to the author's mind is what level can be considered no longer viable as a human individual? With this statement, the author would like to advocate as a previously bed-ridden, unconscious, medically induced coma, and stroke survivor from a brain bleed for greater research to occur. Insofar as it is financially viable, persons in a vegetative or comatose state would be best served by life support, as the author was one who survived on such equipment! Funding for the NIMH (National Institute for Mental Health) is needed to go into finding better options for those of us who may not display typical behavior but show life nevertheless! To bring this section to a close, there must be a balancing act initiated between the federal wing of the government, possibly the National Institute of Mental Health, and the private sector such as the churches, civic organizations, and other volunteer positions to accept the slack of treating these persons.

Currently, a person with a brain injury who is released from hospital care is expected to be "well" and therefore is expected to serve as a functioning individual in a society devoid of any helps or aids. Unfortunately for many, this is precisely the point at which suicide, depression, and forsakenness take hold. May it never be so again! Hopefully, the church in conjunction with the points of introduction (Veterans Administration, Social Security, the Brain Injury Association of America, etc.) can bridge the gap between the brain injured, the medical personnel, and the local churches and civic organizations to smooth the transition to a new homelife.

The Beggar

The rich man in the biblical account was virtually oblivious to the existence of the poor person. In this author's opinion, the notice of the beggar in first century Israel is a close parallel to the recognition of the brain-injured of today. As the appropriate classification of brain injury is still in a relative state of infancy, further advocacy on the part of the brain injured needs to be done. Having one to stand with you often provides more of a feeling of solidarity and support than any amount of funding or political action could warrant! The primary difficulty with this, however, is that most persons with this condition cannot enumerate their plight much less fight for it! The concern for the whole community of persons affected by brain trauma is the need for someone to act as a voice for the brain-injured, who can list and fight for their needs, their wants, and their place in society. Utilizing classification tools of today possibly can serve as a means of discovering the needs and a voice for the brain injured.

The more precise Rankin Scale is provided as well, to grant information to multiple parties as to the patient's quick determination for triage. Developed for quick triage, the Rankin rating helps ER nurses quickly triage persons by both the severity of pain they are displaying and the consciousness they are exhibiting. The modified Rankin Scale (mRS) is used to measure the degree of disability in patients who have had a stroke, as follows:

Modified Rankin Scale with stroke customization	Rating
No symptoms at all	0
No significant disability despite symptoms; able to carry out all usual duties and activities	1
Slight disability; unable to carry out all previous activities, but able to look after own affairs without assistance	2
Moderate disability; requiring some help, but able to walk without assistance	3
Moderately severe disability; unable to walk without assistance and unable to attend to own bodily needs without assistance	4
Severe disability; bedridden, incontinent, and requiring constant nursing care and attention	5
Dead	6

*Chart above attributed to (Christensen, 2014)

The classifications are merely a means of quick triage to the appropriate medical team. If the patient literally has only minutes before permanent debilitating brain injury happens, the triage team may be remiss to summon the attending neurosurgeon in time. This is precisely why a quicker triage mechanism for brain injury may be beneficial to the smaller community hospital.

For an example of this employ, consider the classification of a traditional brain hemorrhage in the admission of a patient to an ER. Typically, the patient would be admitted into the ER, triaged to the attending surgeon, and then on to the attending neurosurgeon for treatment of a traumatic brain injury. Yet with someone who has undergone an AVM rupture, the cerebral deficiency has not been caused by an impact to the skull.

As such, the treatment of this condition is immediately more complicated. Now also consider for the attending surgeon in an emergency room, his focus is largely on brain impact caused by accidents. Further, "Particularly young children seem to bear a higher risk for haemorrhage from their AVM. Treatment of paediatric AVMs can be achieved safely in experienced hands with a high rate of complete elimination and good clinical outcome" (Steina et al., January 2018). Yet, "we identified 238 patients with a mean follow-up period of 13.5 years (range, 1 month–53.1 years.) The average annual risk of hemorrhage from AVMs was 2.4%. Furthermore, "according to this long-term follow-up study, AVMs with previous rupture and large size, as well as with infratentorial and deep locations have the highest risk of subsequent hemorrhage. This risk is highest during the first few years after diagnosis but remains significant for decades" (Juha A. Hernesniemi, Natural History of Brain Arteriovenous Malformations: A Long-Term Follow-Up Study of Risk of Hemorrhage in 238 Patients, 1 November 2008). As this author reads the study, the risk of rebleed is lifelong, potentially increasing, and until properly dealt with (eradicated), contains a recurrence risk for the duration of the patient's life.

If one were to consider, for instance, a child who has impacted his cranium from a fall, what would be the process of treatment? First the patient would be admitted to the ER. Following triage, the attending physician would likely page the resident neurosurgeon to investigate further the impact on the patient's skull. For the particular instance, the situation would be well in hand, and the treatment by the doctors, nurses, and ER staff would remedy the situation. The patient would later be admitted to a room for monitoring and released.

Now we take the same occasion with an eighteen-year-old college student who had suddenly passed out while watching a movie in his dorm with friends. The patient was unconscious at the time that the medical personnel picked him up from his dorm room. Thoughts of a possible drug overdose, a common collegiate misdeed, likely shuffle through the minds of the treatment personnel. Yet with each minute, the patient's vitals are dropping, with his ICP, or intracranial pressure, climbing. This has happened, as this was the author's story. For my situation, the ICP was not relieved until two holes were drilled into my skull to relieve the pressure. By this time, initial brain damage had already probably occurred, as elevated brain pressure causes damage to the organ integrity of the brain! What would have happened if from the initial triage of the patient, the ICP levels were checked as an initial check-in process? In how many other instances are persons subjected to mis-triage simply because the treatment personnel are not aware of this small possibility of change with the patients' treatment? It is with this introduction to a possible fine-tuning of the medical triage process that we may be able to change the very future of some of the patients admitted into the ERs of tomorrow.

The Other Sister

Before we venture too deep into the treatment specifics, let us draw back to this author's personal and not professional experience. Recalling a fictional plot from a movie from my growing up—*The Other Sister*—it dealt with the awkward and unsettling behavior of someone who has limited cognitive reasoning ability. The film served as a reminder to the public that love seldom fits into a pristine box. Without spoiling the film, essentially the question the viewer is left with after seeing the film is what is love? The film chronicles love as it exists between two characters—Carla and Daniel. In the climax of the film, the trouble exists that the general public neither gets nor wants to get involved in the awkwardness that is love between mentally challenged individuals. To be certain, the author is not trying to use a movie example as a test proof positive case showing the public doesn't understand mental and neurocognitive challenges. What the author does wish to show is specifically that the public often does not show any true kindness or compassion as it misses so much of the general awareness that is found in a brain-injured person.

To turn the page to a more reliable example, let us turn to the Christian scriptures in Luke 16:19–31 and consider the cold and calculating rich man and Lazarus. Lazarus is spoken of to the positive in all occurrences of the scriptures. Moreover, his troubles are shown by written record as part of God's use as an example of how one is to live with unfortunate earthly circumstances. Though you are not given what precisely befell him, we are told that Lazarus and the rich man passed from this earth to the next eternal state. Now for the rich man, who lived a luxurious lifestyle on this side of eternity with no thought of eternal destination of Lazarus. For that matter, the rich man showed little concern for anything other than his own levity and comfort.

Contrast the rich man's life with that of Lazarus, who certainly had a rougher life. As Lazarus passed into eternity as well, Lazarus was comforted because of his relationship with the Savior. As the rich man passed into eternity, his immediate existence went from luxury to terror. Even in Hades, we are told in Luke 16:24–31:

> And he cried out and said, "Father Abraham, have mercy on me, and send Lazarus so that he may dip the tip of his finger in water and cool off my tongue, for I am in agony in this flame." But Abraham said, "Child, remember that during your life you received your good things, and likewise Lazarus bad things; but now he is being comforted here, and you are in agony. And besides all this, between us and you there is a great chasm fixed, so that those who wish to come over from here to you will not be able, and *that* none may cross over from there to us." And he said, "Then I beg you, father, that you send him to my father's house—for I have five brothers—in order that he may warn them, so that they will not also come to this place of torment." But Abraham said, "They have Moses and the Prophets; let them hear them." But he said, "No, father Abraham, but if someone goes to them from

the dead, they will repent!" But he said to him, "If they do not listen to Moses and the Prophets, they will not be persuaded even if someone rises from the dead."

The reason for this shift was at its base simplistic. Lazarus had trusted in the Savior Jesus Christ for his well-being and thus was ushered into his eternal rest and refuge. The rich man had trusted in his wealth and posterity to protect him for its endurance. For the rich man, the opulence was burned up in the unquenchable fire that is reserved for the sons of disobedience as they rejected the Savior Jesus Christ.

For a lesser but more contemporary example beside biblical text, consider again a Hollywood example that came out several years ago entitled *The Other Sister*. In the film, the antagonist is played by Elizabeth Tate. The protagonist is portrayed by Juliette Lewis, who is acting as the mentally handicapped sister. The story calls into question what love effectively is. More precisely, it attempts to pin down that quality of human emotion that we quantify or qualify as love.

The movie can be summed up in the statement of the leading character, Ms. Carla Tate: "No matter how long I wait I can't be a painter, and I can't play tennis, and I'm not an artist. But I know how to do something, and I can love" (*The Other Sister*, IMDb). Before the reader thinks this book is advocating the political leanings of the movie or actors and actresses, that is not the intent. The use of this film is merely to point out the need for humanity to feel, express, and enjoy love. Perhaps this was the same problem that the rich man had as well. We are only told that in the afterlife, he pleaded with Lazarus to extend the same charity that he withheld. Only problem being that once the curtain of death has closed on them both, no further help can be offered.

The similarities between Jesus's love for Lazarus and Carla's untethered love is depicted as absurd, embarrassing, uncensored, and, at times, unrestrained. It *looks* awkward to us. It *feels* unfamiliar, but at the same time, what it looks, and feels is seldom what it *is*. In other words, as the writer of Colossians admonished, "Therefore no one is to act as your judge in regard to food or drink or in respect to a festival or a new moon or a Sabbath day—things which are a mere shadow of what is to come; but the substance belongs to Christ."[10] Let's break it down further to today.

Again, in *The Other Sister*, one of the most perfunctory turning points in the movie is the wedding of Carla and her new husband, Daniel. During the scene with the exchanging of the vows, Carla and Daniel, in their haste to get hitched, have a less than normal wedding. In their excitement to go through the steps of a formal ceremony, the procedures and processes of a normal wedding decorum are trampled as both Carla and Daniel are largely working through the perceived expectations of the attendees rather than their love for one another. At the point of exchanging vows, the couple's devotion to one another is expressed, and it becomes a beautiful, memorable mien. Then as they exit the church, Daniel has a surprise gift of a local marching band performing in the street. "This is my present for my bride," Daniel exclaims. Why would such an odd and unusual token be gifted? It was to express Daniel's unique, unselfish, unashamed, and certainly unorthodox love for the one to whom he has pledged his life. Yet Daniel's gift is largely misunderstood by most persons attending.

Now for Christ and Lazarus, Christ comes to the tomb of Lazarus and weeps after Lazarus passes away. We see the emotion of Christ as He was told of the death of Lazarus a few verses before. The shortest verse in the entirety of scripture is found here in John 11:35: "Jesus wept." But Christ is not weeping only because He was unable to converse with Lazarus any longer. Moreover, I believe that Jesus wasn't even crying on account of Lazarus dying alone. In the surrounding text we see some of the crowd that gathered with Martha to mourn, saying effectively, "Could not this man, who opened the eyes because of the unbelief of the Jews and those surrounding the family of Lazarus, open everyone else's?" Yet just as Daniel confessed his love for his bride time and again, seeking out unique ways of telling her exactly who she was in his eyes, so is Christ bellowing His love for His bride for all to hear. "As has just been said: 'Today, if you hear his voice, do not harden your hearts as you did in the rebellion'" (Hebrews 3:15). Therefore, let me ask more precisely, could not this Man change your malady into a victory?

To return to the present day, it is this author's belief there is some good news in the diagnosis of ICR, or intracranial rupture. Within children, "With the advances of neuroimaging, the diagnosis of cerebrovascular disease (CVD) is made relatively easy and many lesions are detected before producing symptoms" (Abu-Arafek & Mack, 2017). Thus, much like

MALFORMATION

Lazarus and the treatment of a more lasting issue of His eternal rest rather than just simply treating the symptoms, we arrive at a more holistic treatment selection. This would include a new section of treatment for the brain-injured. And as we do so we can then remember the words of Carla from the movie, "No matter how long I wait, I can't be a painter, and I can't play tennis, and I'm not an artist. But I know how to do something, and I can love" (Marshall, 1999). Perhaps in the treatment of those diagnosed with an aneurysm or AVM, society could merely recognize their existence in love, to validate their being and enumerate their plight.

CHAPTER 3

Direction?

◇◇◇◇◇

Thus far we've seen the need to define the disorder of AVM such that it can be classified and dealt with. We've seen that the condition of cerebral AVM is different from a traditional TBI because it occurs from within the cranium rather than being brought on the individual from impact or injury. We then looked at reintroducing the AVM condition to the general populace by including testing for AVM in a general triage setting. From there, we moved to view the cost of AVM and the estimated change this would create in modern medicine in the United States. Then we looked at the life expectancy adjustment made to the lives of survivors. Finally, we saw the weight and impact of recognizing that we effectively were wrong about labeling brain injury as only having a mild or moderate effect on a person's life. Instead, it has both a permanent and devastating impact on the person's life and the lives of those who take care of the injured person. Let's review the traditional treatment options and as such, their impact on the general populace. For this section, the author will be using his own records to a large extent due to HIPAA (Health Insurance Portability and Accountability Act), and the Social Security filing for public disclosure of medical records is protected.

Medical Research Effects

As of 2018, the US Department of Health and Human Services has $9 million dedicated to research and support for the traumatic brain injury wing of the disability filings for the US government. While it is beneficial that money is allocated for its study, it is worth noting that no increase had been given to this portion of the budget since 2015.[15](Administration for Community Living (ACL), 2018, US Department of Health and Human Services.) While $9 million is helpful for survivors, considering that the estimated cost of brain injuries for the lifetime collectively of the individual per a study in 1985, some 30 years later is approximately $37.8 billion, $9 million is definitely not enough. The cost for medical procedures, job loss, and care is estimated to be in the hundreds of thousands of dollars per patient based on a study done by MJ Ashley: "Direct costs range from $67,504 to $114,231 per patient" (Humphreys I, 2013). For the average family of four in Virginia, the lifetime cost of a traumatic brain injury in no way amounts to the wages earned. "According to the Census ACS 1-year survey, the median household income for Virginia was $68,114 in 2016" (Department of Numbers, 2017). For those who wish to hold off the mathematics exercise, that comes to the best-case scenario of a person being confined to his or her home, bereft of employment, and applying for Social Security, and looking at doctor and patient bills of $67,504 at a minimum! However, due to relative institutional ignorance of this problem, the patient is left with a long wait and many conversations that both the patient, Social Security workers, and other personnel seem unfamiliar with, or in the worst case, unwilling to have.

Social Security Filing Effects

A more complete approach to treatment including church and parachurch organizations would likely be the best option. As the United States was originally created largely by Christian men and women, however, they endeavored to establish the Social Security government organization. In response to service in the Civil War, "The Civil War Pension program began shortly after the start of the War, with the first legislation in 1862 providing for benefits linked to disabilities 'incurred as a direct consequence of … military duty.'" (United States Government, 2018) Now before we deal with Social Security's founding, we must trace the history of the system briefly to see the need for its intervention at this juncture.

---

[15] https://www.hhs.gov/about/budget/fy2017/budget-in-brief/acl/index.html#f2.

MALFORMATION

Organizational History of SSA

Committee on Economic Security (1934)

This committee was established by President Roosevelt in June 1934 (Executive Order No. 6757) to develop a comprehensive social insurance system covering all major personal economic hazards with a special emphasis on unemployment and old age insurance. The committee's legislative recommendations were presented to the president in January 1935 and introduced to Congress for consideration shortly thereafter. A compromise Social Security Bill was signed by the President on August 14, 1935.

Social Security Board (1935)

A three-member board was established to administer the Social Security Act. It was responsible for old age insurance, unemployment compensation, and public assistance titles of the Social Security Act. The chairman of the board reported directly to the president until July 1939 when the board was placed organizationally under the newly established Federal Security Agency. The original Social Security Board consisted of the three-member board, an executive director, three operating bureaus, five service bureaus and offices, and twelve regional offices.

Birth of the Bureaus (1935)

The Bureau of Federal Old-Age Benefits, renamed the Bureau of Old-Age Insurance (BOAI) in 1937, was created in December 1935 and was the forerunner of today's Social Security Administration. The bureau was responsible for Title II of the Social Security Act, and its functions included: the maintenance of wage records;

supervision of field offices; examination and approval of claims, including related claims functions (for certification of payments recovery of excess payments, and hearing and deciding appealed cases); and the making of actuarial estimates.

First Field Offices (1936)

It was apparent from the beginning that the scope of the Title II program (old age benefits) would require considerable decentralization. The first step in this direction was the establishment of twelve regional offices attached to the Social Security Board with regional representatives for each program. The Bureau of Old Age Insurance concurrently began to establish field offices in October 1936 for public contact and one hundred were in operation by February 1937.

President's Reorganization Plan No. 1 (1939)

This established the Federal Security Agency (FSA), and the Social Security Board became a part of that agency. The FSA also administered the programs of the US Public Health Service, Office of Education, National Youth Administration, and Civilian Conservation Corps. The US Employment Service and the Bureau of Unemployment Compensation were consolidated into the Bureau of Employment Security under the Social Security Board. The only administrative change was the transfer of the general counsel and personnel functions to a central function under the FSA administrator. The FSA administrator permitted the Social Security Board to continue its program in an independent manner. The Bureau of Old Age Insurance was renamed "Bureau of Old-Age and Survivors Insurance" (BOASI) when the president signed the amendments to Title II of the Social Security Act on August 10, 1939, which provided benefits for dependents and survivors of insured workers, and made other major changes. In 1940, a Control Division was added to handle the increased claims load resulting from the 1939 amendments. Finally, a Training Section was established in the Director's Office to take over the complete training program, a part of which had previously been handled by the Social Security Board.

Establishment of Area Offices (Payment Centers) (1942)

Because of the wartime scarcity of space in Washington and a marked increase in the benefit rolls, the central offices of the Bureau of Old Age and Survivors' Insurance were moved to Baltimore in 1942. At the same time area offices were opened in Philadelphia, New York, Chicago, San Francisco, and New Orleans for the certification and recertification of claims. The Control Division was replaced by the Claims Control Division and the old Claims Division by the Claims Policy Division. The adjudication of claims was shifted to the field offices, leaving the responsibility for claims review in the Claims Control Division and its area offices.

Establishment of Social Security Administration (1946)

The president's reorganization Plan No. 2, effective in July 1946, abolished the Social Security Board and placed its functions under the newly established Social Security Administration (still under FSA.) The FSA administrator established the position of commissioner to head the Social Security Administration (SSA.) Several administrative functions (i.e., personnel, procurement, information services, etc.) from the Social Security Board were incorporated into SSA at this time.

Changes in Regional Offices (1948)

In August 1948, following the transfer of the regional offices from the Social Security Administration to the Federal Security Administration, new SSA regions were established. Also in 1948, a Division of Management Planning and Services was created within the Bureau of Old Age and Survivors Insurance to address problems created because of tremendous growth in the size of the bureau.

Department of Health, Education and Welfare Established (1953)

The Federal Security Agency was abolished and its functions transferred to the new Department of Health, Education and Welfare (HEW.) The Bureau of Federal Credit Unions was transferred to the Social Security Administration, and the commissioner's position was designated as a presidential appointee requiring Senate confirmation.

Establishment of Division of Disability Operations (1954)

A modified (disability) freeze program, the precursor of the present disability program, was enacted as a part of the 1954 amendments. The Division of Disability Operations was founded to provide unified program, policy, procedural, and operational leadership for this new program.

Division of Social Security in Two Parts (1963)

On January 28, 1963, a reorganization in HEW retained the old-age, survivors, and disability program functions in the Social Security Administration and established a new Welfare Administration to administer five federal-state programs (the Children's Bureau, Bureau of Family Services, the Special Staff on Aging, and the Juvenile Delinquency and Youth Development Staff.) The Bureau of Hearings and Appeals, the Office of the Actuary, and the Division of Program Research continued as units of SSA. The Bureau of Federal Credit Unions was still affiliated with SSA but only for administrative support. This split effectively made the old BOASI and other legislated social insurance programs into the modern-day Social Security Administration.

Program Bureaus Established (1965)

The 1965 amendments not only increased the scope and complexity of OASI and DI programs but established the Health Insurance Program (Title XVIII), which became known as Medicare. A reorganization was effected which established four program bureaus (Retirement and Survivors Insurance, Disability Insurance, Health Insurance, and Federal Credit Unions.) A centralized recordkeeping operation, the Bureau of Data Processing and Accounts, was established to service all programs as well as a single field organization. Five functional staff units with agencywide responsibility for program evaluation and planning, actuarial functions, public affairs, management and research functions were also established. Also at this time, the regional presence was enhanced by the establishment of the ten regional commissioners who served as the commissioner's representatives and were responsible for evaluating and coordinating the agency operations. It is notable that the regional commissioners were not delegated "line authority," so they might retain their objectivity and detachment.

Bureau of Supplemental Security Income (SSI) Established (1973)

The 1972 amendments created the Supplementary Security Income (SSI) program and a new bureau was established in 1973. There remained only four program bureaus, however, for the Bureau of Federal Credit Unions left the agency in March 1970.

1975 Reorganization of SSA

The commissioner of Social Security announced a reorganization of the agency in January 1975. The new organization significantly reduced the span of control of the commissioner by consolidating eleven functions into only five functions and by placing the regional commissioners under an associate commissioner for Program Operations. The regional commissioners did receive line authority (through the associate commissioner for Program Operations) at this time for all cash benefit operations. Significant changes included: (1) the establishment of four associate commissioners for Operations, Program Policy and Planning, External Affairs and Management, and Administration; (2) creation of a new policy and regulation-making organization; (3) creation of a commissioner-level organization dedicated to the long-range improvement of SSA's automated systems; and (4) the creation of a centralized program evaluation and quality assurance program.

HEW Reorganization (1977)

This reorganization established the Health Care Financing Administration (HCFA) and abolished the Social and Rehabilitation Service (SRS.) HCFA received Medicare (Bureau of Health Insurance) from SSA, which had implemented and run the program since 1965. SSA received the responsibility for the Aid to Families with Dependent Children (AFDC) and the commissioner of SSA became the ex-officio director of the HEW Office of Child Support Enforcement (OCSE).

Some policy functions also transferred to HCFA but other functions (i.e., computer support and field office services) continued to be performed by SSA. SSA also received cash assistance functions from SRS, which encompassed Cuban and Indochinese refugee programs and the US Repatriate Programs.

Functional Reorganization of SSA (1979)

A newly appointed commissioner of Social Security announced a reorganization along functional lines. The intended results were to: (1) improve the communications, policy development, and decision-making processes; (2) eliminate duplication; (3) elevate the field organization back into the mainstream of headquarters activities; and (4) consolidate systems functions. Two deputies were created, one for operations and the other for program policy issues. An Executive Secretariat was created to enhance communications and ten associate commissioners along functional lines "to provide program direction and leadership." This reorganization was followed by a reorganization for the field structure under the regional commissioners. Unlike the 1975 reorganization, which was never fully implemented, it was completed in less than a year.

Organizational Realignments of SSA (1980–83)

Fine-tuning by succeeding commissioners, who found the span of control too broad under the 1979 reorganization, was implemented over the next four years. Efforts to modify the organization to make it more responsive to changing mission requirements resulted in the following changes: (1) the consolidation of the public information and governmental affairs functions; (2) the abolishment of the associate commissioner for Operating Policy and Procedures; (3) the establishment of four deputy commissioners including one for systems and another for management and assessment; and (4) the creation of six new associate commissioners, including two for systems requirements and integration functions; three for the RSI, SSI, and DI programs, and one for the field.

—Taken from https://www.ssa.gov/history/orghist.html

The Civil War Pension program began shortly after the start of the War, with the first legislation in 1862 providing for benefits linked to disabilities "incurred as a direct consequence of. . .military duty." Widows and orphans could receive pensions equal in amount to that which would have been payable to their deceased solider if he had been disabled. In 1890 the link with service-connected disability was broken, and any disabled Civil War veteran qualified for benefits. In 1906, old-age was made a sufficient qualification for benefits. So that by 1910, Civil War veterans and their survivors enjoyed a program of disability, survivors and old-age benefits similar in some ways to the later Social Security programs. By 1910, over 90% of the remaining Civil War veterans were receiving benefits under this program, although they constituted barely .6% of the total U.S. population of that era. Civil War pensions were also an asset that attracted young wives to elderly veterans whose pensions they could inherit as the widow of a war veteran. Indeed, there were still surviving widows of Civil War veterans receiving Civil War pensions as late as 1999! (United States of America, 2018)

From the brief history above, you can see the struggle to create a system within the government by the people and for the people that would care for the people who cannot care for themselves alone. This was carried to further realization through Social

MALFORMATION

Security from the Civil War pension program in 1862. For a more contemporary example, veterans who have returned from the Iraq/Afghanistan conflicts are recorded as from the U.S. Department of Veteran's Affairs, We will return to this subject in the next section. First, however, we must broach the topic of Social Security. The Social Security Administration was originally to provide benefits to the disabled. With the legacy of the Social Security Administrations being traced back to Civil War days, the question then remains for the reader today as to how to leverage this program to aid themselves. Thankfully, the determination process has been streamlined in the Social Security office's Blue Book. Please see the appendix: "Redemption" for more information on various filing options for Social Security.

Filing for disability benefits within Social Security in the state of Virginia is precipitated by the patient or patient's caretaker contacting the Social Security office. They can be reached online at www.ssa.gov or by contacting 1-800-772-1213 (TTY 1-800-325-0778.) Alternatively, you may contact your local DARS (Department of Aging and Rehabilitative Services) agent for Virginia residents. Following this, you will potentially be assigned a caseworker who will then obtain the information to further direct you to employment services, disability, and other government programs available. The reason for this entire agency is the betterment and facilitation of individuals with a secure living despite having challenging circumstances befalling them. For further information regarding this program or those available in your state, see www.ssa.gov and https://secure.ssa.gov/ICON/main.jsp to locate your local office. Further, the Ticket to Work program is a government program to aid disabled persons with the option to work. More information can be found at https://choosework.ssa.gov/mycall/. Overall, your local Social Security office will have the best options for filing for and obtaining information regarding disability.

One final item of note, per the Social Security Blue Book's definition, to be included, you must display a minimum of two of the four criteria below:

"11.18 Traumatic brain injury, characterized by A or B:

A. Disorganization of motor function in two extremities (see 11.00D1), resulting in an extreme limitation (see 11.00D2) in the ability to stand up from a seated position, balance while standing or walking, or use the upper extremities, persisting for at least 3 consecutive months after the injury.

or

B. Marked limitation (see 11.00G2) in physical functioning (see 11.00G3a), and in one of the following areas of mental functioning, persisting for at least 3 consecutive months after the injury:

1. Understanding, remembering, or applying information (see 11.00G3b(i)); or
2. Interacting with others (see 11.00G3b(ii)); or
3. Concentrating, persisting, or maintaining pace (see 11.00G3b(iii)); or
4. Adapting or managing oneself (see 11.00G3b(iv).)." (Social Security Administration, 2018)

While the overall application process and audit for applicants is straightforward, many opt for legal representation to handle this portion of the claim. This can be a stressful and time- consuming process collecting doctor's data to add to the application. Therefore, it is advisable to consider the time constraints within this process. Typically, this process can take months to even years. Based on the administration's guidelines, a five-step determination process is utilized to determine your eligibility for Social Security:

1. Are you working? If you're working and your earnings average more than a certain amount each month, we generally won't consider you to be disabled. The amount changes each year. For the current figure, see the annual Update (Publication No. 05-10003.) If you're not working,

or your monthly earnings average to the current amount or less, the state agency then looks at your medical condition.

2. Is your medical condition "severe"? For you to be considered to have a disability by Social Security's definition, your medical condition must significantly limit your ability to do basic work activities—such as lifting, standing, walking, sitting, and remembering—for at least 12 months. If your medical condition isn't severe, we won't consider you to be disabled. If your condition is severe, we proceed to step three.

3. Does your impairment(s) meet or medically equal a listing? Our list of impairments (the listings) describes medical conditions that we consider severe enough to prevent a person from completing substantial gainful activity, regardless of age, education, or work experience. If your medical condition (or combination of medical conditions) isn't on this list, the state agency looks to see if your condition is as severe as a condition on the list. If the severity of your medical condition meets or equals the severity of a listed impairment, the state agency will decide that you have a qualifying disability. If the severity of your condition doesn't meet or equal the severity level of a listed impairment, the state agency goes on to step four.[8]

4. Can you do the work you did before? At this step, we decide if your medical impairment(s) prevents you from performing any of your past work. If it doesn't, we'll decide you don't have a qualifying disability. If it does, we'll proceed to step four.

5. Can you do any other type of work? If you can't do the work you did in the past, we look to see if there's other work you can do despite your impairment(s.) We consider your age, education, past work experience, and any skills you may have that could be used to do other work. If you can't do other work, we'll decide that you're disabled. If you can do other work, we'll decide that you don't have a qualifying disability"[16]

If you decide to take the next step toward disability filing, please understand, being disabled does not make you disabled for God. Rather, it effectively is *enabling* for His purposes in a whole new world of encouragement and inspiration to others! There are many who are utilized greatly because of their disability. To overview this process, in the

[16] https://www.ssa.gov/pubs/EN-05-10029.pdf Disability Benefits.

next chapter we will go through just a sampling of worldwide, statewide, and citywide organizations that may be available to you now that you are disabled. As this author has been counseled, he now passes on to you, the determination of disability is only one of ability to perform the normative work-related tasks. This does not impede your ability to do anything. It only hones your selection of tasks you can do. Rather than seeing your disability determination as a conquest or defeat, it is this author's challenge to inquire of the Lord what you *can* do after being freed from the normal eight to five routine. Some suggestions for this can be found in the appendix: "Redemptive Workers" section of this volume.

CHAPTER 3.5

Redirection

———————————⟡———————————

Perhaps at this juncture you need to sit a moment and consider all that has taken place. Not being familiar with your specific case, I may have brought up many questions that will not be answered in this volume. Though intended to serve as a guidebook for brain injury, my story is only one of thousands, as is yours. Truly the only fact that can be promised is that your case will not be like my own! Again, this narrative is not intended to guide you to do things exactly as I have. It may be guiding you to do quite the opposite! Instead, my story is meant to merely share my experience, along with the hard lessons that have been learned along the way. Often, I have told others that mistakes are memories. What you do with those memories can be used by the Lord if yielded to Him to help others. My story is also intended to help form in your mind the right questions to ask in response to the scope of your life thus far.

My life, as my wife will tell you, is an open book before God and the world. As such, I believe it would be beneficial now to tell two different sections of what happened in my life to direct me to this point. First is the story of my conversion to Christianity that led through the brain bleed, which led to meeting my wife and fathering the children we now have. This story began in high school in New Brockton, Alabama. I was a successful high school student and a straight A honor roll recipient. Coupled with being a business owner partner with my friend Travis and cofounder of Practically Perfect Computers, I thought I had my life planned out. The only omission in my life was the only One that matters for eternity, that of following my Savior Jesus Christ.

On the beach

I remember a summer in the late 1990s riding down with the youth group to Panama City Beach for our annual youth group's beach trip. Our youth minister at that time, Fox, told us to go out on the beach at night and pray by ourselves. I recall going to find a cool spot in the sand and commence praying. As odd as it sounds, I remember opening my prayer in the typical fashion as taught in Sunday school. However, instead of the peace of the beach and the cool of the night, this sudden terror overcame me, revealing essentially: "I don't know you." Now if you've ever been on the beach at night, you know sudden dread and terror doesn't usually equate with a cool summer night on the beach. Regardless, I remember running over to Fox (our youth minister) and confessing to him I needed to personally know this God who I had claimed to know since I was six.

In the belly

Now for the next number of years, there was a constant wavering between faithfulness to the tenets of Christianity and obedience to my flesh and failures. It reminds me, in retrospect, of the story of Pinocchio. Do you ever wonder what it would be like to be in the belly of a whale for a week? In 1940, Walt Disney dazzled audiences with *Pinocchio*, the story of a wooden puppet who granted a true life to an elderly cobbler. I'll spare you the details, but for the purpose of this book, there is a scene where Monstro, the aquatic beast from below, swallows Pinocchio, Geppetto, and Jiminy Cricket. During this interlude, the character has a brief time to overview his short life on earth, consider the value of the love of his caretaker, and confess his sorrows to Jiminy. Before long, but without spoiling the movie, Pinocchio makes it out on dry land.

Rewind a little further to back to around 793–753 BC to the true story of Jonah. This brief record likely was where Monstro's tale originated. Now if we turn in the Bible to the book of Jonah, we find the same thing— God's prophet swallowed by an aquatic beast! To the self-proclaimed biblical scholar, I realize that it was literally a דג or fish and that the current taxonomy of sea creatures doesn't have a beast large enough to swallow a man and preserve him whole. I'll leave the biblical scholars to wrestle with that one. What swallowed Jonah has little to do with why it swallowed Jonah. Moreover, the interesting subject to mention here is the direct correlation with the prophet Jonah's brief interchange with God. Taken from the biblical book of Jonah 2:8–10, we read:

> "Those who cling to worthless idols turn away from God's love for them. But I, with shouts of grateful praise, will sacrifice to you.
>
> What I have vowed I will make good.
>
> I will say, 'Salvation comes from the LORD.'
>
> And the LORD commanded the fish, and it vomited Jonah onto dry land."

This is hardly the introduction you want to levy when moving to a new town. Yet there is a dangerous if not deadly mistake being taught, preached, advised, and generally obeyed in culture today. The idea that in Disney's *Pinnochio,* Pinnochio's friendly cricket Jiminy Crickett sang:

> "If your heart is in your dream No request is too extreme When you wish upon a star As dreamers do
>
> Fate is kind." (Sharpsteen, 1940)

If you have been advised something along these lines from a wayward preacher or friend, allow me to be the first to apologize. Fate is not kind; dreamers can be forced back to slumber, and your request at times may be too extreme. This is the bad news. The better news is that your life is not normal, never will be normal, and can never be normal again. Isn't this exceptional news? Consider when you take this look at your life now, let me encourage you to view it as a wonderful gift. If you have been through brain trauma, you have been through one of the most severe, medically challenging, difficult situations imposed upon the body—and survived. You probably feel isolated, misunderstood, ignored, and a host of other negative emotions. Let this be an encouragement; you are loved by God and are a miracle in the making! Moreover, as you are tossed out, or better said tossed up, on the beach, there is a mountain on the horizon.

As C.S. Lewis penned in *Mere Christianity*: "A man who changed from having Bios (death) to having Zoe (life) would have gone through as big a change as a statue which changed from being a card stone to being a real man. We are the statues and there is a rumor going around the shop that some of us are someday going to come to life" (*Mere Christianity*, 1940, 159). As often is found in this life, "I lift up my eyes to the mountains— where does my help come from? My help comes from the Lord, the Maker of heaven and earth" (cf. Psalm 121:1–2). If you pit the words of Pinocchio, "Fate is kind" versus the words of Jonah: "What I have vowed I will make good. I will say, 'Salvation comes from the LORD,'" it would stand to reason we need to lift our eyes to Him and forget the puppet to call for help from on high. Let's turn briefly to the mountain on which I'm referring, to find this God Who calls for us to draw near.

On the mountains

In my own life, fast-forward some two to three years later following high school that God brought me low again after enrolling at Auburn University. Unfortunately, the rupture of an arteriovenous malformation, or AVM, in my brain caused me again to refocus my gaze. Diverted from Him because of college trappings and chasing the elusive dollar, I was at this time in 2000 a freshman at Auburn University, enrolled as a software engineer. It was approximately two weeks before final exams to become a sophomore. I remember having an A in calculus 3, a hard-fought battle to be sure, and physics as well. This time, I felt as though I was on a mountain. I felt as though I had climbed to the then heights of academic success. I thought I had scaled the cliffs of the financial aid system and stood there victoriously. Oh, if I had only recognized that at this time, just as the times before, Christ was preparing me for battle, not introducing me to a welcome party. Specifically, He was introducing me to a traveling party. My journey took an odd turn as I was studying for my calculus 3 test. I remember suddenly experiencing a tremendous headache. This was such a weighty trauma that I recall standing up in the dorm there at

MALFORMATION

Auburn, throwing up, passing out, and next waking up in the University of Alabama at Birmingham, some one-hundred-plus miles away.

For those not acquainted with the Christian Scriptures, God tends to lift us out of our comfort zone to place us in His provision. As Nahum prophesied to the next generation in Israel concerning Nineveh, rest, peace, and provision did not coincide with Nineveh's rebellion from God. Previously the people of Nineveh repented and turned at the preaching of Jonah. Now Nahum was written later to declare a message of judgment for the people of Israel because the next generation did not heed the Word of the Lord declared previously by Jonah.

1 The oracle of Nineveh. The book of the vision of Nahum the Elkoshite.

2 A jealous and avenging God is the LORD;

The LORD is avenging and wrathful.

The LORD takes vengeance on His adversaries, And He reserves wrath for His enemies.

3 The LORD is slow to anger and great in power,

And the LORD will by no means leave the guilty unpunished. In whirlwind and storm is His way,

And clouds are the dust beneath His feet.

4 He rebukes the sea and makes it dry; He dries up all the rivers.

Bashan and Carmel wither;

The blossoms of Lebanon wither.

5 Mountains quake because of Him And the hills dissolve;

Indeed the earth is upheaved by His presence, The world and all the inhabitants in it.

—Nahum 1:1–5

Nahum's aim was the same—the worship of the Christian God. Nahum's heritage was like Jonah, a Jewish worshiper of Jehovah God. Even Nahum's drive was the same—to see all peoples worship Jehovah God. Sadly, Nahum's prophesied outcome was completely different. Nahum's task was given after Jonah's preaching had waned from memory in Assyria. Perhaps because of the nation's leaders, perhaps because of the people's insistence on paving their own way, but the nation did not worship God in the days of Nahum.:

Jonah 3:10 "When God saw what they did and how they turned from their evil ways, He relented and did not bring on them the destruction he had threatened."	Nahum 3:19 "There is no relief for your breakdown, Your wound is incurable. All who hear about you will clap their hands over you, for on whom has not your evil passed continually?
Figure 20. Assyria's Nineveh repented approx. 760 BC	**Figure 19B. Assyria'sNineveh destroyed approx. 612 BC**
(BIBLE.CC TIMELINE, 2018)	**(LIVIUS.ORG, 2018)**

Do you understand what Jehovah God was saying to Israel about Nineveh? He is jealous, and as such, if you are not in Him and with Him, you are against Him. Furthermore, if you *think* you are with Him, I encourage you to know for sure you are with Him by His instruction: "By this we know that we love the children of God, when we love God and observe His commandments" (1 John 5:2).

Now for the mountain reference in Nahum 1, consider that the site of the Nineveh excavation lay within the Sinjar Mountains. Nineveh was a well-fortified city for its day, with excavations indicating its protection as the capital of the Assyrian empire, which predates the period of Christ. As described in the Old Testament book of Jonah, God through the reluctant prophet Jonah apparently saved a host of Assyrian persons to claim for Himself a people from every tribe and tongue (Jon. 3:5).

In lieu of this, what might you say regarding this redirection? If you read the brief book of Jonah in the Old Testament, it recounts the disinclined prophet Jonah and his arguing with God as to the value of sharing with *those* people. The irony of the story is that if Jonah had not been used by God to carry the message of salvation to a pagan people, you and I in a similar vein may not either as we are at best a hodgepodge of nations and people groups! As this author is Irish by heritage and not Jewish, someone thought enough of my people to share the good news with them. Akin to Jonah's admonition to share the message of the Jewish God with the pagan people of Ninevah, we are sent to share with those who haven't heard as well! Furthermore, you and I are to take his gospel of Jesus to others just as Jonah was carrying the good news of the Hebrew God to a pagan people who needed Him.

Bear in mind what has been learned from the writings excavated at the site of ancient Nineveh: "Some of these documents showed that Adadmilki or Adadšarru ("Adad the king") was actually the god to whom children, sometimes firstborn, were burned. C. W. Johns, who first published these documents, contended that "burning" is used here in the figurative sense, meaning dedication (Assyrian Deeds and Documents, 3 (1923), 345–6) (The Gale Group, 2008). The horrors of this people in their own pagan worship were largely educed by the belief that by appeasing Molech, the Assyrian deity, the wholesale cultural sacrifice would never occur.

Consider, however, the words of the prophet Jonah, who stated for three days in Nineveh's streets: "Yet forty days and Nineveh will be overthrown" (Jon. 3:4). The peculiar thing about this story in this author's mind is not that Nineveh repented, however. That Nineveh repented was a miracle to be sure, but unlike other cities in scripture that are largely punished and forgotten (see Sodom and Gomorrah), Jonah's targeted city Ninevah gets another whole book devoted to it, which does not end well. (Read Nahum, in the Old Testament for the rest of the story.) Still, in the close of Jonah 4:11 we see God say, "Should I not have compassion on Nineveh, the great city in which there are more than 120,000 persons who do not know the difference between their right and left hand, as well as many animals?" As Jonah pens these words, this author imagines Jonah pensively waiting for the destruction of Ninevah, with a breeze cooling the bothered prophet. This author wonders how often the church has found herself in the same position, sitting comfortably on the hillside when all the while we are meant to be effectively "in the trenches" sharing the good news of Christ with the lost and dying who will, without intervention from the Savior, die and burn in hell.

The Assyrian people were a ruthless collection of warriors. From one archeological find, we read: "I destroyed, I demolished, I burned. I took their warriors prisoner and impaled them on stakes before their cities. I flayed the nobles, as many as had rebelled, and spread their skins out on the piles [of dead corpses?]. Many of the captives I burned in a fire. Many I took alive; from some I cut off their hands to the wrists, from others I cut off their noses, ears, and fingers; I put out the eyes of many of the soldiers" (Time Frame 1500–600 BC, by Time-Life Books) "Assyrian War Bulletin (1000 B.C.)" Consider, the Ninevites were not the people any missionary would want to preach hope to without a divine admonition to do so. Yet it was this very group, that just a chapter after, in Jonah 3:5–10 God declares:

"Then the people of Nineveh believed in God; and they called a fast and put on sackcloth from the greatest to the least of them. When the word reached the king of Nineveh, he arose from his throne, laid aside his robe from him, covered himself with sackcloth and sat on the ashes. He issued a proclamation and it said, 'In Nineveh by the decree of the king and his nobles: Do not let man, beast, herd, or flock taste a thing. Do not let them eat or drink water.' 'But both man and beast must be covered with sackcloth; and let men call on God earnestly that each may turn from his wicked way and from the violence which is in his hands.' 'Who knows, God may turn and relent and withdraw His burning anger so that we will not perish.' When God saw their deeds, that they turned from their wicked way, then God relented concerning the calamity which He had declared He would bring upon them. And He did not do it" Jonah 3:5–10.

As you read these words, imagine this being penned from a prophet who sought to seek the Lord, serve Him diligently, and in Jonah's day, run after God to the fields to chase others with the good news of the gospel (see John 4:35) for today. Only, that wasn't necessarily the case with Jonah. His penchant for initial disobedience led to eventual repentance, but Jonah wasn't the only one who needed reminding of Whom was in charge. Just as the book of Jonah closes with Nineveh repenting and Jonah complaining, the book of Nahum opens and closes detailing the destruction coming to Assyria as a people and Nineveh as a capital. What should this indicate to you or me? That God through His mercy still stayed His wrath to have His Name placed somewhere among the peoples of that pagan nation by redeeming His chosen out of a violent and sinful people.

The problem with Jonah became a similar problem of Nahum as well. Nahum was Jonah's spiritual successor of sorts, prophesying some 150 years later. This time, though, Nahum's message of Nineveh to Israel was effectively, "That's it." Nineveh had survived long enough as a city to repent. They had been sent Jonah who was able to proclaim the hope of salvation. Many of them even repented. Yet now, they had a serious problem. Though a generation had changed, their governing philosophical ideology had not. Effectively as the prophet Jonah was echoing the declaration of Isaiah declared to Israel: "Because this people draw near with their words and honor Me with their lip service, but they remove their hearts far from Me, and their reverence for Me consists of tradition learned by rote" (Isa. 29:13). The spiritual progression of sorts feels akin to many of the countries of today. First spiritual revival by a national speaker or tragedy. Then spiritual decline as the years wane from said event. Finally, spiritual decay as the generation dies off.

One event that is ever fixed on the author's mind is that of September 11, 2001. My wife and I were each in our respective colleges, Dallas Baptist University and Howard Payne University. I recall walking into a public speaking class in the learning center to a group of students huddled around a television set. As I looked on the broadcast, it was a surreal event as we watched together the second airplane crash into the Twin Towers in New York City. No one in the class said anything that I can recall. Partially from shock, partially from terror, our teacher dismissed the class, and we all filtered off to our dorms. The campus was silent that evening as I'm sure the administration scrambled to decide how classes would proceed. The terror of that event led us collectively as a nation to enter a war in Afghanistan, Iraq, and nearby Yemen and others throughout the next twenty years. All of this stemmed from the terror of not knowing what would happen next. Sadly, some two thousand years prior, Jesus had prophesied precisely what would happen in Mark 13:7–10 in situations like this.

> When you hear of wars and rumors of wars, do not be frightened; *those things* must take place; but *that is* not yet the end. For nation will rise up against nation, and kingdom against kingdom; there will be earthquakes in various places; there will *also* be famines. These things are *merely* the beginning of birth pangs. But be on your guard; for they will deliver you to *the* courts, and you will be flogged in *the* synagogues, and you will stand before governors and kings for My sake, as a testimony to them. The gospel must first be preached to all the nations. (Emphasis added to draw attention to the calamities forthcoming.)

The view from the mountains of faith is lofty, clear, pristine, and at times out of touch with the people who are living their life day to day and paycheck to paycheck. For the believer in Jesus, you and I have a God-ordained mission to share the good news of Jesus. Not save people, for that is a process only accomplished by the work of Jesus. Yet the message must be proclaimed, and that is precisely where you and I come in!

Being trained in educational philosophy, this author would seek to remedy the situation through education. Though not the answer to all problems, for Jonah's case, I can see a disconnect between what was being preached and what was being done. To further illustrate, consider a possibly more relatable discussion down to the practical training of educational ideology found by Parkay, Hass, and Anctil for the United States: "The state's (Florida) 1987 English/Language Arts framework tried to overhaul reading instruction by installing curriculum meant to convey 'the magic of language' and 'touch students' living and stimulate their minds and hearts.'" (Parkay, Hass, and Anctil, 2010, 289) Ultimately conveyance of this magic language fell short of comprehension by the students. The problem with this mountaintop teaching was that it was never brought into the trenches where the students were at. A teacher who could relate the information in a middle school fashion was needed.

Though a grouping of students received this mountaintop teaching for a time, it was never installed as a permanent educational fixture. Therefore, the ultimate verdict was reached to compromise and return to a mixture of the old and the new educational practice. "A combination of phonics for beginners and good literature for all was best" (Parkay, Hass, and Anctil, 2010, 290). Now to relate to the Ninevites, their new ideology introduced by Jonah was certainly good, but it was not carried forward in teaching to the next generation. For the believer, always consider the importance of passing on the teaching from mountaintops to the respective valleys below.

For Nineveh initially, "When God saw their deeds, that they turned from their wicked way, then God relented concerning the calamity which He had declared He would bring upon them. And He did not do it" (Jon. 3:10). While the news of Jonah was good, Nahum, written some 150 years later to Israel records: "There is no relief for your breakdown, your wound is incurable. All who hear about you will clap their hands over you, for on whom has not your evil passed continually?" (Nah. 3:19, NASB, 1995). What happened? As this author would concur, there is not a singular nation of persons who are left out of the judgment of God because there is not one person on this earth who has sought to serve the Lord for the Lord's purpose in and of themselves. Yet in agreement with this statement, there is also not a group of persons who are left without the opportunity to accept the forgiveness and love of the Savior Jesus Christ! Do you know why the message of hope was not adopted and passed down? Nineveh rejected the permanent fix—the eternal Hope, Jesus. Just as Jonah and Nahum regarding Nineveh and Jerusalem, respectively. Christians today must proclaim both in their unique sphere of influence here and abroad: Jesus saves!

Christians must proclaim the gospel of Jesus Christ so that the gospel of Jesus will go forward into our respective fields! Perhaps the most difficult yet exciting prospect for me as a brain-injured person is that the doctors, nurses, and treatment specialists are certainly of a different prospectus of many of us (brain-injured). However, the message that the brain-injured has for the rest of the world is that Jesus still saves! Now you and I must gaze upon that point—to life post-injury, and, prayerfully, with an added new hope. To properly redirect, you must relearn how to exist, how to live, and how to thrive in this new mission of life (cf. Jonah 3:10).[17]

CHAPTER 4

Habilitation?

You may be familiar with rehabilitation. There is a general understanding of rehabilitation or rehab. But there is a missing part of our vernacular: simply using habilitation regularly. The simple definition of which is "to make fit."[18] While the doctors, nurses, and medical personnel can acclimate you to your new normal, this new normal is a fluid concept. For instance, in the author's life, he was employed roughly a year after the initial bleed into 2000. Further, he was able to work full time as both an IT worker for around fifteen years and a pastor for five years, until due to his multiple brain injuries, he was forced to quit his job. What do you do if your circumstances are similar? After counsel with colleagues, friends, and family, it was determined that the best option would be to apply for the Social Security Administration filing for disability. Now before misleading you into this process, this is difficult, arduous, exhausting, and mentally taxing. The Social Security workers are going to need your medical records pertinent to your condition. This will include records of doctor's visits, surgeries, medical device implants if included, tests run, and more. Additionally, you will be expected to have access to these records, as well as all treatment facilities in which you were treated. Frankly, it may prove too much for the family and survivor to do.

Also, one can apply for Social Security Disability only if you are disabled by the Social Security Administration standards. Now I would not pretend to be an expert in this field. I had to reapply as my first

---

[18] habilitation. (n.d..) *Dictionary.com Unabridged*. Retrieved January 4, 2018, from Dictionary.com website http://www.dictionary.com/browse/habilitation.

application was denied. Apparently, I was not disabled enough! Yet after then having my neurologist, neurosurgeon, vocational rehabilitation counselor and regular doctor all attest to the fact that I did indeed have prior brain injuries which prevented me from working, I was accepted. Yet being accepted on disability means that my life-long dream of making a big bank and living off the interest on some remote island in the pacific was a pipe dream! Better said, I was and is a realization that my life is not my own. As the Bible tells us "I have been crucified with Christ; and it is no longer I who live, but Christ lives in me; and the life which I now live in the flesh I live by faith in the Son of God, who loved me and gave Himself up for me (Gal. 2:20, NASB).

It can be extremely helpful to keep records and copies of all medical visits and expenses. Many times, the receipts for payment are kept online. For the medical records, a quick phone call to your medical provider can provide you with this information. If you were not aware that this information was needed, it may prove helpful to secure either a lawyer or a legal representative. Alternatively, for Virginia residents, contacting the Virginia Department for Aging and Rehabilitative Services can help expedite and coordinate the gathering of information for the Social Security office. For Virginia, the VADARS office can be located by contacting your regional office at:[19]

Office Name	Phone	City
Disability Determination Services Fairfax	(703) 934-7400	Fairfax
Disability Determination Services Roanoke	(540) 857-7748	Roanoke
Disability Determination Services Norfolk	(757) 466-4300	Norfolk
DRS Southwest District Office	(276) 679-2262	Abingdon
DRS Eastern District Office	(757) 686-4988	Portsmouth

Also, it may prove useful to secure a lawyer who is able to draw together all this data in chronological order to present it before the Social Security Administration. Consider as a section of your life introduction this brief section of text from the Social Security office:

---

[19] https://www.vadars.org/offices.aspx#Administrative, Virginia Department for Aging and Rehabilitative Services, Commonwealth of Virginia

TBI related impairment in function depends on the mechanisms of injury as well as the location and the extent of brain damage. TBI can result in a simple concussion with no impairment in functioning. Alternatively, TBI can result in a mild, moderate, or severe impairment or a devastating irrecoverable vegetative state. Fortunately, the vast majority of TBI cases are mild with limited permanent impairment in functioning. However, at least 20% of individuals sustain moderate to severe TBI which can result in long lasting and significant impairment in functioning, disability and inability to maintain a job. (Social Security Administration)

These individuals are most commonly young men (aged fifteen to twenty-four) with a lifetime of disability and employment limitations, requiring significant support from family and caretakers at a significant cost to society. The CDC estimated that "...lifetime costs can range from $600,000 to $1,870,000 to care for a survivor of severe TBI. The costs associated with caring for Iraq and Afghanistan soldiers who have sustained a TBI are estimated to reach $35 billion over the course of the soldiers' lifetime. Approximately 80,000 individuals develop long-term disability from TBI each year in the US" (MD & PhD, November 18, 2008).

Given this lengthy delay and archaic application process, securing legal representation may prove to be a beneficial purchase. Before that decision is made, however, please consider: "Curriculum-based advocacy training was not superior to a self-directed approach in improving Advocacy Behavior Rating Scale scores. A significant improvement in expression of an advocacy message was observed when intervention groups were combined" (Allen W. Brown, 2015). This the bad news. The good news is that some accommodations are available that may speed up this process while you wait. Of note, studies conducted on young patients show: "Yet, these study designs have to be weighted with caution, as infants 'are not small adults' (Journal of Canadian Academy of Child Adolescent Psychiatry. 2011 Nov; 20 (4): 265-276).

The maturing brain makes key-aspects of AVM characterization difficult to assess, as eloquent brain areas are characterized by a large plasticity in the young patient" (Further, "From our data we suggest that patients' age impacts the clinical presentation. Particularly young children seem to bear a higher risk for haemorrhage from their AVM. Treatment of paediatric AVMs can be achieved safely in experienced hands with a high rate of complete elimination and good clinical outcome" (Stein et al., "Cerebral arterio-venous malformations in the paediatric population: Angiographic characteristics, multimodal treatment strategies and outcome," January 2018).

Church visitation

While researching for this volume, in the course of time, a conversation came up after meeting with a local pastor regarding my disability. Besides the regular affirmation and encouragement offered, one item that stuck with this author was the admonition to consider this new station in life as an opportunity to serve the body of Christ. That seemed rather strange, but he explained that while many members are working their nine to five jobs, which excludes them from serving in any visitation or pastoral role of the church, yet the opportunity may arise that would enable the brain injured to serve as a regular visitation participant who can visit those who otherwise would be missed. If you find yourself bound to the wheelchair or at home, why not write letters or emails? One such service at our facility is that of a bereavement team, who write letters of encouragement or visit families of the community who have recently lost loved ones.

Hospital visitation

Predictably the survivor of the trauma is met with not only the frustration of physical rehabilitation, but in addition, his or her body does not obey the very things the mind tells it to do. This leads to a question: if one is unable to get his or her physical body to do what the mind is commanding, how does one master the spiritual realm? To this focus we will turn, because the core of rehabilitation is first recognizing the root cause of the disorder or disability. "The figures in parentheses are the percentage of people in the study who experienced this particular life event. Some may have had more than one of these experiences at the same time.

- Major life trauma such as a serious accident or abuse (36%)
- Drug or alcohol abuse (28%)
- Death in the family (25%)
- Financial problems (17%)
- Major illness (14%)
- Divorce (11%)
- Childbirth (11%)
- Depression (10%)
- Unemployment (8%)
- Pregnancy (3%)
- No identifiable preceding life event (36%)"[20]

Dr. Archibald Hart, a professional counselor who penned the volume *The Anxiety Cure*, states this regarding trauma and crises (Hart, 1999). Please understand, what I am *not* trying to do is minimize or delegitimize your condition. If you have experienced a brain injury, you have documented, felt, and permanent damage to your brain. What you *also* have, however, is a means of expressing that frustration, confusion, and continuing medical difficulties in a safe environment to doctors and fellow persons who are dealing with different struggles of their own. Brain injury survivors have the challenge of finding out which way was up and now having to find out which way is up, many times daily. They struggle with issues that no one else struggles with. Therefore, a few organizations need to be visited that may help the injured and family members in this journey.

One such example, from a more temporal perspective, is that of the cranial shunt that may have to be installed. For merely a cursory discussion, a study was conducted in 2012 of in-hospital VP shunt procedures done between 1998 and 2000. It was a brief study, conducted on only a small subset of the population. Nevertheless, as it was performed on the cranium, specifically regarding VP shunt, which is a device used to alleviate ICP or intercranial pressure, it bears mentioning. In the study, "Overall, 5955 admissions were analyzed (253 hospitals, 411 surgeons.) Mortality rates were lower at high-volume centers and for high-volume surgeons" (Edward R. Smith, May 2012). This means, of the centers in which there was a high volume of patients, a higher volume of patient deaths was seen. This would

[20] Adapted from Dr. Archibald Hart, *The Anxiety Cure*, 40.

constrain the doctors and nursing staff to more closely attend the initial attention to cerebral AVM patients merely for the purpose of triage. As the patient is correctly diagnosed, he or she can be moved on to the appropriate triage team for more effective treatment.

Congealed with a new proper triage, it is my belief that this offers the most hope, the most challenge, the most promise, and the most volatile challenge for pain in the life of the TBI patient. And please note, I said pain, not necessarily hope. The reason? The decision the survivor makes regarding his or her ultimate state is the subject of the next chapter, but please if nothing else, take the time to reread chapter 3. To set up the remainder of this chapter, let us consider a typical ball game. Whether baseball, football, soccer (or football2 for those from another culture than the author), or another competitive sport, what is definite is the opposing sides. Now for the context of living, me being a sports fan, let's look at this in terms of a good ol' fashioned baseball game.

Visitors

For the visiting team, let's assume that it is you and I. You are in unfamiliar territory. The touches, tastes, smells, and sounds are all foreign. There is no point of familiarity onto which you can grasp. Thus, to what or whom do you cling? As a believer, survivor, husband, and now a father, it is my encouragement to cling to Christ and to allow Him to guide you. There likely is at this interval others who are looking at you to see what you will do. For starters, I admonish you to look up. As the Bible states: "I will lift up my eyes to the mountains; From where shall my help come?"[18] This sounds stable enough. When answered, however, we read: "My help comes from the LORD, Who made heaven and earth." This is, again, a terrifying prospect because it means you will not know where the help will come from if you do not know Him. Conversely, the only guarantee to a believer is knowing Who the help comes from.

Before panic overtakes you, as a father myself I was reminded of the occasional look of terror that reached my daughters' eyes when they were learning to walk. They would struggle and stress to get up on two feet, then wobble over to me and collapse. Yet, without fail, before long they would tear off across the house merely weeks later because they had gained the confidence that led to increased mobility. This could be said of the visitor's side of the team. If a believer, you are not dealing with home court advantage. For a brain aneurysm survivor, the habilitation will be painful. You must learn to live in such a way with your new set of limitations. This is a daunting prospect. However, let me encourage you, if you are in Christ, you and I are "aliens and strangers"19 anyway! For anyone who would say they are home team, let me remind you, as a brain injury survivor, you were born with the disorder, but many of you did not have it fully come to realization until some traumatic incident. As such, at that point—your point of injury, your point of panic, your point of need—Christ is there with His arms outstretched to catch His child. In fact, you *could* see it as your point of entry into this exciting next chapter of your life!

The rules have changed, the teams may have swapped sides, but if you think about basketball or football, they do that anyway at halftime. One organization that has been incredibly helpful to my own family is that of TBIHope, available for free by the methods below:

By email: info@tbihopeandinspiration.com
By phone: 603-898-4540
By Facebook: https://www.facebook.com/tbihopeandinspiration/

Having written for the organization and spoken with David A. Grant, the administrator for this group, they are a fantastic nonprofit organization devoted specifically to the awareness of and devotion to the brain injured.

The converse of being an alien and stranger to this world is being a native. This is one instance in which we want to be extremely precise. To be a home player means that you are comfortable in this state. A home player would say, "Yes, I'm comfortable living in this manner, with these challenges, this cognition, this understanding of reality." If that is you, let us look at what is to come.

Per findings in a study completed in 2013, "nearly 3000 serious head trauma cases found that 52% of survivors (154/100,000 population) were moderate to severely disabled at 1-year" (Humphreys, Wood, Phillips, and Macey, 2013). If a sampling of three-thousand-plus persons finds that more than half of the survivors are on disability within one year, it would stand to reason that if you are beset with this calamity, it would be advisable to secure the appropriate personnel on your side sooner rather than later! It would be advantageous primarily as your health and mental well-being will decline as time and age progress. What can you expect? There are few predictable outcomes. As a point of reference, the author has experienced multiple cranial bleeds, with two occurring in 2000, one in 2010, and a possible microbleed in 2015. For those who trust in Christ, you can expect that He will be your strength and fortress during the battle and medical struggles. Remember, if you are a believer, heaven, not earth, is your home.

And just to be clear on the whole visitors schtick, because I believe it is extremely important to proclaim the truth and not fill your head with empty promises, it will be hard and get harder. As the apostle Paul said in 2 Corinthians 11:23–25:

"Are they servants of Christ?—I speak as if insane—I more so; in far more labors, in far more imprisonments, beaten times without number, often in danger of death. Five times I received from the Jews thirty-nine lashes. Three times I was beaten with rods, once I was stoned, three times I was shipwrecked, a night and a day I have spent in the deep.

To be clear, as a Christian you will face adversity. You will face opposition. You will at times feel as though there is no one in this world that understands you. You will face abandonment, trials, opposition, persecution, and social and societal difficulty. The good news of all this, though, is that you are facing this as an opportunity to show the world that there is hope in the Savior Jesus Christ! As a believer, take these opportunities as chances in your sphere of influence to showcase the love of the Savior and the strength that comes only from a steadfast relationship with Him!

Home

It certainly would not be much of a game if only the visitors showed to play. Therefore, it would be best if you would decide to show up. Now for each person reading this, your effort will look different. For the quadriplegic who can do nothing more than blink to show agreement, that is a start. For those who have suffered lesser forms of disability, it is my assumption that if you have read this far, you are interested in seeing what can be done. That is why I want to introduce in this chapter what will be the discussion for the rest of the book: rehabilitation.

Rehabilitation, at least in a traditional sense, is "the action of restoring someone to health or normal life through training and therapy after imprisonment, addiction, or illness" (Oxford Dictionary). Thus, the survivor of the trauma is met with not only the frustration of physical rehabilitation, but in addition, his or her body does not obey the very things the mind tells it to do. This leads to a question: If one is unable to get his or her physical body to do what the mind is commanding, how does one master the spiritual realm? To this focus we will turn, because the core of rehabilitation is first recognizing the root cause of the disorder or disability.

Dr. Archibald Hart, a professional counselor who penned the volume *The Anxiety Cure* states this regarding trauma and crises:

> I love challenges and thrive on crises. There is never enough time in any day for me to do all I want to. Life is too short, too precious, and full of too many opportunities to be lived halfheartedly, so I pull out all the stops. I have little tolerance for anything that blocks my progress. (Hart, 1999, preface)

Thus, a brain injury survivor has the challenge of finding out which way was up and now having to find out which way is up. But the grit or determination expounded by Dr. Hart is one that hopefully will well up inside of you. It is my belief that this offers the most hope, the most challenge, the most promise, and the most volatile challenge for pain in the life of the TBI patient. And please note that I said pain, not necessarily hope. The reason? The decision the survivor makes with regard to his or her ultimate state is the subject of the next chapter. Please, if nothing else, take the time to read chapter 3.

To challenge yourself to relearn how to walk, talk, read, and write is a humbling, humiliating, frustrating, emotionally debilitating, and altogether messy business. For those in the medical profession, it can be so difficult for the patient to get up from the bed. But once this small victory is gained, you can mark that victory. I intend to be fully transparent here. In rediscovering the use of your faculties, both mental and physical, you may find a new love for reading, new excitement for a game of UNO, a new appreciation for the beauty of the mountains, and any number of missed appreciations simply because of your preoccupation with the business and busyness of life.

How did it feel the first time you took a step? Do you remember the delight, the joy, the sensation of independence coursing through your legs as you took your first few totters across the floor? It is likely you don't because most of humanity cannot remember that far back. However, if you've had to learn again how to walk, you might have a little more empathy for those troublesome toddlers. Point in fact, walking is difficult business! It requires the coordination of your arms, legs, torso, neck, back, pelvis, and a host of other joints and ligaments functioning together in unison to appear normal.

This is precisely what rehabilitation is not. For the many who are in the process of relearning how to walk, it is a humbling experience. "Thirty-two per cent of those working at 2 years were not employed at 5 years. Many students had also become unemployed. These findings suggest the need for intermittent lifelong intervention following TBI" (J. H. Olver, 1996). For the brain injury survivor, it is a frustrating experience! Not only do you remember the freedom and ease at which you used to walk, but paralysis can begin a frustrating descent into depression. Now ancient Gnostics believed you would attain "salvation" through escaping the physical world. This is not unlike the Hindi belief that salvation is attained when one enters Samsara and is detached from reality. Yet, to the brain injury survivor, much of the frustration can come from determining what is reality! As Plato exclaimed in his *Republic,* "The eyes may be confused in two ways and from two causes, namely, when they've come from the light into the darkness and when they've come from the darkness into the light" (Plato, Plato: Complete Works, 1997). The danger survivors face here lies in the determination as to what is reality and what is light and darkness. Thankfully, there is a better Light that can be followed as "For God, who said, 'Let light shine out of darkness,' made his light shine in our hearts to give us the light of the knowledge of God's glory displayed in the face of Christ" (2 Cor. 4:6). After the initial bleed, I can honestly say all I remember are mental photographs and recordings, many of which are quite possibly fabricated in my own mind. So, what is real and what is just the brain trying to piece together the severed connections? Here is where most survivors can lose hope. There must be some mechanism, some individual, some program that involves patience, understanding, and a great deal of mercy on the part of the caregiver.

For me, God placed my loving parents in a position to care for me in 2000 after the initial bleed. I was lovingly encouraged to try, to encourage perseverance, to struggle uphill against what I felt like doing. This was a devastating time of recovery but necessary to return to society. What's worse, it was done to recover back to a grade school understanding of life. Then came the fun part, cognizing that life on this earth would never be the same. Short-term memory, which can be passed off as just forgetfulness, is a persistent reality for every survivor. There have been many who try to empathize by stating something along the lines of, "Ah, it's okay, I forget a name here and there too." And while it's comforting to know that other people struggle with a type of early dementia, its different than forgetting how to drive a car, or forgetting how to tell your left foot to pick up to take the next step, or forgetting where your office is after coming back from a stop at the restroom down the hall. These are realities that many brain injury survivors must deal with. Its more than simple forgetfulness; it is learning to rely on something other than your memory to help you in daily tasks.

To illustrate the point, I share a week in 2005 while working at Dallas Baptist University. I was a network administrator, coming in on a Monday morning for work. I parked the car in staff parking outside the Learning Center at the far end of campus. I started walking into the office like I had done for the past three years. Unfortunately, I had no map. My mind was completely devoid of direction. I walked up the stairs to the second floor of the library called the LC because the signs said, "computer lab ->" to see if anything would register. Nothing. So, after following the signs that pointed to the computer lab, I asked one of the new student workers where my office was; the student worker looked at me as if I had lost my mind. But that is exactly what had happened! When a brain injury occurs, many times the mundane autonomy of the day is gone. Now, you must find your way around your office that you've been working at for years just as if you've never set foot there. And the most frustrating thing is that you know you knew where everything was. It just won't connect. Having been separated from that episode of confusion for ten-plus years, I can look back and laugh. But in the back of my mind, only now am I beginning to see that the confusion, the difficulty finding my way around, and the embarrassment were all a part of God's design.

In 1947, hot on the heels of the close of World War II, a discovery was made that has had a profound impact on nearly every modern version of the Christian Bible. The discovery was a collection of copies of the Septuagint, which included a full copy of the book of Isaiah. The impact of the discovery has been felt even today as most Bible translators can use these transcripts to translate the Hebrew and Greek text into the English many speak today.

The problem with this discovery is that every translation of that time was now subject to the newly discovered text of the cave. The problem came when the excavators attempted to remove the papyri from their vases. "The most famous of these is the complete scroll of Isaiah, which was written sometime between the second century BCE and the destruction of the site in 68 CE. This date was recently confirmed by a radiocarbon examination of a sample of the parchment of the scroll. The books of the Qumran library are regarded as the oldest existing copies of the books of the Bible" (Israeli Foreign Ministry., http://www.jewishvirtuallibrary.org/jsource/Archaeology/Qumran.html). When archeologists found the scrolls, they were extremely well-preserved, yet time and the normal course of aging caused these articles to become very brittle to touch.

There is a fundamental principle to be gleaned from this story. These scrolls were written within the time span of Jesus Christ. These were penned by some hand close to the life of the Savior. Perhaps this isn't exciting to you, but before dismissing, consider the importance. Of the extant copies we have of the classic work *Romeo and Juliet*, we have limited copies to be certain. In 2006, a copy of the first folio of Shakespeare's plays was actioned for 3.5 million pounds. For the American readership, that is $4,853,695! We have *some copies of* the text. But compared to that of the text of the Christian scriptures, timeless, and recording the words and deeds of Christ, can be picked up for >$20 or likely for free from any Christian organization worth the Savior whom it is preaching! The point being, the promised land of a country where God's people could move about freely, express themselves freely, and share the good news of Christ with others freely is upon us. The challenge is that many of us, the author included, are struggling through fighting through the wilderness after the brain injury. We have effectively become visitors to our own home game!

When the people of Israel, hand-selected by God Himself, were struggling through the occupation of their promised land, Canaan, these former slaves were comprised of generations of persons who had known the hardship of the wilderness, the ferocity of the Egyptians, and the wonders of God. Their stories fill the pages of the biblical books of Genesis, Exodus, Leviticus, Numbers, and Deuteronomy. Now, coming into the period of Judges, they had to be refit. Notice what is written in the book of Judges:

> These are the nations the Lord left to test all those Israelites who had not experienced any of the wars in Canaan (He did this only to teach warfare to the descendants of the Israelites who had not had previous battle experience): the five rulers of the Philistines, all the Canaanites, the Sidonians, and the Hivites living in the Lebanon mountains from Mount Baal Hermon to Lebo Hamath. They were left to test the Israelites to see whether they would obey the Lord's commands, which he had given their ancestors through Moses. (NASB, 1995, Judges 3:1–4)

Do you catch the meaning? The Israelites were chosen, through no merit of their own, to inherit the promised land. God *left* the people in the promised land who had rejected Him for the sole purpose of testing (Hebrew סוּת‎ נ‎ ל‎, make a test (1), proved (1), put (1), put to the test.) (Concordance, 2016) Pay attention, as the reason for the testing of the Israelites may have a parallel in your own life. Do you, as a member of the human race, beset with an illness you likely have never heard of, feel entrapped? Take courage because your home is not here anyway!

If anyone in ancient history seemed to deserve a period of rest, it would seem the Israelites would. Yet God chose to use this period to reform the people. Much like James, the brother of Jesus wrote in James 1:2–4, "Consider it pure joy, my brothers and sisters, whenever you face trials of many kinds, because you know that the testing of your faith produces perseverance. Let perseverance finish its work so that you may be mature and complete, not lacking anything." This James probably was the same who went on to pastor the church of Jerusalem through persecution and hardship. He was prepared through adversity for greater leadership. There is a need, however, for you and I to become children of God to submit to His plan. How so? you may ask. We read: "Everyone who believes that Jesus is the Christ is born of God, and everyone who loves the father loves his child as well (NASB, 1995, 1, John 5:1). Consequently, if you would believe that there is a God who loves you, who came to this earth two-thousand-plus years ago, who was murdered for crimes He didn't commit, and was raised from the dead to pay for yours and my sin, you will be saved!

Bringing it back to the day and age of the conquest, the Jews faced a massive undertaking in taking the promised land from its natives. You are no different in that you are an aneurysm survivor. Take courage because you have been chosen by the Lord to undertake this massive conquest, and the results are left for you to declare to others to see and review. For those undergoing recovery, remember you are not merely a prospect for disability claims. This may very well be one option the Lord has provided to you. But you are more than a useless lump of flesh. You are created in the image of God! Your life has permanently changed, true. This permanent change was not a permanent disability, though. It was a God-ordained recommissioning of your life for His purpose.

MALFORMATION

Habilitation requires hardship because usually greater responsibility follows greater adversity. You may be in a circumstance like the Israelites in the days of the conquest of Canaan, being strengthened against your will to prepare you for the victory ahead. You may be like James, the brother of Christ, undergoing trials following failure to recommission you for the victory ahead. Or you may be like many other historical figures who, after failure, comprise another thread in the sad fabric of a surrender flag flown in defeat. By this point, you hopefully have come to some sort of understanding that you are not an accident. You are not a mistake. Your life is not merely a tragedy but *can be* a testimony of what God has done, a victory of what He is doing and will do for those who trust in Him. Your life has taken turns for the worse and for the better. You may find yourself to be in a season much like Job, who exclaimed: "He said, 'Naked I came from my mother's womb, and naked I shall return there. The LORD gave, and the LORD has taken away. Blessed be the name of the LORD'" (Job 1:21). This being spoken after the loss of his children, his fortunes, his livestock, and for all practical purposes his wife as well. Nevertheless, remember what the apostle Paul wrote to the Roman believers "For we know that God causes all things to work together for the good of those who love God, for the good of those who are called according to His purpose" (Rom. 8:28).

Can you imagine what went through the disciples' minds the night of Jesus's death or the days after? Here was Peter, a successful fisherman who had left a likely lucrative family fishing business to follow Christ, now out of touch with the fishing crowd and out of fitting for the fishing business. Or perhaps Levi the tax collector, already hated by both Jew and Gentile alike, cast aside by his own rabbi? Or perhaps Simon the Zealot, member of a religious sect bent on overthrowing the Roman government. What were these men to do with their leader killed? My point is that none of these men were the cream of the crop of society. Yet God used them mightily. What about you? Feel bewildered in your new life? Too much life and not enough time? Friend, we are only guaranteed a moment ago. Everything else is a gift.

The setback you have endured may not be overcome in full this side of heaven. The sobering news of life is that everyone, without exception, will die anyway. The question then is how you and I will live *before* we draw our final breath. If you have considered the cost of surgery, the cost of rehab, and the continuing costs of medicine and medical devices, it may be too much. Again, allow me to remind you, *this is not your home anyway.* You and I are only passing through for a very brief time in the scope of eternity. What we must be prepared for, and expecting, is what our lives in the scope of eternity will look like. Now consider the people of Israel as it stands today.

> *The war was fought along the entire, long border of the country: against Lebanon and Syria in the north; Iraq and Transjordan - renamed Jordan during the war - in the east; Egypt, assisted by contingents from the Sudan - in the south; and Palestinians and volunteers from Arab countries in the interior of the country.*

> *It was the bloodiest of Israel's wars. It cost 6,373 killed in action (from pre-state days until 20 July 1949) almost 1% of the yishuv (the Jewish community) - although that figure includes quite a number of new immigrants and some foreign volunteers.*

> *In the First Phase (29 November 1947 - 1 April 1948), it was the Palestinian Arabs who took the offensive, with the help of volunteers from neighboring countries; the yishuv had little success in limiting the war - it suffered severe casualties and disruption of passage along most of the major highways.*

> *In the Second Phase (1 April - 15 May) the Haganah took the initiative, and in six weeks was able to turn the tables - capturing, inter alia, the Arab sections of Tiberias, Haifa and later also Safed and Acre, temporarily opening the road to Jerusalem and gaining control of much of the territory allotted to the Jewish State under the UN Resolution.*

> *The Third Phase (15 May - 19 July), considered the critical one, opened with the simultaneous, coordinated assault on the fledgling state by five regular Arab armies from neighboring*

countries, with an overwhelming superiority of heavy equipment - armor, artillery and air force.

On 31 May the Haganah was renamed the "Israel Defense Forces". The IDF suffered initial setbacks, including the loss of the Etzion Bloc in Judea, the area of Mishmar Hayarden in the north and Yad Mordehai in the south, but after three weeks was able to halt the offensive, to stabilize the front and even initiate some local offensive operations.

The Fourth Phase (19 July 1948 - 20 July, 1949) was characterized by Israeli initiatives: Operation Yoav, in October, cleared the road to the Negev, culminating in the capture of Be'er Sheva; Operation Hiram, at the end of October, resulted in the capture of the Upper Galilee; Operation Horev in December 1948 and Operation Uvda in March 1949, completed the capture of the Negev, which had been allotted to the Jewish State by the United Nations. (Lorch, 2013)

The people of Israel, like thousands of years ago, are seeking rest and a means of finding a land to call home. Hopefully, prayerfully, and eagerly, it is this author's hope that you will find the rest and rehab in the Savior and not the medicines and therapies alone. In the next chapter, we need to look at, in detail, what I have deemed re-rehabilitation. As we looked at how in this chapter to make this life a home for the brief time we are here, now we will turn to looking more specifically at this habilitation in a more eternal framework, which should have some implications in this life as well.

CHAPTER 4.5

Re-Rehabilitation

The thought of rehab may be a daunting task. The thought of entering another form of rehab in addition to this carnal rehabilitation may be the most distant ideal from your mind but bear with this chapter. The doctors, nurses, caseworkers, speech therapists, and all other medical personnel are working to see you rehabilitate. Knowing this should encourage you. Couple with this the notion that your family and friends are as best as possible hoping for your recovery as well. A third group for many readers is the local congregation of believers with whom you may be associated. Rethinking rehab with a spiritual component in mind is the aim of this chapter.

With the twenty-first century opening with many servicemen and women returning from the Iraq/Afghanistan conflicts, rehabilitation has jumped to the forefront of study. Bearing this in mind, schools have sought to meet this need by offering degrees specifically in rehabilitation. One such example is the Department of Special Education, Rehabilitation, and Counseling at Auburn University. With its programs, it seeks to produce competent workers for the growing field of persons who have significant mental and cognitive challenges.

As was recorded by Dietrich Bonhoeffer during the German invasions that precipitated World War II, "All Christian prayer is directed to God through a Mediator, and not even prayer affords direct access to the Father. Only through Jesus Christ can we find the Father in prayer" (Bonhoeffer, D., 1937, 181). Do you understand what is wrong with the traditional concept of prayer? In order that the needy be heard by the Lord, they must offer their pleadings through the auspices of the Son. Whether intentional or not, the pleadings of the hurting must be directed at the only One who can mend those broken hearts. The primary problem with the current cultural view of prayer seems to be the same as that of millennia ago. The person lets out a cry for help, and the first one to answer must be God. Yet for those who are saved by the only One who can, Jesus should know that seekers must beware!

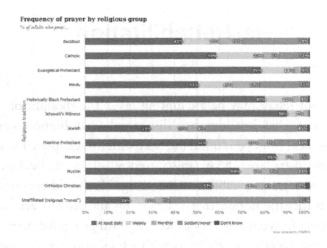

Frequency of prayer by religious group

The cultural view of prayer in the Pew research poll shown finds that among the average American, 58 percent of the population pray daily. Granted this includes the Buddhist, Muslim, Hindu, and Jewish populations as well. However, the underlying truth remains, there is an ingrained desire within our being to be heard. Understanding that the Divine is present is a mandate. Of primary importance is the Divine Son of God. His name is Jesus Christ, the Divine child of Mary and God—the only One who can save us from our sins as He is the Only One born into this earth with the Divine hand of God and the mortal flesh of humanity through Mary. Further, without delving into a whole systematic theology of the triune God, this Jesus is the only One whom you and I must confess is our salvation. We do this as shown by the only Word of God—the Bible. In Romans 10:8–10 we are told:

> "But what does it say? "THE WORD IS NEAR YOU, IN YOUR MOUTH AND IN YOUR HEART"—that is, the word of faith which we are preaching, that if you confess with your mouth Jesus as Lord, and believe in your heart that God raised Him from the dead, you will be saved; for with the heart a person believes, resulting in righteousness, and with the mouth he confesses, resulting in salvation."

Surely you have questions and objections. Therefore, at this point, I plead with you to get a Bible for yourself. Read the gospels of Matthew the tax collector, Mark the wayward missionary, Luke the doctor turned missionary, or John the beloved writer of the Gospel by his name. They all tell the story of Jesus Christ through the eyes of quite different persons. Read of His perfect life. Read of His death on the cross. Read of His resurrection. Read of His plan to return. Read in Acts of the birth of the church and the reason Christianity has for two-thousand-plus years thrived amid tremendous persecution.

Before you are caught up in the culture's inherent objections against Christ, consider that the weight of proof lay on the side of the believer in Christ rather than the agnostic or atheist. As Dr. Ken Ham from the Answers in Genesis organization states: "Ultimately, love, reason, knowledge, logic, and morality are all impossible to explain in a purely materialistic universe that exists by chance" (Answers in Genesis, 2018). To hearken back to the ancient text in Acts 1:3, "He presented Himself alive to them after his suffering by many proofs, appearing to them during forty days and speaking about the kingdom of God." The "He" in the text is the Jesus of the New Testament. The setting of the text is an upper room, which in the first days of the early church would have been meeting in secret following the murder of Jesus. The reason for doing this was to flesh out together what they had just heard, seen, and been a part of so that they could share with others. Little did they know that their gathering would be the catalyst for the largest religious movement that is still ongoing this very day.

Consider the apostle Paul, formerly Saul of Tarsus, who moved from persecutor of the church to a writer of nearly half of the New Testament through his miraculous conversion on the road to Damascus. Consider Maewyn Succat, otherwise known as Saint Patrick, a fourth century saint of the church who sought his captors to become saved. After being kidnapped by pirates and left in Ireland, he returned to that very same country to preach the good news of Jesus to his captors. Consider Clive Staples Lewis, an injured World War I veteran agnostic turned early twentieth century apologist, who wrote among others *The Lion, the Witch, and the Wardrobe* to the children and penned *Mere Christianity* for the masses. Consider time after time and person after person the growing chorus of voices who testify and proclaim, Jesus is Lord! This is the rebirth of the faithful, the birth of the church, and the convincing of the believers would lead to their giving their lives for this cause and more specifically for their Savior.

Rebirth ...

The title for this section is somewhat misleading. The chapter is **Re-Rehabilitation**, but how would you advise to label a new way of reacclimating the patient to reality? Having been in a rehab facility—HealthSouth (Now Encompass Health Corp.) in Dothan, Alabama—I know what it means to go through intensive physical and mental rehabilitation. Further, going through the rigorous physical training brought on by having a retired colonel as a father, I understand rehab! In all seriousness, though, this perhaps stands as a reminder to what you need to be expecting for successful re-rehab, or perhaps better said **Rebirth**. Typically, a rehab program is aimed "to restore to good health or useful life, as through therapy and education" (Dictionary.com, n.d.). The medical definition of rehabilitation is especially important. As measured by most rehab facilities, rehabilitation of a person is seen as "successful" if noticeable improvement is achieved through therapy and education. Note the twofold purpose through therapy for the short term and education for the long term. The reason for deeming this section as Re-Rehabilitation is to consider that the process of rehabilitation must be revisited with a slightly wider definition of success. "If intelligence could be assessed directly, we would be able to measure the neurochemical changes and neurobiological changes that occur in the brain. As educators, we rely instead on indirect measures or tests to estimate intelligence" (Cohen and Spenciner, 2011,

327). Proffered a bit wider, in this author's opinion, it would behoove us to add the small caveat of true rehab to determine the proposed destination of the individual postinjury. Thus, **"Re-Rehabilitation"** includes **"Rebirth"** in view of the individual's eternal destination.

In a discussion for teachers of the disabled it was stated, "Perceptions of disability encompass a range of emotions for family members: embarrassment and shame, guilt and blame, grief and acceptance" (Cohen & Spenciner, 2011, 62). While the parents or guardians of the individual are sifting through these emotions, undoubtedly the individual himself is to some extent mentally languishing as well. Because of this it would be advisable to develop a personalized plan of attack with the family and, if possible, the individual, to work on together with other members of the immediate family to achieve victories in his or her new state of being.

To give an injunction at this point would be advisable. What is *not* being done here is giving an ultimatum. Rather it is the crafting a policy or set of strategies to which the patient can refer. It is the creation of these outside of the patient's mind to refer back to it. Regarding this, consider the moral stages of learning that are typically seen in human development. As the author's intent, as well as the premise for this book, is the restoration of the person to a functioning member of society, we must decide what *kind* of person we are attempting to re-create.

From the pages of Parkey, Hass, and Antcil we read, "We have stated the theory of the just community high school, postulating that discussing real-life moral situation and actions as issues of fairness and matters for democratic decision would stimulate advance in both moral reasoning and moral action" (Parkay, Hass, & Anctil, 2010, 156). Now if we trace the origins of education back to the Jewish point of learning, it would prove helpful to who is responsible for the injured party. You may read in Proverbs 22:6: "Train up a child in the way he should go, even when he is old, he will not depart from it." Considering that many of those who are brain-injured are returning soldiers from the battlefield, the prospect of returning to their parents may no longer be possible. What then is the missing component that would lend the soldier to return to society and deter self-injury? Let us consider a possible cultural concession someone beyond the military medical personnel who could see to the soldier's long-term care.

PAUL MCMONAGLE

At is this point, the scripture again springs to life. If the soldier has returned to the United States, he is covered by the VA and other medical workers for most of his temporal needs. Yet the missing X factor or missing component of rehabilitation in this author's view needs to be a caring community of persons who can relate to the individual's struggle without judgment. This is the point at which a community meet-up of like-minded persons would be helpful. Perhaps in a small community this would not be possible. However, organizations utilizing curriculum such as Celebrate Recovery might be helpful. Though the curriculum for Celebrate Recovery was originally created for church use, a parachurch organization or other community meet-up would be helpful as well.

Considering this prospect, let us briefly review a few observations about points of information. First, we find the total number of veterans using the VA health-care system. According to a summary chart, in 2019 there were 404,060 people alive who have returned from war categorized as having a mental disorder. This data constitutes the Iraq war from the 1990s presided over by President George Bush to the more recent conflict in Iraq/Afghanistan presided over by Presidents Bill Clinton, George W. Bush, Barack Obama, and Donald J. Trump. From the above, the sheer number of mental disorders is staggering. For the injured, there is a 52.3 percent incidence of mental trauma. Now to further complicate matters, the CDC opted to lump traumatic brain injury into the mental disorders category. This means that having a brain injury, which is physical damage to the brain, is included in the mental disorders category! I do not wish to wade into the murky waters of reason for categorization. To be quite honest, I think the medical professionals are doing a great job overall in all the varieties of issues that cause the human body and mind to decay! Yet for the issue of brain injury, the need for a more workable fix is an absolute. The reason for this incident frequency may be the change of combat to which the soldiers are often exposed.

For instance, based on a conglomeration of the World Health Organization and the leaks from the Wikileaks organization, "Taking the WikiLeaks data into account, the IBC (Iraq Body Count Project) now estimates that at least 150,000 have died violently during the war operation, 80% of them civilians." (Conflict Casualties Monitor 2020) That falls within the range produced by an Iraq household survey conducted by the World

130

Health Organization—and further erodes the credibility of a 2006 study published in *The Lancet*, which estimated over 600,000 violent deaths for the first three years of the war (Bohannon, 2010). This war referred to in *The Lancet* was the most recent Iraq conflict. However, if you factor in the Iraq war in the 1990s under the leadership of President Bush, the Iraq/Afghanistan conflicts under Presidents Bush and Obama, and the Iraq conflict under President Trump, the toll on the US military has been grave. Without wading too deep into uncharted or untested waters, or charging the political poles of the readership, the issue in this author's mind is one of those who returned home. How are those veterans being treated?

With the horrible events on September 11, 2001, the United States saw the largest attack ever on her shores. The natural reaction to this attack was to attack back. The unfortunate problem was the attack was launched primarily against a country that contained the attackers when it possibly should have been targeting a specific ideology. However, looking back at this strategy, launching an offensive against a specific segment of the population among a war-torn culture already proved to be a difficult endeavor. For example, the use of the IED or improvised explosive device meant the soldier was unable to identify the assailant, the weapon, and the words being spoken by the attacker.

The additional challenge to the returning soldier or the recovering aneurysm survivor is treated medically in the same manner. Both are given treatments recommended by the post-traumatic stress disorder regimen to allow the individual to grasp reality. Then, following completion or coupled with the PTSD treatment, medical practitioners also treat the physical training to rehabilitate any loss of dexterity, mobility, or use of limbs. This can be a complicated and time-consuming process. Nevertheless, there is a missing factor in this equation that this author believes would be beneficial not only for the recent conflicts but also to stave off any suicidal tendencies for any future conflicts. To this topic we turn.

Post-Traumatic Stress Disorder (PTSD) Treatment

To briefly deal with the more common treatment diagnosis regimens undergone by soldiers and others dealing with traumatic brain injury, let us touch on two distinct yet interrelated conditions, the first of which being PTSD, or post-traumatic stress disorder. Per one study concluded in. "There have been many reports of PTSD in the news and even used as an explanation for illegal and deadly activity such as the Fort Hood shooter and others. The lesser-known fact about the Fort Hood shooting is the truth that the shooter suffered from a traumatic brain injury. As to answering the "why he did it,", the author will not attempt to speculate. The one fact that can be expressed is: "About 12% of 2,235 respondents reported a history consistent with mild TBI, and 11% screened positive for PTSD" (Schneiderman AI, Understanding sequelae of injury mechanisms and mild traumatic brain injury incurred during the conflicts in Iraq and Afghanistan: persistent postconcussive symptoms and posttraumatic stress disorder., 2008)). Consider briefly the life of a military veteran of the most recent conflicts—Iraq and Afghanistan.

With the conclusion of both the Iraq and Afghanistan conflicts, the U.S. servicemember now has the blessed opportunity to serve in a more domicile matter than active combat. Although this may prevent active combat exercise, with the recent and ongoing mental combat strain placed on many a veteran the risk of suicide has increased! Consider the more recent survey, completed January 31, 2018, by the National Academy of Sciences, Engineering, and Medicine. Per the results of this study, there is a rate of suicide elevated 35/100,00 as opposed to the regular civilian 15/100,000. This means that suicide prevalence is over twice the rate of the general population. Considering that a TBI is a lifetime altering of the way your brain functions, the medical and counseling communities need assistance in developing a transition from military service to civilian life. From this data, we see that the PTSD rate of the military veteran population is at minimum twice that of the nonveteran population. Moreover, that is at its lowest point of correlation. However, the generalized anxiety was also elevated. Therefore as a country we must innovate and invent or even rediscover treatment options that have been shelved over time.

Per coverage of the tragedy, it is noteworthy that one outcome of the Fort Hood shooting has been the creation of a future mitigation treatment on-site. "The Fort Hood Intrepid Spirit (program) provides evidence-based interdisciplinary assessment and intensive outpatient care for Service Members with complex medical conditions with the goal of fostering optimal outcomes" (Intrepid Spirit Center/TBI Clinic, 2018).

MALFORMATION

The outcome of the tragedy was an action that has since the event been an attempt to modify the process to prevent future occurrences. As the center has undoubtedly seen many more patients with no outcome as tragic as the shooting in Fort Hood, one must assume the treatment of these persons must be to some extent successful.

With the last of the Iraq/Afghanistan veterans returning at the close of the conflict in 2015, now the US population is at a crossroads. Do traditional methods of dealing with stress and combat situations postwar gravitate toward a normalized life? As studies are still ongoing, it would be best to hold any judgment. Instead, this author does counsel you to consult with your team of treatment personnel from your doctor for medical injuries. Further, seeking a psychiatrist for psycho-prescriptive solutions is possibly advisable. Finally, one typically excluded member of the treatment team, yet personally crucial, is your local church family, which adds therapeutic value both for input and outflow of counsel.

The road is long to be sure, but there is value in community. Also, if you are not from the military but nevertheless have suffered a traumatic brain injury, do not despair; neither was the author! One purpose of seeking a treatment outside of the military is just this. There are others who need help, assistance, and accommodation that you may be able to provide in the situation that you are in. One prospective avenue of treatment often left out of military mitigation, although available for thousands of years, is that of the church.

Further, this is not limited to military patients. The author is not affiliated with the US military, although he is grateful to the men and women who serve! As you have already seen the effect of TBI/ABI/HBI on the general populace, what overarching treatment options are out there that need to be included? It is this author's suggestion, based on twenty-plus years of study, research, corresponding with medical professionals in the field, and personal experience that your treatment need not be left up to just one side of the equation. Perhaps better said, the *team* of treatment personnel should assess and set forth your course of treatment with you in the mix of planning. This team includes possibly your general practitioner, your neurologist(s), your neurosurgeon(s), your physical rehabilitation specialist(s), your home health-care worker(s), your psychologist/psychiatrist, your counselor(s), and your pastor(s).

Process

To spare the gory details, birth is a messy business. For a guy being a participant only in the start of the child's life, ultimately the nine-month ordeal of childbirth is largely on the shoulders of the mother. Pain is involved, risk is involved, and there are moments of utter terror and gut-wrenching agony. Coupled with the messy after-effects, there is little reason this author personally could see in going through with the ordeal save one or two small—six-and seven-pound—reasons (the children of my wife and I). I would hope that in the writing the sarcasm comes through. In retrospect, our children were two of the best decisions we ever made! Granted, the process of birth is agonizing but at the same time beautiful. After consulting with my wife, I can validate the process of childbirth was notoriously difficult to say the least. Yet for both of our children, God took the final sting of death on the cross as valid punishment for our historic disobedience in the garden through Adam and Eve. Furthermore, through His mercy, He created one of the most beautiful, celebrated events in the lives of any young couple.

How does this relate to brain injury? In the process of childbirth, the mother is going to discover strengths and abilities that she never knew she had all through the pains, horrors, and agonizing times of child carrying. Akin to the horrors of an AVM rupture, the pain will be incredible. The agony will likely place you to the point of passing out. The difference is the outcome, however. With a mother, you are blessed with the life of another staring at you with joy, need, and love in his/her eyes. With a brain bleed, you are left as a person who likely will be a shell of the former self. The need of the care and repeated affirmations of love must be restated and restated to the point of breaking. The only bonds of love that can withstand this constant barrage is that of love of something greater than themselves. This is not palliative care. This is love that starts beyond this earth. As we shall see, the love of Someone greater than themselves.

In childbirth, the husband will never experience the pain of delivery. This husband who underwent the brain bleeds will never experience the terror of childbirth because generally he is clueless as to the pain his wife went through. This is not to say the husband is worthless. But I was clueless as to the pain and daily tugging, nausea, and aching that Leslie (my wife) was subjected to.

The child wanted to get out of the womb, and the mother at some point wants out of the pain of carrying a growing being inside her womb!

All of this brings us to the thesis of the chapter: The growing process, however, is the point. The process of childbirth prepares the mother for the delivery of the child. The process of delivery prepares the mother for the eventual release of the child into the world. The process of the brain bleed likewise should not be the point of focus but the path leading the person after the bleed to other survivors. Though you will come to a point in your child-rearing that you can no longer have any other influence over the child than a phone call or a letter, your lasting words of encouragement, instruction, and wisdom will be with the child for his or her duration on earth. Therefore, why not likewise leave a lasting, edible mark of encouragement and hope on the brain-injured soul! Just as you would a child, who is learning and growing, spend some time encouraging those who are wrestling with brain injury. Likewise, the process of recovery from a brain bleed *could* be one of growth, recovery, reinstatement of affirmation for the individual, and a reestablishment of the person to a valued member of society at large.

As an example that hits even closer to home for those who maybe are not parents or are from the opposite sex, Christ told His disciples: "Therefore go and make disciples of all nations, baptizing them in the name of the Father and the Son and the Holy Spirit, teaching them to obey everything I have commanded you. And remember, I am with you always, to the end of the age" (cf. Matt. 28:19.) The *parting* of Jesus and the disciples was to be completed with Christ temporarily with an expectation of a holy eternal reunion in heaven. But the *process* of this parting coming about was a tremendously painful series of events. It involved the loss and betrayal of one of the disciples (cf. Acts 1:18.) It involved the effective relearning most of everything the disciples had ever been raised in from their Jewish heritage (cf. 2 Corinthians 3:11). It involved the salvation of a Jewish betrayer (cf. Acts 9:17), a Jewish doctor (cf. Colossians 4:14), an Italian soldier (cf. Acts 10:1), a Roman Catholic priest (Maewyn Succat), an Irish atheist (Clive Staples Lewis), and hosts of millions of others!

This brings us to you. Reading this volume, you may have come from any number of places, stations, and circumstances. But here's the good news: God knows your life. God planned your life. And now Jesus is bringing you to this point to make an eternal decision.

CHAPTER 5

Prisal?

—————◦◦◦◦◦—————

Prisal: the action of taking something as a prize of war.[21]

As an avid movie aficionado, one of my favorite movies is *We Were Soldiers*. With my father being a retired veteran of both Vietnam and Desert Storm, I recall during my adolescence and young adult years inquiring various times as to why the United States went to Vietnam. Perhaps from too much media, perhaps just collegiate inquiry, but my young mind could not wrap around why the United States would want to involve us in conflict thousands of miles away for a people we had no vested interest in to topple a dictator or rescue an ethnic group from persecution. These were not unworthy actions, but they did seem, from the viewpoint of an ordinary citizen, a waste of the United States' limited capital reserves. Yet with the years came a glimmer of wisdom in seeing that the action of taking a people back was akin to liberating a prisoner of war. They were exercising their innate desire to become free.

As a brain aneurysm survivor multiple times over now, it has become apparent that my life is meant for a purpose, for a reason, for a time, and as such, I must continue. Further, it should become clear that you are here for this reason, for this time, and so you must continue as well. If you're reading these words, you have been granted life and breath for this day. If one reaches this point of logic, lucidity, or languish, then that is at least a start. Now turn to the outside world. You gaze upon a whole realm of persons who go about their day largely oblivious to the hidden pitfalls that

———————————————

[21] https://www.merriam-webster.com/dictionary/prisal, Merriam-Webster Dictionary, 1/10/2020.

may befall them. What can you do now that you couldn't before? Here we reach a crucial interval in our read. If you were not a skilled language worker, why not try it again? Did you know, and studies support, that "the likelihood of heightened emotional distress associated with increased awareness is relatively low due to positive social support and adaptive coping strategies" (T. Ownsworth, 2006). In yet another study: "The patient improved the major components of the second language, including vocabulary. Within the 6 months, the subject was gradually capable of learning additional and more complex lexical items." (Disabil Rehabil., 2008; 30 (18):1397–407, Połczyńska-Fiszer, Mazaux).

From the author's own perspective, he had only learned two semesters of Spanish in high school. Nevertheless, after the first and second brain bleed, he finished five semesters of Greek and three of Hebrew postinjury! Being a math-minded person, analytical before the bleed, lent itself instead to be more language prone after the bleed. This is not to say that language was a proverbial "breeze." What did happen instead was that my thinking was shifted to include the previously untapped portion of psyche that more naturally included language acquisition. Moreover, the same could be said of you! If you have no expectations placed on you because of your injury, could you achieve more than anyone ever dreamed possible?

Let us consider what you can do now. Perhaps you were a musician, but the lack of dexterity in your fingers from paralysis may have crippled that profession. What other job or hobby has always piqued an interest? For me, I had always dreamed of writing words of encouragement to others but never could arrange the time and place to do so because of my rotating work schedule. Now, I am afforded this opportunity because of my disability. What dreams, what passions, what connections have you never made because you lacked either the time or opportunity to correspond? If you are reading this, you may be at that awkward juncture in your life where you are wondering, What now? Well, let's peer into that window a bit to find some exciting things in store!

As employment full time or part time may no longer be within your abilities, what do you do with the time you have? First, let me allay some of your fears. Per one study of AVM of HHT patients: "Two hundred twenty-five/407 (55 %) of respondents were included creating HHT- (n = 225) and control groups (n = 225) of equal size. Two hundred thirteen/225

(95 %) of the HHT group had not been screened for organ involvement of the disease prior to death. The life expectancy in parents with HHT was slightly lower compared to parents without (median age at death 73.3 years in patients versus 76.6 years in controls, p0.018.)" (E. M. de Gussem, 2016) With this only being a 3.3-year regression of normative life expectancy of 82, this is certainly not horrible news![21] If you have been chosen to attack this beast of brain injury be aware, it has come to this author's attention that to conquer this dragon, you must first venture into its lair.

To interrupt our regularly scheduled heavy discussion, let's take a moment to picture something a bit more humorous. In *Monty Python's Quest for the Holy Grail*, there is an image of a horrendous, hopefully humorous, beast of Aaaaarrrrrrggghhh!!!!!!! This was a popular film from my upbringing. It was hardly serious yet speaks to what you and I are trying to accomplish here. In the movie, as the knights of the round table, led by King Arthur, seek the holy grail, they are met by the monstrous beast on the way to the grail. Certainly not a scary image, yet it does illustrate a fact that this author wants to utilize as a jumping-off platform. Though careful distinctions have been given to traumatic brain injury and acquired brain injury, there is currently no defined category of classification for certain types of brain injury. "After adjustment for other variables, patients with mental illness waited 10 minutes longer to see a physician compared with other patients during noncrowded periods (95% confidence interval [CI] 8 to 11), but they waited significantly less time than other patients as crowding increased (mild crowding: –14 [95% CI –12 to –15] min; moderate crowding: –38 [95% CI –35 to –42] min; severe crowding: –48 [95% CI –39 to –56] min; $p < 0.001$.)" (Clare L. Atzema, 2012). Do you see the complications? If a patient *looks* to be fine but is suffering crippling and debilitating manifestations of cerebral trauma, they *may* be suffering a brain bleed. And remember, this can affect any age, but particularly 18- to 24-year-olds are susceptible! Moreover, while waiting in a hospital bed to see a doctor may be suitable for some, with a brain injury, minutes of waiting could be the difference between life and death. Therefore, what can you do?

What you could do is simply support initiatives to get the word spread about the existence of a research group beyond the AVM community. Consultation with your general practitioner and possibly your neurosurgeon is recommended at this juncture. Resources such as the *Handbook of Venous Disorders: Guidelines of the American Venous Forum* give some information regarding this deformity. "Quite often, a docile-looking AVM lesion progresses dramatically into an explosive condition following an ill-planned therapeutic intervention" (Gloviczki, 2008, 584). Withholding judgment, consider the following ill-planned therapy:

> Of 977 AVM patients, 155 ARUBA-eligible patients had microsurgical resection (71.6% surgery only and 25.2% with preoperative embolization.) Mean follow-up was 36.1 months. Complete obliteration was achieved in 94.2% after initial surgery and 98.1% on final angiography. Early disabling deficits and permanent disabling deficits occurred in 12.3% and 4.5%, respectively, whereas any permanent neurological deficit (modified Rankin Scale score ≥ 1) occurred in 16.1%. Among ubAVM of Spetzler–Martin grades 1 and 2, complete obliteration occurred in 99.2%, with early disabling deficits and permanent disabling deficits occurring in 9.3% and 3.4%, respectively. Major bleeding was the only significant predictor of early disabling deficits on multivariate analysis ($P<0.001$.). (Johnny Wong, Alana Slomovic, George Ibrahim, and Ivan. Radovanovic, Microsurgery for ARUBA Trial (A Randomized Trial, 2017))

The study effectively says that patients experienced permanent and disabling aftereffects 9.3 percent of the time. If you consider a nearly 10 percent chance of disability versus a 90 percent success rate, what follows in this author's mind would be to operate! Unfortunately, the medical team does operate often with minimal patient medical history to guide their decisions. Again, this author implores that if you are uncomfortable with the treatment decision, ask for explanation. Yet, this laity written resource possesses far from the expertise the medical treatment team can offer in diagnosing and determining your best course of medical action. What I can do is encourage that if you don't understand, ask questions, and get answers!

MALFORMATION

What do I do now?

From the ARUBA study results, researchers determined for the first time the effects of brain injury on a sample of the AVM population. Another study recorded: "As a clear sign, treatment of the AVM anomaly was extremely successful! A success rate of 94.2 by way of angiography is extremely promising" (ARUBA Study). Conversely, however, for those who elected to go without surgical intervention, the results were far more dire. In a follow-up study to the ARUBA trials the authors persisted: "What is certain is that an active intervention means an immediate risk" (Mohamed Samy Elhammady, 2017). Though the study result is encouraging in and of itself, further it is noted: "Interestingly, a recent multicenter retrospective radiosurgical series from 7 international institutions in 509 ARUBA-eligible patients 39 (mean follow-up 86 months) showed an AVM obliteration rate of 75%, with a post radio surgery latency hemorrhage rate of 0.9% per year" (Johnny Wong, Alana Slomovic, George Ibrahim, and Ivan Radovanovic, Microsurgery for ARUBA Trial (A Randomized Trial) of Unruptured Brain Arteriovenous Malformation)– Eligible Unruptured Brain Arteriovenous Malformations, 2017). The study results and the outlying future of brain injury patients are promising. Regardless of the brain injury field, a 75 percent success rate is to be celebrated! Furthermore:

> Intracranial vascular diseases are not common in children, but when suspected they should be fully investigated, monitored, and treated. Headache can be the presenting symptom, and therefore, a full clinical history and examination should be obtained in all patients with headache and particularly in those with any red flags that may suggest a cerebrovascular disease (CV). (Abu-Arafeh I., 2015, 1530–38)

Again, there is some good news regarding pediatric AVM occurrence although "particularly young children seem to bear a higher risk for hemorrhage from their AVM. Treatment of pediatric AVMs can be achieved safely in experienced hands with a high rate of complete elimination and good clinical outcome" (Cerebral arteriovenous malformations in the pediatric population: Angiographic characteristics, multimodal treatment strategies and outcome, January 2018, 164–68). As seen in another surgery, however, "At 14 months after this treatment the AVM was believed to be obliterated. The patient had a new intracranial hemorrhage 59 months after radiosurgery. Renewed angiography showed an obvious AVM outside the previously irradiated area" (W. Y. Guo, "Even the Smallest Remnant of an AVM Constitutes a Risk," 1993). Conversely, "Between 5% and 12% of all maternal deaths during pregnancy and puerperium are attributable to hemorrhagic stroke, which harbors a maternal mortality of 35% to 83%" (Jose L. Porras, Wuyang Yang, Philadelphia, & Law, 2017). In summary, if you are a younger patient, it would be best to consult your doctor as to the when of operations. Per study after study, the risk of bleed is higher as you approach the late teens to early twenties. As this author would advise, once you have been diagnosed, it is imperative to consult with your doctor for the best treatment options. And note, I said treatment options, as time after time and study after study indicate simply waiting for something to happen is not viable! Whether it be the results from ARUBA or other studies, get it treated! Perhaps it would be an appropriate time to ask what you can do now.

What can I do now?

With the understanding that the bleed is not an end but sometimes rather a turning point, the question should be, "What can I do now?" Perhaps you had a catastrophic bleed that blindsided you. Perhaps you had a minor bleed that only partially affected you. The point is this section's question is phrased in such a way for you to determine your next step, not your final arrangements. From sometime in my church youth group upbringing, I can recall an action acronym that has provided instruction in a three-letter word, JOY. The breakdown is the order of priorities in your life, which should be Jesus, J, Others, O, and Yourself, Y. Keep this as a memorable device as you weigh lofty decisions in light of Christ. And, as we have already outlined the application for the Social Security Administration's benefits, the first item you will need to concentrate on is recovery. Yet remember: Jesus, others, yourself. As you strive to follow

Jesus, you will find your life will be sheltered in His embrace. Then as you soak in His deep-swell healing balm for your ailment, you will both find others to minister to as they are ministering to you! Without revealing names and addresses, I can recall many a person both professional and personal that my wife and I would have never met were it not the divine hand of the Lord! I recall my rehab counselor, who just happened to be a faithful follower of Jesus Christ. I recall the church groups my wife and I joined as we were moved about the United States following the leading of the Lord. I recall the friends who led us to deepen our faith in Him as we found time after time the comfort and security of Him. Thus, I will say surround yourself with persons and personalities who will encourage, strengthen, and challenge you. This will strengthen your person in multiple ways.

As the author can recall his speech therapy sessions, understand you will have to relearn many tasks. In one assessment, "a trend observed was that greater awareness of deficits was associated with more favorable outcomes in the areas of self-care, safety, and independence" (Tamara Ownsworth, 2006). To avoid sounding trite, you really can do anything you aspire to do if you surround yourself with the means to succeed in Him (Jesus). Yet it likely will not be in the same *manner* you did before. Again, only as a personal example, when the author was recovering from his second bleed, he was asked to merely write on a piece of paper with a pencil. After weeks of rehab at HealthSouth in Dothan, coupled with speech therapy from a licensed speech therapist, he was challenged to write on a piece of paper. It *seemed* simple. Yet when he asked from his brain that his hand perform the function, it would not oblige. Fast-forward twenty years later, and that very same patient is now a published author with Westbow Press (https://www.westbowpress.com/en), a bachelor's degree graduate from Dallas Baptist University (https://www.dbu.edu), a seminary and educational specialist graduate from Liberty University online (https://www.liberty.edu/), and a regular blogger (https://malformationblog.wordpress.com/). Time heals a lot that otherwise seems immovable!

Let us not forget though that the Lord gives and takes away. I cannot drive any longer. I cannot see much any longer (I walk with a seeing eye cane). I cannot dance any longer of course I rarely did anyway. I cannot retain information any longer unless I am actively taking notes even in polite conversation. However, through making relatively miniscule steps to utilize the tips, tricks, and techniques in this day and age, you can remedy some of the deficits that either have or will come up!

Though you may see the doorway through this path as being dark and terrifying, there is hope in Jesus! When one who has been through school, has driven, and has played football, racquetball, and other sports can't write his name, you have a problem. That is the point at which again you have a choice. On the one hand, some perverse means of eugenics might weed out the less desirable genetics from humans. Hopefully, however, humans has moved past this. Therefore, we are left with the only option being to treat the condition. But the real question is *where* the treatment starts. It would be this author's suggestion, based on the many articles, books, and days he has experienced, to suggest beginning with a reevaluation of what you have. If you consider what you have been left with, then you have a starting point. But before mourning only the losses, consider the gains! "Our intent is not to discourage patients with TBI or their families and caregivers, but rather to emphasize that TBI should be managed as a chronic disease and defined as such by health care and insurance providers." (Masel, 2010) The author suggests we look with our childhood outlook. Without admonishing widespread cultural regression, allow me to explain.

Interestingly enough, "Young infants often act as though they do not think that objects are permanent. Preschoolers believe that rearranging objects can change their number and assert that the wrongness of an act depends on how much damage resulted" (Miller, 2011). For any person, regardless of condition, ailment, or upbringing, the scope of possibilities is laid out before them. Yet, for the brain-injured community, this scope is limited because of their abbreviated life span. With this possible limitation, what will you do with the time you have left? What if you approached your new life as a preschooler, always discovering, often becoming aware of things you *can* do rather that the rehab routine of finding what you *can't* do? One caveat, however, should be noted. Instead of seeing all that is missing as failed and irredeemable, what if it were merely a starting point? Just as the author could step down the stairs the wrong way and fall to his death, so could any person regardless of his or her station. Instead of dreading possible calamity, why not rejoice in the present as a gift of another day! There are many positions of influence, encouragement, and aid that you might be able to fulfill if you embrace your new station in life.

To again bring the discussion to more tangible terms, one such example that bears exhibiting is Ms. Joni Erickson Tada. Her organization Joni and Friends and her zeal for reaching the forgotten yields another avenue to reach the lost in a somewhat neglected population of every ethnic demographic. Being the forefront of the Christian Institute on Disability, the organization Joni and Friends has Ms. Tada, who is a world-renowned speaker, author, and encouragement to a large portion of the disabled community. In a sense, she is one empowering agent of the disabled to achieve God's greatness for His glory. Ms. Tada's corner of the church citizenry is a unique vantage as it seeks to reach the lost, the hurting, and those who feel shunned for their infirmities. Better said in her and the gospel's own words, "Joni and Friends is answering the call in the Gospel of Luke 14, 'invite the poor, the crippled, the lame, the blind and you will be blessed … make them come in so my house will be full'" (Joni and Friends, 2018). You can gain ideas to utilize your disability to promote the grace of God to a segment of the population that otherwise would never be touched!

From another author, Dr. Sandra Wilson, we read, "Deception flows in two directions: inward (as we try to convince ourselves) and outward (as we try to convince others) that we are strong and invincible instead of weak, wounded, and easily hurt" (Wilson, 2001, 33). As this author recalls, Jesus sought this very audience for His own. As a matter of fact, the Bible records in numerous places that God was searching for this very type! For example, in John 9:1–3 we read: "As [Jesus] passed by, he saw a man blind from birth. And his disciples asked him, 'Rabbi, who sinned, this man or his parents, that he was born blind?' Jesus answered, 'It was not that this man sinned, or his parents, but that the works of God might be displayed in him'" (John 9:1–3 NLT). The Bible records that in this instance, the man was not disabled because he had done anything wrong specifically, but rather so that Christ might use this instance to display His goodness through this man's life.

Having briefly reviewed this example, the question now turns to you. Perhaps you have been beset by test after test and failure after failure. If you have the results, and you have seen the faces of disappointment, disgust, and disapproval, what can you do? What about turning from those who ridicule and put forth these negative emotions and instead turn to the One who made or allowed you to be put in this place? Perhaps it is this condition that God will uniquely use to draw others to Himself, to encourage others who are watching, and to correct the wrong thinking of those who would say you can do nothing!

When Christ was in His final days before the crucifixion, He foretold the brief future in John 12:31–33:

> Now judgment is upon this world; now the ruler of this world will be cast out. "And I, if I am lifted up from the earth, will draw all men to Myself." But He was saying this to indicate the kind of death by which He was to die.

Do you see what He was saying? Christ, aware that His life was nearly finished, aware of the wheels that were already turning behind the scenes to put Him to death, confessed that His purpose on this earth was never for His own but rather for His Father. It was for God's glory that Christ came, was born, lived a perfect life, died on a sinner's cross although He was perfect, and was raised in three days. This was to show the world that humankind can never be perfect in and of ourselves. But, if we cling to Christ, call out to Christ, confess to Christ our need of Him, and come to Christ in repentance, you and I can be made whole in Him. For more information, please read appendix: "Redemptive Workers."

What should I do now?

The question of "what *should* I do" is deeply personal and hardly something this author wishes to delve into in his own life, much less yours. Not knowing your specific situation, it would be helpful in this volume to touch on what this author believes should be done generally at this point. First, recognize that your survival was for a reason. This cannot and should not be missed. As the university where I met my wife Dallas Baptist University says in its "mission verse" in Jeremiah 29:11.

MALFORMATION

*"FOR I KNOW THE PLANS THAT I HAVE FOR YOU,'
DECLARES THE LORD, 'PLANS FOR WELFARE AND
NOT FOR CALAMITY TO GIVE YOU A FUTURE
AND A HOPE.'"*

While this is inspirational, motivational, and seems like something you slap on your locker, weight-room door, or bumper, the quote garners a great bit of meaning in the context. The passage is by the hand of Jeremiah to the exiles of Israel. The weeping prophet, as Jeremiah is called, penned these words of hope. The people of Israel had been carried off into exile. Their country was devastated by war. Their children and wives were sold into slavery. Their hope of peace and security on earth was all but destroyed. Yet in this environment God spoke words of encouragement that speak even today.

This should be a volume of hope for you. Though the title of the chapter has somewhat fallen from common use, "prisal" is, again, "the action of taking something as a prize of war" (Merriam-Webster, 2018). This old word is perfect for the subject! If you look in the Biblical book of Judges we read an oft-overlooked but gem of knowledge that highlights this word's value:

> *"1These are the nations the LORD left to test all those Israelites
> who had not experienced any of the wars in Canaan 2(He did
> this only to teach warfare to the descendants of the Israelites who
> had not had previous battle experience.)" Judges 3:1-2*

Just like the Jewish people, whose youthful introduction to war came at the hands of the peoples they were all too familiar with such as the Philistines (remember David and Goliath?), they had to learn war. You and I are in a battle for sanity and cognition. As this author can attest, the battle for keeping organs is a real ordeal as well. Having lost my appendix, gallbladder, and part of my small intestine, undergoing gamma knife twice, enduring a craniotomy, and enduring a shuntectomy, I understand some of the medical struggles! Moreover, my vision is deteriorating daily, reminding me that this world is not my home. I understand that this life is fleeting. However, I am reminded "That Jesus was flesh was visible face, but that He bore our flesh is a matter of faith. 'To this man shalt thou point and say, Here is God' (Luther)" (Bonhoeffer D., 1997, *Cost of Discipleship*. 277). Even more clearly and succinctly said, apostle Paul states: "I have been crucified with Christ; and it is no longer I who live, but Christ lives in me; and the life which I now live in the flesh I live by faith in the Son of God, who loved me and gave Himself up for me" (Gal. 2:20). Therefore, I beg you—I implore you—you must make the hard decisions now so that as the days progress you will have a Savior and plans subject to His changing.

Based on the wealth of data forthcoming coupled with the studies that have already taken place, there is a tendency to become overwhelmed. Regular individuals, not withstanding being a brain injury survivor, *can* tend to even consider suicide as an option. In fact, "the incidence of suicidal thoughts was 0 percent compared with 6.9 percent for those who'd sustained a single TBI and 21.7 percent for those who'd experienced more than one TBI (p=.009.) A similar pattern was found for suicidal ideation within the past year—0 percent for those who had not had a TBI, 3.4 percent for a single TBI, and 12 percent for those who had more than one TBI (p=.04.) A second TBI made a major difference—researchers initially broke out the groups into the number of TBIs, but "it didn't change the results" (Jessica L. Mackelprang, July 2014 (7)). I have experienced three bleeds. That would place me in the 12 percent bracket and in the 100 percent for *contemplating* suicide. Quite honestly, I have contemplated suicide before. One item of note, however, for me was that the antiseizure medicine I had recently switched to revealed itself as the culprit in my instance. After consulting with my doctor, I was switched to another medication, and I was fine. I did not mention the specific type because I do not wish to tarnish the reputation of any medication because I had adverse reaction. Everyone's chemical makeup is different, so please consult your doctor. But one simple fact that is sometimes missed is the chemical reaction of the medications that have little to do with your actual opinion of life. Again, part of the point of this volume is to direct you to ask the right questions to the right persons to get the right answers!

Again, I switched from one popular antiseizure medication to another, and suicide was no longer on my mind. That is why it is so important to consult the doctor at the first instance you have thoughts that would end your life: "However, as it is written: 'What no eye has seen, what no ear has heard, and what no human mind has conceived'—the things God has prepared for those who love Him" (1 Cor. 2:9). Consider the risk of suicide for others who have vocational stress as well as a brain injury.[22] From data collected in 2001, "The increased risk of suicide among patients who had a mild traumatic brain injury may result from concomitant risk factors such as psychiatric conditions and psychosocial disadvantage. The greater risk among the more serious cases implicates additionally the physical, psychological, and social consequences of the injuries as directly contributing to the suicides" (Teasdale TW, 2001: 71). Also, "during 2008–2017, the national age-adjusted rate of fall-related TBI deaths increased by 17%, from 3.86 per 100,000 persons to 4.52 (Table 1), representing 17,408 fall-related TBI deaths in 2017 (Peterson AB, Kegler SR. Deaths from Fall-Related Traumatic Brain Injury—United States, 2008–17, *Morb Mortal Wkly Rep 2020* 69:225–30. DOI: http://dx.doi.org/10.15585/mmwr.mm6909a2external icon). Though not wishing to surmise and jump to conclusions, I do believe that the lack of a hopeful vision for their future led some to despair, which led to the decision to end their lives. Therefore, it is so important to invest your life in the body of Christ, the local church. Here you may find Christ, find others who deal with varying struggles and issues, and ultimately you can play a part in serving the larger body of Jesus!

Suicide is never the answer. Yet within that three-year period after injury especially, please see a counselor if you have thoughts of ending your life. Though suicide due to depression is certainly a temptation, other factors may need to be factored in (Ursano, Stein, Kessler, and Heeringa, 2017). So many persons with so many different experiences and persons from all walks of life wish to hear *your* story, to see how God has worked in *your* life. If you end your life, you will miss out on imparting the hope, peace, joy, and grace that could be given to you and work through you to give to others! In short, go and tell! With data from the Institute for Social Research at the University of Michigan helmed by Saundra Schneider, "ICPSR (Inter-university Consortium for Political and Social Research) stores, curates, and provides access to scientific data so others can reuse the data and validate research findings. Curation, from the Latin 'to care,' is the process that ICPSR uses to add value to data, maximize access, and ensure long-term preservation" (Schnieder, 2018, https://www.icpsr.umich.edu/web/pages/datamanagement/index.html).

[22] https://www.cdc.gov/mmwr/preview/mmwrhtml/00049117.htm.

As the results speak to the inevitability of death ever on the mind of the researchers, what about the mind of the victim? What if the victim, instead of focusing on the "can't do" side of life, focuses instead on what he or she *can now do?* The author wants to be cautiously optimistic here on your behalf. If you've ever considered writing, what about writing now? If you've ever wondered about a certain language or culture, why not study it and master it? As someone who formerly was an engineering mind, acing calculus, physics, and the like, it soon became clear that concentrating on language and culture was not to my benefit preinjury. However, *after* injury, I was able to take five semesters of ancient Greek and master (at least get a master's degree) with the ancient language in tow. I was able to take three semesters of ancient Hebrew and become fairly proficient in that as well. This was in part due to my new skills acquired through teaching my brain to pursue a new and exciting never before explored path prior to injury! Again, to rescue from the abstract, I am writing about neuroplasticity.

One of the more recent developments and promising findings of neurological trauma has been that of neuroplasticity. "Neuroplasticity is the quality of neural structures to change, primarily through the change in the interconnections of the nerve cells that constitute the structures" (Shihui Han, 2011, 2). Further instance: "Brain reorganization takes place by mechanisms such as 'axonal sprouting' in which undamaged axons grow new nerve endings to reconnect neurons whose links were injured or severed. (MedicineNet.com, 2018, p. Definition: Neuroplasticity) To assuage the unease regarding the technical lingo, our brains become young again! As evidence, consider a study completed in 1998 of 119 patients with AVM; 115 patients initially presented with rupturing. "In 54 patients (47%; 95% confidence interval [CI], 38% to 56%) the incident hemorrhage resulted in no neurological deficit, and an additional 43 patients (37%; 95% CI, 28% to 46%) were independent in their daily activities (Rankin 1). Fifteen patients (13%; 95% CI, 7% to 19%) were moderately disabled (Rankin 2 or 3), and 3 (3%; 95% CI, 0% to 6%) were severely disabled (Rankin 4)." (Andreas Hartmann, Henning Mast, J. P. Mohr, and Hans-Christian Koennecke, 1998). Thus, the plans for what should be done should at least in part rest on validating your family's well-being and preparing for the costs of your own well-being in an expedited fashion.

What? Rather than why?

Lest this chapter leaves you feeling defeated or deflated, or at the very least perplexed, allow this to be an encouragement. If you are alive, you have options. To avoid sounding trite, you could write. A wonderful group, which does take guest submissions, is HOPE After Brain Injury. The organization, led by David Grant, offers resources from a Facebook group and meetings in the northeast United States, as well as contacts within the Brain Injury Association. The basic term of note is, get involved. To the extent that you are able, take this disability as a chance and opportunity to effect change in the culture around you to become aware of brain injury. Also, other avenues of writing may pique your newfound interest!

Consider your life is a gift. Christ's mercy has given you breath today. If you are drawing breath, you have been offered God's mercy to hear Him and respond. The life you live can be great if you turn to Him and respond. The clear, concise, and only answer is Christ. So long as you respond affirmatively to Him, your life can then be a journey of finding out the "what" rather than the "why" of life. You can find out what He has for you to do rather than the why. "What does He have in store?" rather than "Why did this happen to me?" "What would He have me do" rather than "Why can I not do what I used to" will be the aim. "What would He have me become in following Him" rather than "Why should I trust Him?" would be the thrust of your life. It becomes a lifelong pursuit of Him to ask *what* rather than *why* and as such, a story full of the "whats" of joy rather than the "whys" of despair. To hearken back to the story of Jonah, he should have been asking the "what" of "What do You want me to say to them" rather than the "why" of "Why do I have to go!" The Lord knows I have been there, and perhaps you have too!

CHAPTER 5.5
Reprisal

———◆◇◆———

Reprisal: the regaining of something (as by recapture)

The overall action of this book is to take back the pain of injury for those who are brain injured. The good news, for the time being, is that of recapturing a life that otherwise would be lost. In sifting through numerous sources and resources, I came across a perfect word that captures the essence of the chapter: *reprisal*. The word is relatively unused in most civilian sources but nevertheless very poignant. The meaning is so relevant to the subject at hand—life after brain injury. The definition of reprisal gives some clue to its intention from the previous chapter. With "prisal" being used in the previous chapter as "the action of taking something as a prize of war," what then is reprisal? Again taking a military tone, it means "to regain or recapture something that is lost." (Merriam-Webster Dictionary, 2020) Implied in the definition is conflict. For those with a brain injury, though, that is one of the most obvious statements of all time. Some of you will have to fight to walk. Rehab helps, but some twenty years after the initial injury, I still misstep. You will have to fight to use your left side or right side. Some twenty years after injury, I must "wake up" my left side when it just goes numb or to sleep. You will have to fight to find words, as they are trapped in your head but refuse to come out of your mouth. Some twenty years after injury, I still fight to find words that otherwise would come naturally for a "normal person." We are at war, and the next movement should be on our side in an all-out offensive against the forces of the evil one!

It is this second act that we will focus on here—to retake the time, retake the relationships, and retake the physical, mental, emotional, and spiritual deficits that thus far have held us back. Reprisal is an act of war, but our enemy is not ourselves or our treatment team. Our enemy is that of the deceiver—Satan himself—and sin. The deception then follows along the lines of "whatever is not from faith is sin" (Rom. 14:23). When you or I attempt to return to the cultural definition of normal, likely we will be shocked and set back. You likely cannot return to "normal." What you *can* turn to is the Savior of the world who will show you how you can be utilized by Him to reach out and share your story with so many who are hopeless and aimless without Him.

Now the prospect of recapturing enemy territory may scare you. It certainly did me as I recovered from my bleeds. Each time I experienced a bleed, I felt as though a part of my past identity had died a horrible death. Of course, little did I realize that the Christian notion of salvation contains an admonition to do the very same thing! As the apostle Paul wrote some two thousand years ago, "I have been crucified with Christ and I no longer live, but Christ lives in me. The life I now live in the body, I live by faith in the Son of God, who loved me and gave himself for me" (Gal. 2:20 NIV). For those unfamiliar with crucifixion, it was a horrendous, cruel, and intentionally painful process. That is why it was reserved for criminals only. Moreover, Roman citizens were exempt from this punishment, even for murder. And such was exactly what humanity wanted to happen to Christ, the Savior of the world because He was our propitiation, or appropriate appeasing sacrifice.

This fact allows us to point out a few matters that may have been ignored in previous discussion. First, the life you live as a survivor is one of statistical obscurity. You are an enigma, an exception to the rule, but as I and many others of a believing body would say, you're a miracle! If you venture back into the world after recovery without realizing the amazing odds that you have bested, then you will miss out on possibly one of the biggest blessings of the ordeal. Do not consider yourself a failure or a disappointment. Instead, consider yourself a special forces agent to be used of God for a specific purpose! Sure, there may be many that will not understand you. Yet for the millions of other brain-injured persons you could be hope that there is a life yet to life. You were not supposed to live. Statistically you and I should be dead. The wonderful challenge is that we are not! Fittingly then, the decision needs to be made *by* you, not *for you* daily, What am I to become today? To return to the concept introducing this chapter, we must take back through war the loss to the enemy. The enemy, however, is not our brains or even the disease. It is Satan who is causing us to think that the injury, our abilities, and our new life station are worthless! Accordingly, we must choose daily to take in faith our fight to the enemy, Satan, and as such, charge forward in Christ!

You and I are now approaching our destination. It is that uncomfortable spot in the morning or evening that invites farewells, goodbyes, and a host of other emotions. Yet your journey is only beginning. In sharing together on this trip, we have been up the mountains of injury, scaled the cliffs and crags of medical treatment, stepped through the swamps of different treatment options, and descended to consider a variety of venues for answers. In hopes that this book has found some point of correspondence with your life, let me finish this volume in the further discussion of the original French meaning of the word as to reprehend with force with a story from Israel that perhaps will give greater clarity to both the word *reprisal* and the meaning of its selection.

Of reprisal, there was a historical example from the diary of the Israeli prime minister of the time, Moshe Sharett, in response to the Ma'ale Akrabim massacre of March 17, 1954. For those unfamiliar, "The Ma'ale Akrabim massacre was an attack on an Israeli civilian passenger bus, carried out the night of 16–17 March 1954. Eleven passengers were shot dead by the attackers who ambushed and boarded the bus. Four passengers survived, 2 of whom had been injured by the gunmen" (Isracast, 1954 1:29 am). As covered by Israeli news:

> On the night of 16 March, a bus operated by the Egged Israel Transport Cooperative Society on an unscheduled journey carrying 14 passengers made its way from Eilat to Tel Aviv. As it was climbing up the steep grade, it was ambushed by gunmen who shot and killed the driver as well as passengers who tried to escape; they then proceeded to board the bus and shoot and pilfer from the remaining passengers. The male driver, eight male passengers and two female passengers were killed. The four survivors

were a five-year-old girl, Miri Firstenberg, after one of the soldiers riding the bus defended her with his body, two Israeli soldiers and a woman. (Hagen, 1954)

As was briefly commented by a local official in Israel, "Committing a severe responsive act to this bloodbath would only obscure its horrors and put us in an equal level with murderers of the other party. We should rather this instance to accept the compromise to raise political pressure on the world powers, to have them exert unprecedented pressure on Jordan" (Sharett, 17 March 1954) (Caplan, 2015). The delicacy of political arrangement of the Middle East in the 1950s could be mirrored today with AVM awareness. Allow me to explain.

You see, concerning the modern AVM awareness, you and I have a similar choice regarding AVM as Israel in the 1950s. We can allow the formidable conglomeration of medical professionals, psychologists, psychiatrists, nurses, and doctors to treat those of us who have been diagnosed with this neurological disarrangement as a stereotypical head trauma. Then, consequently watch the numbers of those with brain AVM consistently pass away an estimated seven years before the average patient in the ER. Or perhaps you and I can attempt to change the medical practices to allow for a better future for those suffering with and those who will suffer in the future the trauma of AVM. It should be noted, this is rarely the fault of the treatment team! I am not advocating a storming of the towers of medical treatment practices to overthrow the practices of treatment. Personally, I am alive in part because of the doctors, nurses, and medical professionals! Instead, the suggestion I would make is simply that more of an awareness on the part of the medical professionals be made to the rest of the public regarding AVM. When was the last time you saw a poster or advertisement suggesting checking for a history of brain bleeds in your family? While stroke has gained footing due to the FAST campaign (for more info go to www.stroke.org), virtually no global or national campaign has been arranged for AVM. With the recent COVID outbreak, was any effort given to alert the at-risk population of brain AVM survivors? Currently an estimated "6.5 million people in the United States have an unruptured brain aneurysm, or 1 in 50 people" who have the potential for a disabling or fatal brain bleed. (Brain Anyeurism Foundation, 2020) The need to take "back the land" is ripe for reprisal!

I believe that good news rests in the near future, however. The national Brain Aneurysm Foundation has been pushing awareness using the "Stop the Pop" campaign. You can visit www.stopthepopnow.org to obtain quick facts and data about the nature of AVM awareness and advocacy. Moreover, you can visit https://www.joeniekrofoundation.com/ for another organization driving awareness and advocacy for brain aneurysm awareness. The reason these two organizations are suggested is because both are nationally recognized, federally funded, and aggressively targeting the treatment and diagnosis of brain AVM. Though there are some local and even individual-sponsored fund-raising efforts, the public consensus as to AVM's existence seems to be a blank stare and a general shrug of the shoulders! For the author's own life, I would not have known of the existence of AVM much less the full name arteriovenous malformation. The very name it would seem suggests some sort of premed student's flash card ritual and not a real-life problem. "The best estimates for new detection of an AVM are 1 per 100,000 population per year (about 3,000 new cases detected per year in the U.S.) (Sen, n.d.). Yet prior to reading this book, how many times have you heard about AVM? Public awareness is one of the most important changes in culture that would bring additional financing and research to mitigate this problem.

If you wish, like many in Israel in the 1950s, to allow abuse of this travesty to go unnoticed and forgotten, then merely do nothing. Much like the ancient Israelis in various points in Bible times, you will see your people swept away, with little that can be done because of the general ignorance and specific negligence of the populace to recognize this condition. Still, it would be the conviction of many, including this author, that as you have the designation of the condition and medical means to ascertain proper testing for this condition, now is the day and age for its treatment and care.

Now if after working through reading this book you've been encouraged, fantastic! It was intended to be an informative, uplifting, and encouraging vignette into what could be yours or your loved one's next leg of the story. If after reading this book you've been confused or frustrated by the lack of clarity and seeming confusion as to an answer to the questions you came into the book with, let me offer one final plea—revise your questions! The first question you and I need answered, and many would say the only question that really needs answering is, "Who is this Jesus to you?" If He is a good man and nothing more, then you are lost, and as such the confusion likely will become an overbearing burden and, to that end, it is our hope you will find peace in Jesus Christ.

Second, what are you doing to cope with this malformation? More generally, you may not have an arteriovenous malformation but some other malady. I am reminded of Jesus's words to the disciples, before His crucifixion in John 16:33: "These things I have spoken to you, so that in Me you may have peace. In the world you have tribulation but take courage; I have overcome the world." Now there are not a great many support groups for AVM survivors. However, I would suggest checking with your local hospital as often they may have an AVM support group in your area. One such example is the Brain Injury Support Group of Southwest Virginia at https://www.vadars.org/cbs/biscis.htm. This site, as well as many others regarding brain injury, will give you both validation of your disorder and hopefully inclusion into a community quite literally of like-minded persons.

Third, and perhaps one of the most constantly challenging questions is, "What are you going to do with your life now?" With grade-school-aged daughters at the time of this writing, my wife and I are constantly challenged by the "whys" of parenting. Sometimes, these "whys" are legitimate questions with which she and I must wrestle. "Why do we make lights out at 9:00 p.m. a mandate?" "Why do we go to church even though the friend across town doesn't anymore?" Or perhaps more challenging, "Why would God allow x?" I am bracing myself for the third question, but just as He has done in the past, God will provide the answer at the right time and often not. Just be aware, sometimes His answer is His embrace. Remember God told the sons of Korah, "Cease striving and know that I am God; I will be exalted among the nations, I will be exalted in the earth" (Psalm 46:10). We are not to understand all His ways just as we cannot hope to see all that He is doing this side of heaven! That is why He asks us to follow Him, not meet Him.

To be clear, what I mean is if God wanted you and I to simply meet Him in heaven, He would leave instructions on how to get there and then effectively abandon us. Instead, He beckons us through His Son Jesus's words "I am the way, and the truth, and the life; no one comes to the Father but through Me" (John 14:6). As we surrender to Jesus, He simultaneously commissions us saying "Follow Me, and I will make you become fishers of men" (Mark 1:17). So then, as you maybe have seen, Jesus does not simply save us for an eternity, but also for the service of sharing the good news in this life so that Jesus saves us with others for the remainder of our lives on this earth! If the God of the universe wishes a relationship with me and you now and for an eternity, it would be in my best interest to answer an emphatic "yes!". How about you? After all, He created everything. This is not the time to wrestle with my belief or unbelief as I heard His voice! Moreover, if you have read His Word, you have heard His voice as well! As it says elsewhere in scripture: "Today, if you hear his voice, do not harden your hearts" (Heb. 4:7).

For more precise language, a seldom-used word, *reprisal*, needs to be dredged up from yesteryear. Its original meaning was "seizing property or citizens of another nation in retaliation for loss inflicted on one's own." Moreover, from multiple cultures it carried the idea of recompense. Stemming from the Anglo-French *reprisaille* (14c.), from Old French *reprisaille* (Modern French *représaille*), from early Italian *ripresaglia*, from *ripreso*, past participle of *riprendere* "take back," from Latin *reprendere*, earlier *reprehendere* (see reprehend), these cultures all represented the word as a means of taking back what was stolen away. What's more, for all these cultures, all members of said cultures had a sense of necessary recompense for loss in the context of the modern "making it right."

The reason for tracing this word in so many languages is to see the depth and weight of certain aspects that words have in our common cultures. France, Italy, and all Latin languages understand the notion of taking back by force. The modern word we have in English is largely unused. Yet the meaning is so important as to be effective agents in change of our culture for the good, you and I have a mission ahead of us. What is more, few are tasked with the mission, but that is precisely why it is so exciting! You and I can follow a freshly cut path that has only recently been blazed by the Savior, as formerly those with brain injury simply died! Now, countless others could follow to eternal life! We can serve the Savior and seek reprisal to take back the ground that was lost by so many and serve!

The battle

The battle we are looking into is the war of words and deeds between the doctors, nurses, patients, and their families. Remember, none of the aforementioned are the enemy, however. Satan is the enemy. This is not to say the players, whether perceived on your side or the opponents' side, are striving to rule the day. Instead, consider that the battle is against Satan and his forces. They are seeking to "steal, kill, and destroy (John 10:10a). Conversely, Jesus said later in the verse, "I came that they may have life, and have it abundantly" (John 10:10b). That in and of itself should give hopefully a refined perspective on who the good guys and the bad guys are. We must also remember, "no wonder, for even Satan disguises himself as an angel of light" (2 Cor. 11:14). That lends itself to remind, "For our struggle is not against flesh and blood, but against the rulers, against the powers, against the world forces of this darkness, against the spiritual forces of wickedness in the heavenly places" (Eph. 6:12). Do you catch the drift? The medical battles you are facing do not only reside in the present. They started thousands of years ago when Satan rebelled and fell. The battle thus is not one of just misdiagnosis or mistreatment. It is an eternal quest for mastery of your soul. The AVM in question is merely one more distraction to occupy your time until it is too late!

The medical treatment team is seeking to bolster your survival. The nursing staff is on your side. Family members, friends, and coworkers are on your side. Thus, they would all be on the good side. The doctors sometimes have different "weapons," if you will, to attack the infirmity. This does not mean they are attempting only to harm your brain but rather a different attack at the source of conflict—namely, the soul.

With the players and conflict now properly defined, now we can consider weighing the advantages and tactical data that has been gleaned. First a study completed in 2018 records, "The TENP individuals showed a recovery from the trauma over the follow-up, and that was accompanied with increased brain microstructure integrity in fiber tracts primarily involving corticostriatal networks. These changes may contribute to the psychological resilience to a severe life stress that led to PTSD in quake victims" (Linghui Meng, January 1, 2018). Specifically, for brain trauma patients, there are three dominant forms of stroke from the American Heart Association.

Figure 26. Types of stroke (American Stroke Association, 2018)

Within these types, various pitfalls and dangers exist. For each, it is strongly recommended that you consult with your medical team to properly diagnose and treat the condition. However, as is the conviction of this author, the more information you can glean about the condition, the better you can frame the discussion and inquire as to exactly what is being done to treat the illness. Moreover, what this indicates is a truth stated in different terms some two-thousand-plus years prior. First Corinthians 9:22 says, "To the weak I became weak, to win the weak. I have become all things to all people so that by all possible means I might save some" (NASB, 1995, 1 Cor. 9:22). The battle is not against your nurses, your doctor, your family, or even your disease! The battle is against the enemy, who wants for you to die, suffer, and burn in hell for eternity, and that is not what God wishes for anyone!

To illustrate, let's look briefly at a golden gem from the scriptures found in Judges 3:1–2.

"Now these are the nations which the LORD left, to test Israel by them (that is, all who had not experienced any of the wars of Canaan; only in order that the generations of the sons of Israel might be taught war, those who had not experienced it formerly.)"

To be clear, the people of Israel by this time were no longer former Egyptian slaves, as that generation had died out. Now the Jews were being taught war to take the promised land! Nevertheless, they were led out of Egypt, into the promised land, which had inhabitants already in it. They then were told to conquer the people because those inhabitants had refused the grace of God. Therefore, God said that those people already in the promised land were going to be used as a means of training, proving, and conditioning God's people because God uses everyone— for His good or their evil if they refuse Him. Yet, those who wish to be used for His glory and His purposes must surrender to Him. They must surrender to what He has in store for them. It sounds difficult, it sounds painful; there will certainly be loss of life and gains of victory. Yet as with life in any business, school, or even leisure activity, we would do well to consider the losses and the gains.

The losses

First from the perspective of loss, a brain injury survivor is going to face cognitive damages and possible physical, sociological, and psychological impairments. From the physical side, a study was released in January 2018 reflecting the impact of disability on the population of patients from Addenbrooke's Hospital, Cambridge Neurotrauma Outpatient Clinic between 2005 and 2013 below. Out of a sampling of 513 patients, some one-fifth of the patients saw a disability occur within one year of the initial TBI. Further, "this study highlights that patients' physical outcome following TBI is a strong predictor of their subjective mental and physical health" (Anastasia Tsyben, 2018). For more distinctions, please consult the data below. The baseline measurement should be a quick application and approval for disability to alleviate the stress on the family and then working with community personnel to coordinate visits, transportation, and possible employment if the patient is both able and willing. For reference, a study was concluded in January 2018 studying the "traumatic brain injury-relationship between functional impairment and health-related quality of life" (Department of Neurosurgery, 2017, Oct. 7). In it, most persons who experienced traumatic brain injury found their health declining to the point of being considered disabled within a seven- to ten-year period following their injury.

The results of the study are alarming, disconcerting, and beg the question, Can something more be done? Per the study's conclusion, "This study highlights that patients' physical outcome following TBI is a strong predictor of the subjective mental and physical health. Nevertheless, there remains tremendous variability in individual SF-36 scores for each GOSE category, highlighting that additional factors play a role in determining quality of life" (Tsyben A, 2018 Jan.). In another study, from 2002, "Death rates were as follows: all causes, 12.9%; all BAVM related, 8.75%; BAVM related during conservative management, 24.6%; and BAVM related during active management, 3.9% (P=0.031.) Mean diagnosis-to-death interval was 10.6 years" (H.T. ApSimon, 2002). What are these factors? What additional weights give value, meaning, and purpose to a survivor postinjury? For one, a brain injury survivor will have a 46 percent higher rate of death. But the loss of normal living ought not be loss of life! Nevertheless, the marker of learning disabilities *may* be reason for checking with your doctor regarding this existence. "One retrospective study demonstrated that approximately two-thirds of individuals with AVM have a history of mild learning disabilities in childhood or adolescence" (National Organization for Rare Disorders (NORD), 2018). This is not to say that the presence of a learning disorder equals an AVM. This *does*, however, indicate that perhaps ruling that outright *may* be a possible query to pose to your doctor.

As with any news, the problems should be followed with the solutions if you have them. One promising treatment of AM is that of embolization. During this is procedure, glue is injected into the spot of AVM after which the blood flow is then redirected to a different pathway along the veins and arteries. Consider the results of a study finished on January 1, 2018—"The neurobiology of brain recovery from traumatic stress: A longitudinal DTI study"—we read, "The TENP individuals showed a recovery from the trauma over the follow-up, and that was accompanied with increased brain microstructure integrity in fiber tracts primarily involving corticostriatal networks. These changes may contribute to the psychological resilience to a severe life stress that led to PTSD in quake victims" (Meng et al., 2018). While the patient may gain a resiliency to certain traumas, only a portion of the story is told in these results. Beyond the mental struggles felt by the brain-injured community, the general community at large does see in brain injured persons a shortening of life in general. Again, in a study released in 2018, "Shortening of LE (life expectancy) in comparison with the GP (general population) is 3.58 years. Estimated shortening of LE by severity for mild, moderate and severe injury were–0.51, 4.11 and 13.77 years, respectively" (Groswasser and Peled, 2018). This is a measured, documented, and valid estimate from TBI patients. As with any statistical estimate for life, your results may vary!

The gains

The battle would be somewhat bleak if the chapter ended there. Conversely, there are positive gains that can be seen for a brain-injury survivor. The first of which being, what considerations have you given to another either vocation or hobby? For this section, the author can only speak from his own experience. However, I have been a business owner, computer technician, network administrator, pastor, and now author. The interesting fact of this was that the pastor opportunity presented itself only *after* the brain bleed. The Lord works in ways beyond what you and I can see. I was not able to devote the time necessary to write this volume until *after* being let go from a computer technician job as well. My point, and perhaps it was better said by a biblical personality far more notable than myself, the apostle Paul, who wrote:

> "But whatever things were gain to me, those things I have counted as loss for the sake of Christ. More than that, I count all things to be loss in view of the surpassing value of knowing Christ Jesus my Lord, for whom I have suffered the loss of all things, and count them but rubbish so that I may gain Christ, and may be found in Him, not having a righteousness of my own derived from *the* Law, but that which is through faith in Christ, the righteousness which *comes* from God on the basis of faith, that I may know Him and the power of His resurrection and the fellowship of His sufferings, being conformed to His death; in order that I may attain to the resurrection from the dead." (Baker, ed., 1995, Philipians 3:7–11)

CHAPTER 6

Conclusion?

The conclusion for this volume feels misleading. If you have trudged through the bayous and swamps, you know that it feels incomplete. It almost feels as if "The Nothing" has gotten us! It is as though there is a sinking feeling of loss that cannot be averted but is nevertheless swiftly coming. To that end, I turn your attention back to the reintroduction chapter. This life will end, but the question of whether it will end well is largely up to you. For the brain injured, I get it. I can't even pretend to have been through *your* story. Nevertheless, I've been through some tests. I've lost my appendix, my gallbladder, part of my small intestine, had my shunt replaced twice, and been through multiple gamma knife treatments. I've had my skull opened and a plate of bone lifted from it. I can understand some of your pain but not *your* frustration or questions. It is impossible at this moment to pretend that this volume will even answer the many questions of life. It is designed to offer the answer to the ultimate question, Who is this Jesus Christ? Yet to that end, I wish to leave you with a brief story of two persons who ended up being bound up in the same brain.

If you are a child of the '80s, you may recall the movie *The Never-Ending Story*. In it, the lead character, Atreyu, was caught up in a book such that he was transported to Fantasia, a fantasy world being swallowed up by "The Nothing." This Nothing, was the literal embodiment of the death of thought and new ideas. Whether you have ever seen the movie, or even more enjoyed the film, it makes a solid argument regarding our *option* to act or merely allow the flow of events to carry us on into "The Nothing." In dialogue between the protagonist and the chief enemy—the wolf G'mork—we witness Atreyu, the young hero, trying to understand why Fantasia is dying and hear this discussion:

Atreyu: But why is Fantasia dying, then?

G'mork: Because people have begun to lose their hopes and forget their dreams. So, the Nothing grows stronger.

Atreyu: What *is* the Nothing?

G'mork: It's the emptiness that's left. It's like a despair, destroying this world. And I have been trying to help it.

Atreyu: But *why*?

G'mork: Because people who have no hopes are easy to control. And whoever has control has the Power. (Petersen, 1984)

Before I suggest watching children's movies as therapy, let me say that this only serves as an illustration. Nevertheless, the foundational truth is valid. People who have no hopes *are* easy to control. Moreover, whoever has control *does* have the power. As it stands, the control of HHT, AVM, and cerebral disorders of this type often go either untreated or undiscovered until it's too late. In this modern age of medicine, and as a survivor of three cranial bleeds myself, this is unacceptable. Considering this, two stories would befit us as we close.

The first is the story of C. S. Lewis. Originally an ardent atheist, Lewis, through the power of the written word, suggests in his book *Mere Christianity*: "When you argue against Him you are arguing against the very power that makes you able to argue at all: it is like cutting off the branch you are sitting on" (Lewis, *Mere Christianity*, 34). What's more, Lewis was an atheist such that he had formerly re-penned the words of Lucretius (*De rerum natura*, 5.198–9): "Had God designed the world, it would not be a world so frail and faulty as we see" (Lucretius). After reading these words, one would be almost convinced of the validity of this statement. And in the soundbite-driven world we live in today, it would seem not an hour goes by that we are not bombarded with breaking news or "this just in" type hysteria. But what I would suggest, and I believe that the Word of God calls us to, is a calmer more even keel. Again, from the Christian scriptures, Jewish king after king and prophet after prophet of yesteryear wrote, with the assailants of ancient Assyria, Babylon, Persia, Greece, Rome, and others looking on, "God is our refuge and strength, A very present help in trouble"(Baker, ed., Psalm 46:1, 1995). What allowed the king of the Jews at the time to pen these words facing almost certain death? Faith in something greater than himself.

Let us rehearse what revisions to procedure we have investigated as a way of drawing to a close. First, from chapters 1/1.5 the testing for AVM, HHT, and OWR syndrome needs to be included in triage for those who complain of a headache or have passed out, due to the abbreviated time that persons suffering from brain trauma have to survive without permanent and irreversible brain damage. Second, from chapters 2/2.5, the cost of care should never completely preclude a person from survival. We are made in the image of God. For those who disagree with that statement, you may marvel at monkeys, but you still are drawing breath instead of offering food for flowers. Also, from chapter 2, your life expectancy, though possibly abbreviated, was not radically changed from the bleed. Based on this, you now have an opportunity to learn new things at a rate and in a manner equaled only by the rapid motor learning of an infant! Third, from chapters 3/3.5, the direction of your life in the past likely will be facing an intersection. This is not a dead end. Fourth, the life you were living is not the life you will live. However, as chapter 4.5 outlines, it can be an exciting adventure with new possibilities to explore. In chapter 5 we looked at how this life *could* look assuming the overall priorities were arranged in the order of Jesus, others, yourself (JOY.) So long as you proceed down a path with the understanding that you are drawing breath for a reason, as "The mind of man plans his way, But the LORD directs his steps" (Prov. 16:9).

If you've recognized the need for a new lease on life, consider the direction you're headed. If you continue to drive, you likely will take a wrong turn down a well-traveled path that leads straight away from your destination. As the Bible says in Matthew 7:13–14: "Enter through the narrow gate. For wide is the gate and broad is the road that leads to destruction, and many enter through it. But small is the gate and narrow the road that leads to life, and only a few find it." On the other hand, you can continue down the path you were already on. To be clear though, ignoring the facts presented could be likened unto staring into the gaze of the Bugblatter beast of Traal.

The Bugblatter beast is, of course, a fictional creature. Yet its use is very poignant. You See that its introduction is meant to highlight the dangers of ignoring the blatantly obvious, and the Bugblatter beast is introduced to the reader as part of a diatribe regarding the use of towels. The caricature of the beast is certainly fictional, but the truth is nevertheless urgent. The Bugblatter beast was used as a literary device to excise both caution and levity. It was truth presented in a humorous manner. The subject, Adams, was attempting to elevate human ingenuity as the highest form of mental capacity on earth, yet with the same breath highlight the glaringly stupid

> A towel, it says, is about the most massively useful thing an interstellar hitchhiker can have. Partly it has great practical value...wrap it around your head to ward of noxious fumes or avoid the gaze of the Ravenous Bugblatter Beast of Traal (a mind- bogglingly stupid animal, it assumes if you can't see it, it can't see you—daft as a brush, but very, very ravenous) ...

decisions sometimes made from bias, prejudice, or religious dogma. Regardless of Douglas Adams's personal religious persuasions, he was after all an ardent atheist; his yearning for humans to think through their temporal and eternal philosophic positions was so true!

An answer of this world

First, hopefully a temporal answer that should at the very least empower you to ask the right questions. As to the disorders of AVM, TBI, or ABI, these are all relatively miniscule percentages of persons affected by the ailment. Because of this, the sad reality is that doctors, nurses, legislators, and facilitators are often so busy treating the cancer patients, the car accident survivors, and the work accidents that they often overlook the AVM. In trying to accommodate and modify the current medical practicum, this author suggests timely inclusion of an addition to the ER triage for AVM, TBI, and ABI. More recently, the author's personal response from the Social Security Administration, as recent as of January 12, 2018, effectively stated that I was initially declined because of lack of medical evidence. This is after I included the surgeries and neurological problems. So, I appealed. With the appeal I included the copious amounts of paperwork stemming from 2000 up the hospitalizations in 2017. I also contacted my local representative in the government to get that person involved as well. I say this to indicate that the burden of proof is against you because of the stringent requirements held for brain-injured persons.

For more of the background, this author initially applied for disability because he could not see. On purview of advice from both my Brain Injury Services caseworker and my assigned worker with the Virginia Department for the Blind and Visually Impaired, my wife and I went through the proper processes of applying for Social Security. After mounds of paperwork, multiple doctor's visits, and multiple caseworkers across a variety of government and private organizations offering their input as to the validity of the claim, the case was reviewed and then denied. To point out, this is merely correspondence within the existing framework of the Social Security Disability office to include this disorder under its umbrella. The first recommendation was to appeal, this time with a lawyer on my side. Legal action aside, possibly other avenues of resolution exist.

For instance, for those living in Virginia, consulting with your local Department of Aging and Rehabilitative Services office may help. If you have a caseworker from the state, that person may be more familiar with your case and as such offer some pull and validity beyond your own in making this case for you. Further, having your doctors, which include your general practitioner(s), neurologist(s), and neurosurgeon(s), can add clout to your side. Any rehabilitation organization you have visited for rehab can add a touch of empathy for your state. Finally, any organizations that you may be familiar with such as Brain Injury Services, Red Cross, Brain Injury Association of America, Joe Neikro Foundation, and others again validate and further weight your side of decision for you! More information can be found in appendix: "Resources." As to the final arrangements for both family and your own, the National Hospice and Palliative Care Organization is the nationwide organization with a vision to allow patients to experience "a world where individuals and families facing serious illness, death, and grief will experience the best that humankind can offer" (NHPCO, 2018). This leads us at this point to the fact that in the United States, according to the Centers for Disease Control, "The lifetime economic cost of TBI, including direct and indirect medical costs, was estimated to be approximately $76.5 billion (in 2010 dollars). Additionally, the cost of fatal TBIs and TBIs requiring hospitalization, many of which are severe, account for approximately 90% of total TBI medical costs" (Centers for Disease Control and Prevention, National Center for Injury Prevention and Control, 2020). Until increased research and success come from detecting the anomaly, the culture must be made aware of its presence. The answer for the interim? Do not beware but *be aware* of those around you who are suffering in silence.

An answer beyond time

As one might imagine, the more concerning problem at hand is that of what happens when you or I pass away. Again, the purpose of this book is to challenge you, to equip you, and ultimately to provide for you resources and tools such that you as a brain-injury survivor can review, revise, and retool to the best of your ability as the days progress. Those questions, nevertheless, will always end. The author of this volume has no illusions about his abbreviated life span. It is my hope and legitimate prayer that you will find some answer in these pages that will be beneficial to you. If you do not have a relationship with Jesus Christ, that can be remedied by giving your heart and life over to Christ. To do so requires you to admit that you are a sinner. I am and have been since birth. As some of the other support frameworks say, "We admitted we were powerless over alcohol—that our lives had become unmanageable" (Alcoholics Anonymous, 2017). Much like Alcoholics Anonymous, I urge you to first admit that you are powerless over your sin in and of yourself. Mind you, not alcohol necessarily but anything and everything that keeps you from following Christ. The only way this can be done is to invite Jesus Christ to be your Lord and Savior. If you need some assistance, please consult the "Redemption" section of this book in the appendix.

If you are willing to admit that you are powerless over sin, therefore by the Bible's standard, because of sin, you are guilty of murdering Christ. At this point, you have achieved the first step of something far more lasting than deliverance from alcoholism! Before this strikes you as odd, let me ask you, have you ever really hated someone? Have you ever looked at a member of the opposite sex to whom you were not married and imagined a physical interlude with that person? How about using expletives or, even worse, the name of the Lord for purposes other than to call on Him? The price we pay for this is death because there is One Who did not do such a thing. His life was perfect, and for this reason, He was killed by you and I in the most horrifying way—crucifixion.

Nevertheless, in three days, contrary to what most believed, even to this day, He arose from the grave. What's more, you and I are told: "After that, He appeared to more than five hundred of the brothers and sisters at the same time, most of whom are still living, though some have fallen asleep" (1 Cor. 15:6). Now beyond what is for me, the obvious next question I ask is What have you done with this truth? What is more, now that you have had the gospel shared with you, you are accountable with what you do with this truth. I share this with you because you can have eternal life and a loving relationship with the Creator of the universe for all time.

When you die, regardless of whether it is from an AVM, stroke, car accident, skydiving, or falling into a singularity of a wormhole (sorry, that was for my sci-fi upbringing), death is real. We all must die. Some will be judged based on what they have done, of which none of us are righteous or fit the bill for entrance into heaven. The good news is that for the others—those who accept Jesus as their Lord and Savior—He pays the bill, and He takes your place. The most freeing news, however, is that if you confess with your mouth that Jesus is Lord and believe in your heart that God raised Jesus from the dead, you will be saved (cf. Romans 10:9–10). It is as simple and secure as that. Let me be clear, though, that if you do not receive Christ, as He has made Himself available to you, you will eventually die and for eternity burn because you rejected Him. Therefore, I strongly encourage you to make three subsequent steps.

First, find a Bible-believing church and get involved. If you have questions, ask them. If you have doubts, great, so do I. But the wonderful truth about the Savior is that His grace, mercy, and forgiveness are not dependent on how much we know or how often we are faithful to Him. Consider the words of the first century Paul writing to young Timothy: "It is a trustworthy statement, "For if we died with Him, we will also live with Him; If we endure, we will also reign with Him; If we deny Him, He also will deny us; If we are faithless, He remains faithful, for He cannot deny Himself"" (2 Tim. 2:13). What I encourage you to do, implore you to do, and if you are brain injured, beg you to do, is find out Who this Jesus is because He can and will make all the difference in your life.

Second, and at least for now a very important second, find another group of persons to involve in your life. You certainly will need a treatment team. Perhaps searching within the Social Security office visits for local support groups. And there is no prerequisite for membership in most. As an example, the Lynchburg brain injury support group meets the first Thursday of each month at 7:00 p.m. in Heritage United Methodist Church at 582 Leesville Road, Room 206, in Lynchburg, Virginia. Ms. Gwen Carwile currently is the contact at 434-239-7053.

Third, get involved in helping others. There are those who are homebound who perhaps do not enjoy the freedoms that so often you and I take advantage of. At the time of writing, this author just within the past year lost his ability to drive. This does not mean he is homebound. Rather he has time now to devote to reaching out online in the Facebook groups, brain aneurysm support groups, and message boards. For those who are still able to walk, perhaps take some time to walk in your area. If you live in a neighborhood, perhaps taking an afternoon stroll will do you good in both health and well-being. Also, get involved in encouraging others. Remember, you are here for a reason. If you have survived, great! There are others just coming out of the initial trauma who need to know there is hope and a future!

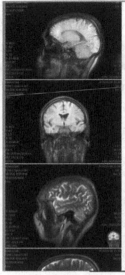

Living with an AVM
By Paul McMonagle

Seventeen years ago, I was diagnosed with a genetic brain disorder. Prior to my diagnosis, I had never heard of an AVM. Is this brain condition an *"irregular, anomalous, abnormal, or faulty formation or structure"* as defined by the medical community? I have asked that question to myself, my family, and my doctors. Most importantly, I asked my God that question.

If this condition was nothing I could have planned, affected, or caused, then why did it happen to me? And if you go down that line of thinking, you will end up in a very dark and depressing place. So, over the last seventeen years that I've lived with this condition, it rather has been a great opportunity to see the grace, the care, the hope, and the love that both has been given to me and is given among those who suffer similar conditions.

The condition of an AVM is one largely shrouded in mystery. AVM's form based on some incorrect gene instructions regarding the construction of faulty blood vessels. It is largely fatal when occurring inside the skull. What should it mean if you have this disorder? Well, rather than lose hope and find despair, I *hope* that you will see it as a gift. This may sound strange, but hear me out. If you are alive to read

Among others, the author happened upon a particular group that may be of interest called TBIHope. Currently managed by David Grant, the group is a wonderful resource for encouragement, connection, and information. The site can be found at http://tbihopeandinspiration.com/. They have a Facebook group, "Brain Aneurysm/AVM Community Together Survivor Support Association (ACT)"; a Twitter screenname, @tbi_hope; a blogger page, http://surviving-brain-injury.blogspot.com,; YouTube collection, https://www.youtube.com/channel/UCZtEisvkV6l7hgJbPYIOnaw; and Pinterest group as well, at https://www.pinterest.com/tbihope/tbi-recovery-motivation/?eq=tbi&etslf=NaN. For the less than tech-savvy, the phone number is 603-898-4540.

Though there are others, I have personal experiences with those mentioned. The point is that there is hope after your injury. You effectively have succumbed briefly to a type of death. As Deidrich Bonhoeffer, noteworthy theologian of yesteryear, said, "If we contemplate the image of the glorified Christ, we shall be made like unto it, just as by contemplating the image of Christ crucified we are conformed to his death" (Bonhoffer, 1959, 343). You have met change. The choice of what to do with your life is dependent on you. Your mental, cognitive, and physical abilities have changed for now. The question is what you will do with this change. There is more to do from the perspective of the injured than ever before, so feel free to get involved. There is more hope and freedom than ever before, so get active! There is more to discover than ever before, so get encouraged! But above and beyond all this, there is a Savior who has allowed this to happen so that you will cry to Him, so ask, and it will be given. My prayer is that you would find Him, find hope, and find your new reason for living. Now, blessings as you go!

CHAPTER 6.5

Reconclusion

In "Reconclusion," a brief story to begin. In January 2018, my wife and I saw *Star Wars: The Last Jedi*. When we got out of the theater, I honestly wasn't all that astounded at the outcome. To spare you the details and the spoilers, the movie has a plot twist. Its significant, but at this point, a movie without a twist is like tea without sugar—it just isn't good until it's made sweet! *The Last Jedi* gave a sense of closure to the story of Luke Skywalker and cemented Rey, Finn, and others in the next generation. This is all well and good, and the movie is enjoyable. But what I want to bring out is something more insidious within the Jedi movie anthology. The movies all are centered around the "force," which, per one of the main character's own discovery, is greatly misunderstood:

Luke Skywalker: What do you know about the force?

> Rey: It's a power that Jedi have that lets them control people and make things float.

> Luke Skywalker: Impressive. Every word in that sentence was wrong.22

To spare you the spoilers Luke has a strange means of dealing with the force shifting and moving without him. Luke becomes a recluse. He is finally located on some obscure island. What happened to the great emperor slayer from *Star Wars: Return of the Jedi*? Simply put, Luke found the reclusive style of life to befit his preference of reality. While this may work for a retired Jedi, this is tremendously dangerous for a brain-injured person. Now if you were a recluse prior to injury, you may find that the recovery process is even more difficult because you *must* reach out beyond yourself to obtain help. I should know because that's me. You can ask my wife, my children, my parents; I am a recluse. I've heard the terms introvert, socially awkward, loner, and any other descriptive terms you want to use. But now I am forced to reach out. This is because I cannot accomplish the tasks that I need to do without enlisting the help of others and admitting my deficiencies. I know this is difficult, but *you too* must reach out. What's more, you cannot expect your friends to know, your family to know, if working your coworkers to know either. They each have troubles all their own. This why it is such a danger that plagues so many. If we consider brain-injured veterans, for example, in the United States it is recorded as of 2010 that 12.4 per 100,000 persons committed suicide. This number is among a population not at war but *after* war. Meaning their battle while on foreign fields has ended, but their lifelong conflict with acclimating with their new challenges proved to be too much. It is as if the coalition between post-traumatic stress disorder, injuries obtained while on the battlefield, and the social aspect of life proved to be an overwhelming force! Consider that the Bible said to all who were trying to do things on their own with no help from others: "For all who rely on the works of the law are under a curse, as it is written: 'Cursed is everyone who does not continue to do everything written in the Book of the Law.'" (Baker, ed, 1995, Gal. 3:10) So, you cannot survive forever apart from Jesus. The good news is you *have* survived up to now.

As one study conducted in India completed in 2018 states:

> Data pertaining to 107 unknown patients were collected. Most patients were found to be males in 3rd decade of their lives with vehicular accidents as the common mode of injury. Patients presenting with Glasgow coma scale (GCS) score <8 at the time of admission had poor outcome and associated with higher mortality. Intra-cranial hemorrhage were predominantly found on CT scan. Only one-third of the patients were discharged after treatment while half of them suffered untimely death. Conclusions: Outcome of these neglected patients is

poorer in comparison to patients who are accompanied by their relatives. Their management from pre-hospital to treatment and discharge from hospital is fraught with challenges. (Ankit Ahuja, 2018)

From a study at the University of South Carolina School of Medicine: "The detection rate in the general population based on prospective data from the New York Islands AVM Study is approximately 1.34 per 100,000 person-years" (Souvik Sen, 2018). The problem, suffice it to say, is real and now uncovered.

If you did not serve in the wars but did serve as one who was a member of society, you and I have a part to play here too. I never served in the US military though my family has served in a variety of divisions. Because of my disability, I would not be fit to serve in any capacity. But if you thought to yourself, *That's unfortunate about those numbers*, then why not do something about it? As such, please view life as a blessing, your future as promising, and your hope fixed only in Him. This is the avenue to the action steps of this book. This author is getting no kickbacks. The purpose of this book is to help the hurting.

Ultimately, you and I will pass away. That is a given. The difference possible between you and I is the assurance of what will happen after. If you have used this book as a type of therapy, let me encourage you to find a group of persons who not only are sharing similar circumstances but also those struggling with other maladies as well. It is estimated that for a male living in the United States, you and I have a lifespan of:[23]

At Age m/f	Additional Life Expectancy (in years)	Estimated Total Years
M 37, F 37	45.0, 48.6	82.1, 85.6

Now the brain-injured community, as you might expect, has a lesser expectancy. That is the bad news. The good news is that due to medical advances, the difference is only seven years, with the average life expectancy of a brain injury survivor being 75 for a male and 77 for a female. What is not included, however, are the compounded medical procedures that likely

---

[23] Life Expectancy Calculator, https://www.ssa.gov/cgi-bin/longevity.cgi

should be expected. From personal experience and medical documentation, the life expectancy of male and female patients is relatively unchanged over the course of a normal life.

> Modern trends in surgical treatment of hydrocephalus are moving towards the greater use of minimally invasive endoscopic procedures and away from routine shunting wherever feasible. Patients with isolated hydrocephalus should have a normal life expectancy, as long as prompt detection and treatment of complications is provided through maintaining appropriate arrangements for long term follow up. (Pople IK, 2002)

Instead of living out your days in despair and dejection, why not find a group of persons who seek your addition for completion! It was Christ Himself who said, "For the Son of Man came to seek and to save the lost" (Luke 19:10).

In reclosing, I want to draw your attention to one more movie that might be worth reviewing. Though our modern sensibilities might make the viewing a little difficult, the story of *Die unendliche Geschichte*, or *The Neverending Story* is a wonderful fairytale to unravel. In the close of the film, the main character, Bastian, is reviewing all that he has seen and done. In a dialogue with the Childlike Empress, the conversation ensues one final time:

> **Bastian**: Why is it so dark?
>
> **The Childlike Empress**: In the beginning, it is always dark.
>
> **Bastian**: What is that?
>
> **The Childlike Empress**: One grain of sand. It is all that remains of my vast empire.
>
> **Bastian**: Fantasia has totally disappeared?

MALFORMATION

The Childlike Empress: Yes.

Bastian: Then ... everything's been in vain.

The Childlike Empress: No, it hasn't. Fantasia can rise anew. From *your* dreams and wishes, Bastian.

Bastian: How?

The Childlike Empress: Open your hand. *[Places the grain in the palm of his hand].* What are you going to wish for?

Bastian: I don't know ...

The Childlike Empress: Then there will be no Fantasia anymore.

Bastian: How many wishes do I get?

The Childlike Empress: As many as you want. And the more wishes you make, the more magnificent Fantasia will become.

Bastian: Really?

The Childlike Empress: Try it.

Bastian: *[starting to smile]* Then my first wish is ...

[The Empress looks up and smiles too, and Bastian is shown riding on Falkor through the sky over a reviving Fantasia]

Bastian: *YEAH!* Falkor, it's even more beautiful than I thought!

Falkor: Like it?

179

Bastian: Falkor, it's wonderful! Falkor, it's like the Nothing never was!

Narrator: Bastian made many other wishes and had many other amazing adventures—before he finally returned to the real world. But that's ... another story.

- www.imdb.com/title/tt0088323/

Do you understand what the close of the movie means? The Childlike Empress is in a position of power and influence. Unfortunately, she does not have the understanding to use these abilities and influence for the purposes of eliciting change around her. She is unaware of the power within herself to motivate others to do great things for others. She is unpracticed with her high station in utilizing her royalty by virtue of her family to exert her Father's wishes throughout the entirety of creation.

Switch the focus now from the childlike empress in *Neverending Story* to the dominion innate within those who have surrendered to the call of Christ on their lives. He has purchased them by His death on the cross (cf. Eph. 2:14–16). He has taken our place on the cross because He desires a relationship with us (cf. Rom. 6:23). He has put to death sin on the cross that you and I might die only once then live for an eternity with Him (cf. 1 Tim. 2:11). He has given us a new life here on earth as well that we can serve Him by serving others (cf. Rom. 6:12–13). He has reconciled us (cf. 1 Cor. 5:20). He has equipped us to fight the good fight against our common enemy Satan (cf. Eph. 6:11). He calls us His children not slaves (cf. Rom. 8:15). All this and a Bible's worth more all because Jesus died and rose for you and me. Yet for all of this and more to take place, one actionable difference is necessary—a personal relationship with the Savior of the world, Jesus Christ. This one-time action seals an eternity of joy and knowing intimately the Savior.

We have seen the conclusion, but now we finally turn to the final pages. The consideration of reconclusion was much like the phenomenon of cinema as of late. If you are a movie aficionado, there often is the after the credits teaser, or additional info. The information given is not meant to box up the story for you but instead to give a slight advantage or an additional insight for those who waited the extra one to two minutes after the credits rolled. You can essentially think of this as the same. The credits have rolled, but the consideration for the remainder of your life will be to consider what you are going to *do* with the information. As my favorite book in the scriptures states: "But beyond this, my son, be warned: the writing of many books is endless, and excessive devotion to books is wearying to the body" (Eccles. 12:12, ibid.). Therefore, what will *you* do?

As you and I have had the opportunity to travel down this road, it is my hope, my aim, and my prayer that you will find your hope in Jesus. Any other search for hope not grounded in Christ, by my belief and far more importantly by the Christian scripture, will fail. Please visit your local Bible-believing church. If they are unfriendly or, more importantly, do not read from the Bible, find another church! Please do not give up. You have made it this far. Your life has been preserved to this point to empower you to do something with it. In brief retrospect, I think it safe to say that Christ has brought you this far. Thank you for journeying together with me. Christ wants to reintroduce you to this life in Him. He wants you to recognize your value, His worth, and the worth of your life in Him. He wants to direct and now redirect your life to chase after Christ to the fields white unto harvest (cf. John 4:35). He wants to make life not only bearable but overflowing, abundant with Him! His rehab includes the community of Christ and the fellowship of persons who do not have it all together! Christ wants you not to think of your life as over but rather just beginning. As you and I follow, it may very well be that the persons we interact with will not understand, and that's okay. You can show them what you know from His Word—the Bible. Just so long as you realize your life is bought with a price, redeemed for a great use by Christ. The venture so far has likely not been enjoyable but meaningful. There is hope in Him! As you close this volume, merely turn the page onto the next chapter of your life. Now onto the next adventure! Grace, peace, and hope in Him! Blessings as you go!

APPENDIX 1

Redemptive Workers

Below is a listing of persons whom the brain-injury patient can likely expect to visit during and after rehabilitation from their injury assembled by the Mayo Clinic.

- **Physiatrist,** a doctor trained in physical medicine and rehabilitation, who oversees the entire rehabilitation process, manages medical rehabilitation problems and prescribes medication as needed.
- **Occupational therapist,** who helps the person learn, relearn, or improve skills to perform everyday activities.
- **Physical therapist,** who helps with mobility and relearning movement patterns, balance, and walking.
- **Speech and language pathologist,** who helps the person improve communication skills and use assistive communication devices if necessary.
- **Neuropsychologist,** who assesses cognitive impairment and performance, helps the person manage behaviors or learn coping strategies, and provides psychotherapy as needed for emotional and psychological well-being.
- **Social worker or case manager,** who facilitates access to service agencies, assists with care decisions and planning, and facilitates communication among various professionals, care providers, and family members.

- **Rehabilitation nurse,** who provides ongoing rehabilitation care and services and who helps with discharge planning from the hospital or rehabilitation facility.
- **Traumatic brain injury nurse specialist,** who helps coordinate care and educates the family about the injury and recovery process.
- **Recreational therapist,** who assists with time management and leisure activities.
- **Vocational counselor,** who assesses the ability to return to work and appropriate vocational opportunities and who provides resources for addressing common challenges in the workplace.[24]

As one might imagine, each therapist can be time consuming and in certain instances costly, which often necessitates transportation and financial compensation. Though the Social Security Administration may be your viable earthly destination for sustenance, other organizations in your local areas are likely available as well.

---

[24] ("Diagnosis," 2018).

APPENDIX 2

Revisited

This appendix is intended to have the author's links and listings to all known agencies or personnel that this author has received help in either the writing of or research of this disorder. While far from exhaustive, it is comprised of over twenty years of personal life with AVM.

Worldwide:

> http://www.avmsurvivors.org/—A worldwide forum written and maintained by personnel interested in AVM disorder. The site sponsor, Bens Friends, specializes in treatment of and awareness of specialized disorders.
>
> https://curehht.org/research/# — "The CureHHT Hereditary Hemorrhagic Telangiectasia (HHT), also known as Osler-Weber-Rendu Syndrome, is an inherited disease that leads to malformed blood vessels in multiple organs of the body and typically begins with nosebleeds during childhood. HHT can result in serious health problems if not promptly diagnosed and treated. Our mission is to find a cure for HHT while saving the lives and improving the well-being of individuals and families affected by HHT" (2018). Please note, it is a specific type of AVM, as there are multiple types of cerebral AVM.

https://curehhtresearchnetwork.org/—Further research participation in research for the HHT community.

https://www2.drexelmed.edu/HHT-ESS/—Drexel University nosebleed severity evaluator for Hereditary Hemorrhagic Telangiectasia.

United States:

http://www.biausa.org/—Brain Injury Association of America

https://www.boston.va.gov/research/Translational Research Center for TBI and Stress Disor ders TRACTS.asp—The Translational Research Center for TBI and Stress Disorders (TRACTS)

http://www.dvbic.org/—Defense and Veterans Brain Injury Center

https://headsup.cdc.gov/ —Center for Disease Control HeadsUp initiative to combat youth sports concussion

http://www.icdri.org/legal/CAP.htm—US Client Assistance Program (CAP) site listings

https://www.ssa.gov/benefits/disability/—Social Security Disability planner

https://www.nhpco.org —National Hospice and Palliative Care Organization, 1731 King St., Suite 100

Alexandria, VA 22314, 703-837-1500 (phone)

703/837-1233 (fax)

186

https://www.ssa.gov/
Social Security Administration Office of Public Inquiries
1100 West High Rise
6401 Security Blvd.
Baltimore, MD 21235
1-800-772-1213 (phone)

National Data and Statistical Center: https://www.tbindsc.org
/Researchers.aspx

The Traumatic Brain Injury Model Systems National
Data Center: http://www.tbindc.org/registry.html

National Association of Guide Dog Users (NAGDU):
http://www.nagdu.org

National Organizations:
Brain Injury Association of America: http://www.biausa.org/

Defense and Veterans Brain Injury Center: http://www.
dvbic.org/

National Data and Statistical Center: https://www.tbindsc
.org/Researchers.aspx

The Traumatic Brain Injury Model Systems National
Data Center: http://www.tbindc.org/registry.html

National Association of Guide Dog Users (NAGDU):
http://www.nagdu.org

National Toll-Free Numbers

National Brain Injury Information Center:
1-800-444-6443

Defense and Veterans Brain Injury Center: 1-800-870-9244

If you are in an emotional crisis, please talk to someone: 1-800-273-TALK (MIRECC, 2018)

Nationally Funded Organizations—Americans with Disabilities Act (ADA):

From the Americans with Disabilities Act, the regions and contact information is below as of 2019:

Region 1—New England ADA

Connecticut, Maine, Massachusetts, New Hampshire, Rhode Island, Vermont New England ADA Center
Address: Institute for Human Centered Design 180-200 Portland Street, Suite 1
Boston, MA 02114
Phone:617-695-1225 (V)*
Fax:617-482-8099
Website: www.NewEnglandADA.org
*Spanish: Ana Julian

Region 2—Northeast ADA Center

New Jersey, New York, Puerto Rico, Virgin Islands Northeast ADA Center (link is external)
Address: K. Lisa Yang and Hock E. Tan Institute on Employment and Disability Cornell University: ILR School
201 Dolgen Hall
Ithaca, NY 14853
Phone: 607-255-6686 (V/TTY)* Fax:607-255-2763
Email:northeastada@cornell.edu   Website:www.northeastada.org
*Spanish: Yessica M. Guardiola Marrero (Puerto Rico)

Region 3—Mid-Atlantic ADA Center

Delaware, District of Columbia, Maryland, Pennsylvania, Virginia, West Virginia Mid-Atlantic ADA Center
Address: TransCen, Inc.
12300 Twinbrook Parkway, Suite 350
Rockville, MD 20852
Phone: 301-217-0124 (V/TTY)
Fax:301-251-3762
Email: adainfo@transcen.org
Website: http://www.adainfo.org

Region 4—Southeast ADA Center

Southeast ADA Center
Address: Burton Blatt Institute Syracuse University
1419 Mayson Street NE
Atlanta, GA 30324
Phone:404-541-9001 (V)* Fax:404-541-9002
Email: ADAsoutheast@law.syr.edu
Website: http://www.adasoutheast.org
*Spanish: Emily Rueber

Region 5—Great Lakes ADA Center

Illinois, Indiana, Michigan, Minnesota, Ohio, Wisconsin

Great Lakes ADA Center

Address:University of Illinois at Chicago
Institute on Disability & Human Development (MC 728)
1640 West Roosevelt Road, Room 405
Chicago, IL 60608
Phone:312-413-1407 (V/TTY) *
Videophone:312-767-0377**

FAX:312-413-1856
Email:adata@adagreatlakes.org
Website:www.adagreatlakes.org
*Spanish:Ancel Montenelli
**ASL:Shannon Moutinho

Region 6—Southwest ADA Center

Arkansas, Louisiana, New Mexico, Oklahoma, Texas

Southwest ADA Center

Address: TIRR Memorial Hermann Research Center
1333 Moursund St.
Houston, TX 77030
Phone:713-797-7171 (V)*
Fax:713-520-5785
Email:swdbtac@ilru.org
Website:http://www.southwestada.org
*Spanish: Diego Demaya

Region 7—Great Plains ADA Center

Great Plains ADA Center
Address: University of Missouri
100 Corporate Lake Drive Columbia, MO 65203
Phone: 573-882-3600 (V/TTY) Fax:573-884-4925
Email: adacenter@missouri.edu
Website: http://www.gpadacenter.org

Region 8—Rocky Mountain ADA Center

Colorado, Montana, North Dakota, South
Dakota, Utah, Wyoming
Rocky Mountain ADA Center (link is external)

Address: Meeting the Challenge 3630 Sinton Road, Suite
103 Colorado Springs, CO 80907
Phone:719-444-0268 (V/TTY)
Videophone:719-358-2460** Fax:719-444-0269
Email: adainfo@adainformation.org
Website: http://www.rockymountainada.org
**ASL: Paul Simmons

Region 9—Pacific ADA Center

Arizona, California, Hawaii, Nevada, Pac. Basin

Pacific ADA Center Address:555 12th Street, Suite 1030
Oakland, CA 94607-4046
Phone:510-285-5600 (V/TTY) Fax:510-285-5614
Email: adatech@adapacific.org
Website: http://www.adapacific.org

Region 10—Northwest ADA Center

Alaska, Idaho, Oregon, Washington
Northwest ADA Center
Address: Center for Continuing Education in
Rehabilitation University of Washington
6912 220th St. SW, Suite 105
Mountlake Terrace, WA 98043
Phone:425-248-2480 (V)
Videophone:425-233-8913**
Fax:425-774-9303
Email: nwadactr@uw.edu
Website:www.nwadacenter.org
**ASL: Michael Richardson

State-Funded Organizations (Alabama/Texas/Virginia):

http://www.rehab.alabama.gov/—ADRS—Alabama Department

of Rehabilitation Services—Created by the Alabama Legislature in 1994, the Alabama Department of Rehabilitation Services (ADRS) is the state agency that serves people with disabilities from birth to old age through a "continuum of services"("Alabama Department of Rehabilitation Services," 2018).

https://www.asbisg.org/—"Educate the public about neurological impairments, who the people are, where to go and how they happen."

Phone: Toll-free TBI helpline exclusively for OEF/OIF veterans and families Veterans Helpline: 888-VET-1TBI (888-838-1824)

Additional TBI help, call Veterans with TBI Outreach: 617-204-3662

SAVE (Statewide Advocacy for Veterans' Empowerment) Team: 1-888-844-2838

800-628-5115

https://www.twc.state.tx.us/find-locations

Email: customers@twc.state.tx.us

http://bisswva.org—Brain Injury Services of Southwest Virginia

https://vadars.org/—VADARS—Virginia Department for Aging and Rehabilitative Services

"The Virginia Department for Aging and Rehabilitative Services, in collaboration with community partners, provides and advocates for resources and services to improve the employment, quality of life, security, and independence of older Virginians, Virginians with disabilities, and their families." (State of Virginia, 2018).

City-Funded Organizations (Lynchburg, VA):

https://vadars.org/—Lynchburg, VA DARS - The Department for Aging and Rehabilitative Services, in collaboration with community partners, provides and advocates for resources and services to improve the employment, quality of life, security, and independence of older Virginians, Virginians with disabilities, and their families.("https://vadars.org/downloads/DARS2014E-flier.pdf," 2018)

http://www.lacil.org/index.html—LACIL—The Lynchburg Area Center for Independent Living (LACIL)—For those living in or around the Lynchburg, VA, area, this organization "encourages and supports people with disabilities who desire to live happily within their community."

Military Organizations:

https://www.dol.gov/vets/ahaw/—America's Heroes at Work—Veterans Hiring Toolkit

https://www.dol.gov/veterans/findajob/—Site dedicated to helping veterans find a job http://www.nrd.gov/—National Resource Directory for wounded, ill and injured service members, veterans, their families and those who support them

https://www.ptsd.va.gov —PTSD: National Center for PTSD

http://afterdeployment.dcoe.mil/—Wellness resources for the military community

Facebook Groups:

https://www.facebook.com/ groups/134820625466/	AVM (Arteriovenous Malformation) Awareness
https://www.facebook.com/groups/avm. aneurysm.network/about/	Brain Aneurysm/AVM Support Group by The Joe Niekro Foundation
https://www.facebook.com/groups/avm. aneurysm.network/	AVM & Aneurysm Network
https://www.facebook.com/groups/ SurvivingSurvivingHeadTrau maSupport	Surviving-Surviving, head trauma support for survivors & family members
https://www.facebook.com/groups/ BAAVMCT/	Brain Aneurysm/AVM Community Together Survivor Support Association (ACT)
https://www.facebook.com/groups/ BrainAneurysmandAVM/	Brain Aneurysm/AVM, TBI & Concussion Awareness and Support Group
https://www.facebook.com/groups/ fightbrainaneurysm/	FIGHT BRAIN ANEURYSM
https://www.facebook.com/groups/ BISfam/	Caregivers and Family of ABI/TBI Survivors

https://www.facebook.com/groups/aneurysmavm/	Brain Aneurysm/AVM Support Group by The Joe Niekro Foundation
https://www.facebook.com/groups/536778616342822/	Arteriovenous Malformation (AVM) Support

APPENDIX 3

Redemption

Of the many organizations that have proven useful in this process, one has provided a more lasting impression than any other for the purposes of sharing the hope that is inside—The Pocket Testament League. Intended to introduce you to the Word of God, it is an organization founded by Ms. Helen Cadbury. "The ministry began in 1893 as the vision of a teenage girl named Helen Cadbury, daughter of the president of Cadbury Chocolates. She was so excited about sharing her faith that she organized a group of girls who sewed pockets onto their dresses to carry the small New Testaments her father had provided. The girls called their group 'The Pocket Testament League'" (Pocket Testament League, 2018). This is, again, not an advertisement for evangelizing with the PTL or an admonition to go shopping for some Cadbury eggs! It is, however, an opportunity for you to see that one grade school girl's fervency for sharing the good news can blossom into a worldwide phenomenon. More information can be obtained at www.ptl.org.

The Cadbury story is captivating to say the least. From John Cadbury's humble beginnings as son of Richard Tapper Cadbury and as one of ten children in Bristol, England, "growing sales of John Cadbury's 'superior quality' cocoa and drinking chocolate meant, that in 1831, a small factory was rented in Crooked Lane, Birmingham, and John Cadbury became a manufacturer of drinking chocolate and cocoa, the foundations of the Cadbury manufacturing business as it is known today" (Cadbury Corporation, 2018). John fathered Helen Cadbury, who per their Christian upbringing, sought a way to carry the good news of Jesus into her day-to-day life. She devised a method of carrying the gospel of John by means of sewing an inner pocket into her dresses and handing out these gospels. The organization born out of this endeavor became the Pocket Testament League. This is a voluntary organization and is in no way affiliated with a particular church or denomination. Furthermore, the author does not necessarily endorse the statement made by Read Carry Share apart from the gospel message and those found in the scriptures. Read Carry Share is merely an organization this author has been affiliated with for over twenty years since my first introduction to it at Dallas Baptist University from a classmate. It is a means to get the gospel to the nations from the casual introduction of the gospel from your pocket!

> Romans 10:9-10: "If you declare with your mouth, 'Jesus is Lord,' and believe in your heart that God raised him from the dead, you will be saved. For it is with your heart that you believe and are justified, and it is with your mouth that you profess your faith and are saved".

Now if you are wondering what this gospel is, it is really simple to understand, but eternally impactful for your life. You see, we are told in the Gospel of John that there was a man named Nicodemus, who was an expert in the Jewish law, which *should* have meant he would know how to be saved. But like most of the Jews and the world then and today, Nicodemus missed the means of salvation. In John 3:10–17 we read:

> "You are Israel's teacher," said Jesus, "and do you not understand these things? Very truly I tell you, we speak of what we know, and we testify to what we have seen, but still you people do not accept our testimony. I have spoken to you of earthly things and you do not believe; how then will you believe if I speak of heavenly things? No one has ever gone into heaven except the one who came from heaven—the Son of Man. Just as Moses lifted the snake in the wilderness, so the Son of Man must be lifted up, that everyone who believes may have eternal life in Him. For God so loved the world that he gave his one and only Son, that whoever believes in him shall not perish but have

eternal life. For God did not send his Son into the world to condemn the world, but to save the world through Him."

This means it is as simplistic as ABC.

A: Admit that you are a sinner. This means that you have broken God's commands.

B: Believe that Jesus came to pay for all the sins you and I have or will commit.

C: Confess that Jesus is the only way to God, to heaven, and to have eternal life.

To view the full presentation, please visit: https://www.ptl.org/sharing/umbrella/

Courtesy of ReadCarryShare.org and the Pocket Testament League.

If you have decided to follow Jesus Christ and receive Him as your Lord and Savior, welcome! You have embarked on a journey that will last forever! Remember, we all die. But only some of us will truly live with Christ forever in eternity with Him if we have confessed with our mouth Jesus is Lord and believed in our heart that God raised Jesus from the dead (cf. Romans 10:9–10)! If this is your circumstance, please reach out to a local church in your area who believes the Bible and preaches Jesus Christ. Also, please write to https://twitter.com/mcmalform or mcmalform@gmail.com Finally follow the blog at https://malformationblog.wordpress.com.

APPENDIX 4

Relate

Paul Shawn McMonagle psmcmonagle@gmail.com

Facebook: www.facebook/com/randombeggar

Twitter: https://twitter.com/randombeggar

Email: mcmalform@gmail.com

Blog: https://malformationblog.wordpress.com/

Website: https://www.themalformation.com (coming 2nd quarter 2021)

ADDITIONAL CONTACT INFORMATION

University of Alabama at Birmingham: Thomas Novack—https://www.uab.edu/medicine/tbi/contact

Craig Hospital: Cindy Harrison-Felix—https://craighospital.org/contact

Miami University: Doug Johnson-Greene—http://people.miami.edu/profile/djgreene@miami.edu

Iowa University: Flora Hammond—https://medicine.iu.edu/faculty/20302/hammond-flora/

Harvard University: Joseph Giacino—https://connects.catalyst.harvard.edu/Profiles/display/Person/91704

The Mayo Clinic: Allen Brown—https://www.mayoclinic.org/biographies/brown-allen-w-m-d/bio-20054281?_ga=2.137556080.1579695087.1517329789-1622064450.1515098440

The Kessler Foundation: Nancy Chiaravalloti—https://kesslerfoundation.org/aboutus/Nancy%20Chiaravalloti

Wayne Gordon—http://icahn.mssm.edu/profiles/wayne-a-gordon

Tamara Bushnik—https://med.nyu.edu/faculty/tamara-bushnik

John Corrigan—https://wexnermedical.osu.edu/find-a-doctor/john-corrigan-phd-17846

Amy Wagner—(412) 648-6666, akw4@pitt.edu

Tessa Hart—(215) 663-6677

Mark Sheerer—msherer@bcm.edu https://www.bcm.edu/people/view/mark-sherer-ph- d/b21f134f-ffed-11e2-be68-080027880ca6

Jeffrey Kreutzer—(804) 327-1166 jeffrey.kreutzer@vcuhealth.org

Jeanne Hoffman—http://www.uwmedicine.org/bios/jeanne-hoffman

GLOSSARY

AVM. arteriovenous malformation. "Normally, arteries carry blood containing oxygen from the heart to the brain, and veins carry blood with less oxygen away from the brain and back to the heart. When an arteriovenous malformation (AVM) occurs, a tangle of blood vessels in the brain bypasses normal brain tissue and directly diverts blood from the arteries to the veins. - https://www.stroke.org/en/about-stroke/types-of-stroke/hemorrhagic-strokes-bleeds/what-is-an-arteriovenous-malformation"

ARUBA. "A Randomized Trial of Unruptured Brain Arteriovenous Malformations" – "The ARUBA study: where do we go from here?" - J Neurosurg 126:481–485, 2017, https://www.ncbi.nlm.nih.gov/pubmed/29040773

craniotomy. "A craniotomy is the surgical removal of part of the bone from the skull to expose the brain. Specialized tools are used to remove the section of bone called the bone flap. The bone flap is temporarily removed, then replaced after the brain surgery has been done" – Johns Hopkins, "Craniotomy" https://www.hopkinsmedicine.org/health/treatment-tests-and-therapies/craniotomy.

CCU. "Critical Care Unit" – "Mayo Clinic's critical care doctors treat people who need advanced monitoring and care. The full spectrum of critical care services is provided by doctors and other medical professionals specially trained in critical care (intensivists) who are present in Mayo Clinic hospitals 24 hours a day, 365 days a year" https://www.mayoclinic.org/departments-centers/critical-care/sections/overview/ovc-20399554.

gamma knife. "A type of radiosurgery (radiation therapy) machine that acts by focusing low-dosage gamma radiation from many sources on a precise target. Areas adjacent to the target receive only slight doses of radiation, while the target gets the full intensity" Medical Author: William C. Shiel Jr., MD, FACP, FACR https://www.medicinenet.com/script/main/art.asp?articlekey=12192.

hereditary. "(of a characteristic or disease) determined by genetic factors and therefore able to be passed on from parents to their offspring or descendants. Ibid.

hydrocephalus. Hydrocephalus is a condition in which an excess of cerebrospinal fluid accumulates in the cavities of the brain known as 'ventricles.' https://www.medtronic.com/us-en/patients/conditions/hydrocephalus.html

ICU. intensive care unit. "The intensive care unit is a designated area of a hospital facility that is dedicated to the care of patients who are seriously ill" William C. Shiel Jr., MD, FACP, FACR, https://www.medicinenet.com/script/main/art.asp?articlekey=3891.

ischemic stroke. "Ischemic stroke occurs when a vessel supplying blood to the brain is obstructed. It accounts for about 87 percent of all strokes" 2020 American Heart Association, Inc, https://www.stroke.org/en/about-stroke/types-of-stroke/ischemic-stroke-clots.

intraventricular hemorrhage. "When IVH occurs, the blood vessels of the brain bleed into nearby ventricles." Cerebral Palsy Group. https://cerebralpalsygroup.com/cerebral-palsy/causes/intraventricular-hemorrhage/

SAH. subarachnoid hemorrhage. "Subarachnoid hemorrhage (SAH) is a life-threatening type of stroke caused by bleeding into the space surrounding the brain. SAH can be caused by a ruptured aneurysm, AVM, or head injury. One-third of patients will survive with good recovery; one-third will survive with a disability; and one-third will die." https://d3djccaurgtij4.cloudfront.net/pe-sah.pdf

schemic stroke. "Hemorrhagic Stroke (Bleeds.) Occurs when a weakened blood vessel ruptures. The two types of weakened blood vessels that usually cause hemorrhagic stroke are aneurysms and arteriovenous malformations (AVMs.)" https://www.stroke.org/en/about-stroke/types-of-stroke

shuntectomy. "Hydrocephalus is a condition in which an excess of cerebrospinal fluid accumulates in the cavities of the brain known as 'ventricles.'"

ventriculoperitoneal (VP) shunt. "During this surgical procedure, a small drainage tube is implanted to relieve the pressure of hydrocephalus. Hydrocephalus is a condition that develops when excess cerebrospinal fluid builds up within the ventricles of the brain" University of Alabama at Birmingham Medical Center https://neurosurgicalassociatespc.com/ventriculoperitoneal-shunts-for-hydrocephalus/

BIBLIOGRAPHY

Abu-Arafeh I., M. K. (2015.) *Headache: Comorbidity with Vascular Disorders.* Switzerland: Springer International Publishing. doi:978-3-319-54726-8.

Agency for Healthcare Research and Quality. (2013.) *Statistical Brief #146.* 2013: Healthcare Cost and Utilization Project.

Aki Laakso, M. P. (2011, February.) "Risk of Hemorrhage in Patients with Untreated Spetzler-Martin Grade IV and V Arteriovenous Malformations: A Long-Term Follow-up Study in 63 Patients." *Neurosurgery,* 372–78. doi: https://doi.org/10.1227/NEU.0b013e3181ffe931.

Alcoholics Anonymous. (2017, December 1.) *Alcoholics Anonymous Step 1: Admit Powerlessness.* Retrieved from Recovery.org: https://www.recovery.org/topics/step-1-aa/.

Allen W. Brown, A. M. (2015.) "A randomized practical behavioral trial of curriculum-based advocacy training for individuals with traumatic brain injury and their families." *Brain Injury* 29, no. 13–14, 1530–38.

Alzheimer's Association. (2018, February.) "Traumatic Brain Injury." Retrieved from Alzheimer's Association: https://www.alz.org/dementia/traumatic-brain-injury-head-trauma- symptoms.asp.

American Art Therapy Association. (2018, February.) "About the American Art Therapy Association." Retrieved from American Art Therapy Association: https://arttherapy.org/about/.

American Heart Association/American Stroke Association. (2017, April 26.) "Ischemic Strokes (Clots.)" Retrieved from American Stroke Association: http://www.strokeassociation.org/STROKEORG/ AboutStroke/TypesofStroke/IschemicCl ots/Ischemic-Strokes-Clots_ UCM_310939_Article.jsp#.Wn3mCKinHcc.

American Stroke Association. (2018, February 15.) American Stroke Association. Retrieved from Types of Stroke: http://www. strokeassociation.org/STROKEORG/AboutStroke/TypesofStroke/ Types-of- Stroke_UCM_308531_SubHomePage.jsp.

Anastasia Tsyben, &. M. (2018.) "Spectrum of outcomes following traumatic brain." *Acta Neurochir*, 160:107–15. doi: I 10.1007/s00701-017-3334-6.

Andreas Hartmann, M., Henning Mast, M., J.P. Mohr, M., and Hans-Christian Koennecke, M. (1998.) "Morbidity of Intracranial Hemorrhage in Patients with Cerebral Arteriovenous Malformation." *Stroke*, 931–34.

Ankit Ahuja, S. V. (2018.) "Outcome of traumatic head injury in unknown patients." *Int Surg J* 5:633–37.

Answers in Genesis. (2018, January 18.) "How do we know there is a God?" Retrieved from Answers in Genesis: https://answersingenesis. org/is-god-real/how-do-we-know-there-is- a-god/.

A Stefani MD And, P. P.-S. (2014, February .) "Medical management with or without interventional therapy for unruptured brain arteriovenous malformations (ARUBA): a multicenter, nonblinded, randomized trial." *The Lancet*, 614–21.

Auburn University. (2018, February 27.) "Rehabilitation and Disability Studies Mission."

Retrieved from Auburn.edu: http://www.education.auburn.edu/department-of-special- education-rehabilitation-and-counseling/rehabilitation-disabi lity-studies-mission/.

BA Foundation. (2018, February.) "Early Detection and Screening." Retrieved from Brain Aneurysm Foundation: https://www.bafound. org/about-brain-aneurysms/diagnosis/early- detection-and-screening/.

Baker, K. (1995.) *NASB Study Bible.* Grand Rapids, Psalm 46:1–2: Zondervan.

Beecher JS, L. K. (2017, July.) "Delayed treatment of ruptured brain AVMs: is it ok to wait?"

Journal of Neurosurgery 7, 1–7. doi:10.3171/2017.

Bohannon, J. (2010, October 29.) "Leaked Documents Provide Bonanza for Researchers."

Science, p. pp. 575.

Bonhoeffer, D. (1937.) *The cost of discipleship.* New York: MacMillan.

Brain Aneurysm Foundation. (2018, January.) "Brain Aneurysm Statistics and Facts." Retrieved from Brain Aneurysm Foundation: https:// www.bafound.org/about-brain- aneurysms/brain-aneurysm-basics/ brain-aneurysm-statistics-and-facts/.

Brinjikji W, K. D. (2012.) "Hospitalization costs for endovascular and surgical treatment of unruptured cerebral aneurysms in the United States are substantially higher than Medicare payments." *AJNR Am J Neuroradiol.* doi:10.3174/ajnr.A2739.

Brothers, T. W. (director.) (1999.) *The Matrix* [Motion Picture].

Bruce E. Pollock, J. C. (1996.) "Factors That Predict the Bleeding Risk of Cerebral Arteriovenous Malformations." *Stroke, 1996* (27), 1–6. doi: https://doi.org/10.1161/01.STR.27.1.1.

Cadbury Corporation. (2018.) "The Story of Cadbury." MELBOURNE VIC: Cadbury Corporation.

"Cerebral arterio-venous malformations in the paediatric population: Angiographic characteristics, multimodal treatment strategies and outcome." (January 2018.) *Clinical Neurology and Neurosurgery,* 164–68.

Charles Antoni, A.-S. R., & COL Michael A. Silverman, M. U. (2012.) "Providing Support Through Life's Final Chapter for Those Who Made It Home." *MILITARY MEDICINE,* 12:1498, 177.

Christensen, B. (2014.) *Modified Rankin Scale.* New York: Medscape. Christopher S. Ogilvy, M. a. (2018, January 5.) "Central Nervous System Vascular Malformations: A Patient's Guide." Retrieved from Massachusetts General Hospital:

https://neurosurgery.mgh.harvard.edu/neurovascular/vascintr.htm#AVM.

Clare L. Atzema, M. J. (2012.) "Wait times in the emergency department for patients with mental illness." *CMAJ* 184 (18) E969-E976.

Clinical Epidemiology Unit and Department of Emergency Services. (2007.) "Ontario EDs misdiagnose 1 in 20 ruptured brain aneurysms." *Stroke: ICES Data.* Retrieved from https://www.ices.on.ca/Newsroom/News-Releases/2007/ Ontario-EDs-misdiagnose-1-in- 20-ruptured-brain-aneurysms.

Cohen, L. G., and Spenciner, L. J. (2011.) *Assessment of Children and Youth with Special Needs.*

Cole SG, B. M. (2005.) *A new locus for hereditary haemorrhagic telangiectasia (HHT3) maps to chromosome 5.*

Concordance, E. S. (2016.) *Strong's Exhaustive Concordance.* Baker Publishing. Coronado, V. G., Haileyesus, T. M., Cheng, T. A., Bell, J. M., Haarbauer-Krupa, J. P.

Lionbarger, M. R., … Gilchrist, J. M. (2015, May/June.) "Trends in Sports- and Recreation-Related Traumatic Brain Injuries Treated in US Emergency Departments: The National Electronic Injury Surveillance System-All Injury Program" (NEISS-AIP) 2001–12. (J. M. Bell, C. A. Taylor, and M. J. Breiding, eds.) *The Journal of Head Trauma Rehabilitation* 30, no. 3), 185–97.

CureHHT. (2018, 1 9.) Retrieved from https://curehht.org/: https://curehht.org/.

Ibid. (2018, January 18.) *https://curehht.org/get-involved/raise-awareness/*. Retrieved from Raise Awareness for HHT: https://curehht.org.

DARS. (2018, 1 5.) *https://vadars.org/downloads/DARS2014E-flier.pdf*. Retrieved from https://vadars.org/: https://vadars.org/.

Department of Neurology, B. I. (2018.) "Safety and Costs of Stroke Unit Admission for Select Acute Intracerebral Hemorrhage Patients." *The Neurohospitalist* 8, no. 1, 12–17.

Department of Neurosurgery, A. H. (2017 Oct 7.) "Spectrum of outcomes following traumatic brain injury-relationship between functional impairment and health-related quality of life. *Acta Neurochir (Wien)*, 107–15.

Department of Neurosurgery, Kyoto University School of Medicine. (1999; 9 (3), May 25.) "Do cerebral arteriovenous malformations recur after angiographically confirmed total extirpation?" *Department of Neurosurgery, Kyoto University School of Medicine* (May 25), 606-8507. Retrieved from https://www.ncbi.nlm.nih.gov/pubmed/10369967.

Department of Numbers. (2017.) *Virginia Household Income*. Department of Numbers. Dictionary.com. (n.d.). *http://www.dictionary.com/browse/rehabilitation*. Retrieved from

Dictionary.

Disney, W. (Director.) (1940.) *Pinnochio* [Motion Picture].

E. M. de Gussem, C. P. (2016.) "Life expectancy of parents with Hereditary Haemorrhagic Telangiectasia." *Orphanet Journal of Rare Diseases,* 11:46.

Edward R. Smith, W. E. (May 2012.) "In-hospital mortality rates after ventriculoperitoneal shunt procedures in the United States, 1998 to 2000: relation to hospital and surgeon volume of care." *Journal of Neurosurgery,* 116, no. 5: 90–97. Retrieved from http://thejns.org/doi/abs/10.3171/2012.05.C1.

Faustina N A Sackey, c. N. (2017, May.) "Highlights on Cerebral Arteriovenous Malformation Treatment Using Combined Embolization and Stereotactic Radiosurgery: Why Outcomes are Controversial?" *Cureus,* e1266. doi:http://doi.org/10.7759/curl.

Gamma Knife Radiosurgery. (2018, February.) Retrieved from Columbia Neurological Surgery: https://www.columbianeurosurgery.org/treatments/gamma-knife-radiosurgery/.

Gloviczki, P. (2008.) *Handbook of Venous Disorders : Guidelines of the American Venous Forum, 3rd ed.* Boca Raton, FL: CRC Press.

Groswasser, Z., and Peled, I. (2018.) "Survival and mortality following TBI." *Brain Injury,* 149–57. doi:10.1080/02699052.2017.1379614.

Gunel, M., and Machuk, D. (2013.) "Arteriovenous Malformation." Danbury, CT: National Organization for Rare Disorders (NORD.) Retrieved from https://rarediseases.org/rare- diseases/arteriovenous-malformation/.

H.T. ApSimon, H. R. (2002.) "A Population-Based Study of Brain Arteriovenous Malformation: Long-Term Treatment Outcomes." *Stroke,* 2794–2800.

Hart, A. (1999.) *The Anxiety Cure.* Nashville: Thomas Nelson.

Hasegawa, H. (2018.) "Does Advanced Age Affect the Outcomes of Stereotactic Radiosurgery for Cerebral Arteriovenous Malformation?" *World Neurosurgery* 109 (January), e715-e723. doi:https://doi.org/10.1016/j.wneu.2017.10.071.

Hirotaka Hasegawa, S. H. (January 2018.) "Does Advanced Age Affect the Outcomes of Stereotactic Radiosurgery for Cerebral Arteriovenous Malformation?

Elsevier, e715–e723.

Humphreys I, W. R. (2013.) *Clinicecon outcome res.* Wales: ClinicoEconomics and Outcomes Research.

Humphreys, I., Wood, R. L., Phillips, C. J., and Macey, S. (2013.) *The costs of traumatic brain injury: a literature review.* Wales, UK: Swansea University.

Intrepid Spirit Center/TBI Clinic. (2018.) "Mission and Vision." Fort Hood, TX: US Army Medical Department.

J. H. Olver, J. L. (1996.) "Outcome following traumatic brain injury: a comparison between 2 and 5 years after injury." *Brain Injury,* 841–48.

Jason A. Ellis, M., and Sean D. Lavine, M. (2014 Oct.-Dec.) "Role of Embolization for Cerebral Arteriovenous Malformations." *Methodist DeBakey Cardiovascular Journal* 10(4), 234–39. doi:10.14797/mdcj-10-4-234.

Jefferson, T. (1776.) *Preamble to the constitution.* Philadelphia: United States of America.

Jessica L. Mackelprang, P. a. (July 2014 (7).) "Rates and Predictors of Suicidal Ideation During the First Year After Traumatic Brain Injury." *American Journal of Public Health,* e100- e107.

Johnny Wong, P., Alana Slomovic, B., George Ibrahim, P., and Ivan Radovanovic, P. (2017.)

Microsurgery for ARUBA Trial (A Randomized Trial. *Stroke. originally published online November 17, 2016*, 136–44.

Ibid. "Microsurgery for ARUBA Trial (A Randomized Trial) of Unruptured Brain Arteriovenous Malformation)–Eligible Unruptured Brain Arteriovenous Malformations." *Stroke*, 136–44.

Joni and Friends. (2018, February.) "About Us." Retrieved from http://www.joniandfriends.org/: http://www.joniandfriends.org/about-us/.

Jose L. Porras, B., Wuyang Yang, M. M., Philadelphia, E., and Law, J. (2017.) "Hemorrhage Risk of Brain Arteriovenous Malformations During Pregnancy and Puerperium in a North American Cohort." *Stroke*, 1–6.

Josephus, F. (August 3, 2013.) *Wars of the Jews.* (W. Whiston, trans.) Retrieved from http://www.gutenberg.org/files/2850/2850-h/2850-h.htm.

Juha A. Hernesniemi, M. P. (01 November 2008.) Natural History of Brain Arteriovenous Malformations: A Long-Term Follow-Up Study of Risk of Hemorrhage in 238 Patients. *Neurosurgery, Neurosurgery* 63, no. 5,.5E 823–31. doi:https://doi.org/10.1227/01.NEU.0000330401.82582

(1 November 2008.) NATURAL HISTORY OF BRAIN ARTERIOVENOUS MALFORMATIONS: A LONG-TERM FOLLOW-UP STUDY OF RISK OF HEMORRHAGE IN 238 PATIENTS..

Kanel, K. (2007.) *A guide to crisis intervention*, 3rd ed. Boston: Cengage.

Kang, A. I. (2008, April 17.) "Understanding Sequelae of Injury Mechanisms and Mild Traumatic Brain Injury Incurred during the Conflicts in Iraq and Afghanistan: Persistent Postconcussive Symptoms and Posttraumatic Stress Disorder." *American Journal of Epidemiology* 167, no. 12: 1446–52.

Khan Academy. (2018, February.) Retrieved from https://www. khanacademy.org/math/pre- algebra/pre-algebra-arith-prop/ pre-algebra-order-of-operations/v/introduction-to-order- of-operations.

King, J. L. (2016.) *Art therapy, trauma, and neuroscience: theoretical and practical perspectives.* New York: Routledge.

Klaus-Dieter Lessnau, M. F. (2018, January 18.) "Osler-Weber-Rendu Disease (Hereditary Hemorrhagic Telangiectasia.)" Retrieved from https://emedicine.medscape.com/: https://emedicine.medscape.com/ article/2048472-overview.

Klaus-Peter Steina, B.-O. H. (August 2017.) "Cerebral arterio-venous malformations in the paediatric population: Angiographic characteristics, multimodal treatment strategies and outcome." *Clinical Neurology and Neurosurgery* 164 (2018), 164–68. doi:doi.org/10.1016/j. clineuro.2017.12.006.

Klaus-Peter, S., Bernd-Otto, H., Goerickeb, S., Oezkana, N., Leyrerall, R., Sandalciogluc, E., ...

Muellera, O. (2018, January.) "Cerebral arterio-venous malformations in the paediatric population: Angiographic characteristics, multimodal treatment strategies and outcome." *Clinical Neurology and Neurosurgery,* 164–68. Retrieved from https://doi.org/10.1016/j. clineuro.2017.12.006.

Kwon Y, J. S. (December 2000.) "Analysis of the causes of treatment failure in gamma knife radiosurgery for intracranial arteriovenous malformations." *J Neurosurg*: 104–6. doi:10.3171/jns.2000.93. supplement.

Lenore Hawley, D. G. (2015.) "Improving personal self-advocacy skills for individuals with brain injury: A randomized pilot feasibility study."

Journal of Social Work in Disability & Rehabilitation 15, no. 3–4: 201–12.

Lewis, C. S. (1952.) *Mere Christianity.* New York: HarperCollins.

Linghui Meng, Y. C. (January 1, 2018 .) "The neurobiology of brain recovery from traumatic stress: A longitudinal DTI study." *Journal of Affective Disorders* 225, 577–84.

livius.org. (2018, February 8.) *ABC 3 (Fall of Nineveh Chronicle.)* Retrieved from livius.org: http://www.livius.org/sources/content/ mesopotamian-chronicles-content/abc-3-fall-of- nineveh-chronicle/?

Lorch, N. (2013.) Israel's War of Independence (1947-1949.) In N. Lorch, *The Arab-Israeli Wars.* Jerusalem: Israel Ministry of Foreign Affairs. Retrieved from http://mfa.gov.il/MFA/AboutIsrael/History/Pages/ Israels%20War%20of%20Independenc e%20-%201947%20-%20 1949.aspx.

Lucretius. (n.d..) *De rerum natura* (vol. 5.).

Marian J. Vermeulen, M. J. (2007.) "Missed Diagnosis of Subarachnoid Hemorrhage in the Emergency Department." *Stroke* 38, no. 4. Retrieved from http://stroke.ahajournals.org/content/38/4/1216.short.

Mario Zuccarello, M., & Andrew Ringer, M. (2018, February.) *Arteriovenous malformation (AVM.)* Retrieved from Mayfield Brain & Spine: https://www.mayfieldclinic.com/PE- AVM.htm.

Marks, M. P., L.Marcellus, M., Santarelli, J., Dodd, R. L., Do, H. M., D.Chang, S., … K.Steinberg, G. (March 2017.) "Embolization Followed by Radiosurgery for the Treatment of Brain Arteriovenous Malformations (AVMs.)" *World Neurosurgery* 99: 471–76. doi: https:// doi.org/10.1016/j.wneu.2016.12.059.

Marshall, G. (Director.) (1999.) *The Other Sister* [Motion Picture].

Masaaki Yamamoto, M. M. (1996, May 1.) "Gamma Knife Radiosurgery for Arteriovenous Malformations: Long-term Follow-up Results Focusing on Complications Occurring More than 5 Years after Irradiation." *Neurosurgery, 38*(5), 906–14. doi: https://doi.org/10.1097/00006123-199605000-00001.

Masahiro Shin, M. S. (2011, October.) "Retrospective analysis of a 10-year experience of stereotactic radiosurgery for arteriovenous malformations in children and adolescents." *Journal of neurosurgery,* 779–84.

Masel, B. E. (2010.) "Traumatic Brain Injury: A Disease Process, Not an Event." *Journal of Neurotrauma, 27 no. 8:* 15929-1540.

Mayfield Brain & Spine. (2018, February 23.) *Arteriovenous malformation .* Retrieved from Mayfield brain & spine: https://www.mayfieldclinic.com/PE-AVM.htm.

Mayo Clinic. (2018, January.) *Diseases and Conditions.* Retrieved from "Arteriovenous malformation." https://www.mayoclinic.org/diseases-conditions/arteriovenous- malformation/symptoms-causes/syc-20350544.

Mayo Clinic Traumatic Brain Injury Treatment. (2018, January 8.) *Diagnosis.* Retrieved from "Traumatic brain injury." https://www.mayoclinic.org/diseases-conditions/traumatic-brain- injury/diagnosis-treatment/drc-20378561.

Mcleod, A. 2. (2004 February.) "Shell shock, Gordon Holmes and the Great War." *J R Soc Med* 97, no. 2, 86–89.

MD, A. R., & PhD, J. D. (November 18, 2008.) *Traumatic Brain Injury Assessment and Therapy.* Washington, DC: Social Security Administration. https://www.ssa.gov/disability/professionals/bluebook/11.00-Neurological-Adult.htm

MD, E. K., & Patricia O. Shafer RN, M. (2018, February 26.) "Absence Seizures." Retrieved from Epilepsy: https://www.epilepsy.com/learn/types-seizures/absence-seizures.

MedicineNet.com. (2018, February 5.) "Medical Definition of Neuroplasticity." Retrieved from Medicinenet.com: https://www.medicinenet.com/script/main/art.asp?articlekey=40362.

Meng, L., Chen, Y., Xu, X., Chen, T., Lui, S., Huang, X., ... Gong, Q. (2018.) "The neurobiology of brain recovery from traumatic stress: A longitudinal DTI study." *Journal of Effective Disorders* 225: 577–84.

Merriam-Webster. (2018, February 2.) "Definition of Prisal." Retrieved from https://www.merriam- webster.com/: https://www.merriam-webster.com/dictionary/prisal.

Ibid. (2018, January 8.) Redeem. Retrieved from https://www.merriam-webster.com/dictionary/: https://www.merriam-webster.com/dictionary/redeem.

Meyer, H. A. (1829.) *Meyer's NT Commentary.* Edinburgh: St. Mary's College.

Michael Fralick, D. T. (2016.) "Risk of suicide after a concussion." *Cananadian Medical Journal,* 190, no. 6. doi: https://doi.org/10.1503/cmaj.150790.

Michele Zander, Plaintiff, v. United States of America, Defendant, 786 F.Supp.2d 880 (2011) (US District Court, D. Maryland, Southern Division February 2, 2011.)

Miller, P. H. (2011.) *Theories of Developmental Psychology.* San Franscisco: Worth.

MIRECC. (2018, February.) "Traumatic Brain Injury and Suicide." Retrieved from Suicide Prevention Resource Center: https://www.sprc.org/sites/default/files/migrate/library/TBI_Suicide.pdf.

Mohamed Samy Elhammady, M. a. (Feb 2017.) "The ARUBA study: where do we go from here?"

Journal of Neurosurgery 485.

Mt. Sinai Hospital. (2018, February.) "Anoxic Brain Damage." Retrieved from Mount Sinai Hospital: http://www.mountsinai. org/patient-care/service-areas/neurology/diseases-and- conditions/ anoxic-brain-damage#causes.

National Academy of Sciences. (2018.) *Evaluation of the Department of Veterans Affairs Mental Health Services.* Washington, DC: National Academies Press.

National Association of State Head Injury Administrators. (2018, February 6.) "Traumatic Brain Injury Act of 2008: Overview." Retrieved from https://www.nashia.org/: https://www.nashia.org/pdf/tbiactof_2008_ history_08.pdf.

National Center for Health Statistics. (2018, January 4.) "Mortality Data." Retrieved from National Vital Statistics System: https://www.cdc.gov/ nchs/nvss/deaths.htm.

National Institute of Neurological Disorders and Stroke. (2018, February.) "Arteriovenous Malformation Information Page." Retrieved from National Institute of Neurological Disorders and Stroke: https://www.ninds.nih.gov/Disorders/All-Disorders/ Arteriovenous- Malformation-Information-Page.

National Organization for Rare Disorders (NORD.) (2017.) "Vascular Malformations of the Brain." Retrieved from National Organization for Rare Disorders: https://rarediseases.org/rare-diseases/ vascular-malformations-of-the-brain/.

National Organization for Rare Disorders (NORD.) (2018, February 13.) Vascular Malformations of the Brain. Retrieved from National

Organization for Rare Disorders: https://rarediseases.org/rare-diseases/vascular-malformations-of-the-brain/.

NHPCO. (2018, February.) "About Us." Retrieved from National Hospice and Palliative Care Organization: https://www.nhpco.org/nhpco-0.

Nickalus R. Khan, M., Georgios Tsivgoulis, M. P., Siang Liao Lee, B., G. Morgan Jones, P. B., Cain S. Green, B., Aristeidis H. Katsanos, M., ... Andrei V. Alexandrov, M. (2014.)

"Fibrinolysis for Intraventricular Hemorrhage." *Stroke* 45:2662–69.

North, M. (n.d.) "National Library of Medicine." Retrieved from https://www.nlm.nih.gov/hmd/greek/greek_oath.html.

North, M. (2018, February.) "The Hippocratic Oath." Retrieved from US National Library of Medicine: https://www.nlm.nih.gov/hmd/greek/greek_oath.html.

Nussbaum ES, H. R. (Jan 1995.) "Surgical treatment of intracranial arteriovenous malformations with an analysis of cost-effectiveness." *Clinical Neurosurgery* 42:348–69.

Opko Health. (2018.) *Hereditary Hemorrhagic Telangiectasia Panel.* Gaithersburg, MD: GeneDx.

Parkay, F. W., Hass, G., & Anctil, E. J. (2010.) *Curriculum Leadership.* Boston: Pearson.

Patrick J. Codd, B. A. (September 2008.) "A recurrent cerebral arteriovenous malformation in an adult." *Journal of Neurosurgery* 109, no. 3: 486–91.

Ibid. (September 2008.) A recurrent cerebral arteriovenous malformation in an adult. *Journal of Neurosurgery*, 486–91. Retrieved from http://thejns.org/doi/abs/10.3171/JNS/2008/109/9/0486?journalCode=jns

Petersen, W. (Director.) (1984.) *The neverending story* [Motion Picture].

Plato. (1997.) *Plato: Complete Works* (Vol. Republic VII.) (J. M. Cooper, ed.) Indianapolis: Hackett.

Plato. (2011.) *Republic*. Mesa: Mesa Community College.

Pocket Testament League. (2018, January.) *Helen Cadbury*. Retrieved from Pocket Testament League Home: https://www.ptl.org/about/history.php.

Połczyńska-Fiszer M., Mazaux J. M. "Second language acquisition after traumatic brain injury: a case study." *Disabil Rehabil.*, 2008, 30, no. 18:1397–407. https://www.ncbi.nlm.nih.gov/pubmed/19230178.

Pople IK, 7. (2002.) Hydrocephalus and Shunts: What the Neurologist Should Know. *Neurosurgery & Psychiatry*, i17-i22. doi:10.1136/jnnp-2012-302538.

Public Health Agency of Canada. (2018, February 6.) "Anoxic Brain Damage." Retrieved from Mount Sinai Hospital: http://www.mountsinai.org/patient-care/service-   areas/neurology/diseases-and-conditions/anoxic-brain-damage.

Rector and Board of Visitors. (2018.) "Development of the Gamma Knife." Retrieved from University of Virginia School of Medicine: https://med.virginia.edu/neurosurgery/services/gamma-knife/for-physicians/history-and- technical-overview/.

Riley-Smith, J. (1987.) *The crusades: a short history*. New Haven: Yale University Press.

Roman Liščák, M. V. (June 2007.) "Arteriovenous Malformations after Leksell Gamma Knife Radiosurgery: Rate of Obliteration and Complications." *Neurosurgery*, 1005–16.

SB, B. (January 2002.) "Disturbance of the knowledge representation in patients with arteriovenous malformations of the deep brain structures." *Zhurnal Nevrologii i Psikhiatrii Imeni S.S. Korsakova* 102, no. 9:32–36.

Schnieder, D. S. (2018.) Summer Program in Quantitative Methods of Social Research. Ann Arbor, MI: Inter-university Consortium for Political and Social Research.

Sharett, M. (17 March 1954.) *Diary.* Beersheba.

Sharpsteen, H. L. (Director.) (1940.) *Pinocchio* [Motion Picture].

Shihui Han, E. P. (2011.) *Culture and Neural Frames of Cognition and Communication.*

Munich: Springer Science & Business Media.

Social Security Administration. (2018, January 12.) "Disability Evaluation Under Social Security."

Retrieved from 11.00 Neurological - Adult: https://www.ssa.gov/disability/professionals/bluebook/11.0-Neurological-

Adult.htm#11_18.

Ibid. (2018, January 11.) "Medical/Professional Relations." Retrieved from Disability Evaluation Under Social Security: https://www.ssa.gov/disability/professionals/bluebook/11.00-Neurological- Adult.htm#11_18.

Social Security Administration. (n.d.) "Employment." Retrieved from https://www.ssa.gov/work/.

Solomon, R. A. (2017.) "Arteriovenous Malformations of the Brain." *New England Journal of Medicine*, 1859–66.

Souvik Sen, M. M. (2018.) "Arteriovenous Malformations." Department of Neurology. Richland: University of South Carolina. Retrieved from https://emedicine.medscape.com/article/1160167-overview#a6.

SSA. (2018, 1.) "Disability Planner: Social Security Protection If You Become Disabled."

Retrieved from Social Security: https://www.ssa.gov/planners/disability/.

State of Alabama. (2018, January.) Alabama Department of Rehabilitation Services. Retrieved from Alabama Department of Rehabilitation Services: http://www.rehab.alabama.gov/about-us.

Stein, K.-P., Huette, B.-O., Goericke, S., Oezkan, N., Leyrera, R., Sandalcioglu, E., ... Mueller,

O. (2018, January .) "Cerebral arterio-venous malformations in the paediatric population: Angiographic characteristics, multimodal treatment strategies and outcome." *Clinical Neurology and Neurosurgery* 164 (January 2018), 164–68.

Stein, K.-P., Huettere, B.-O., Goericke, S., Oezkana, N., LeyreraI, R., Sandalcioglu, E., ...

Muellera, O. (2018.) "Cerebral arterio-venous malformations in the paediatric population: Angiographic characteristics, multimodal treatment strategies and outcome. *Clinical Neurology and Neurosurgery*, 164 (January 2018), 164–-168. doi: https://doi.org/10.1016/j. clineuro.2017.12.006.

Ibid. Mueller, O. (2017, August.) "Cerebral arterio-venous malformations in the paediatric population: Angiographic characteristics, multimodal treatment strategies and outcome." *Clinical Neurology and Neurosurgery*, 2018 (164), 165–68. Retrieved from https://ac.els- cdn. com/S0303846717303426/1-s2.0-S0303846717303426-main.pdf?_ tid=ad28e55a- 18b0-11e8-b88f-

00000aab0f27&acdnat=1519400953_7e7bd545de114e27441c3
f2fade91e5b.

Steina, K. P., Huettera, B. O., Goericke, S., Oezkana, N., Leyrera, R.,
Sandalcioglu, I. E., ... Muellera, O. (January 2018.) "Cerebral arteriovenous malformations in the paediatric population: Angiographic
characteristics, multimodal treatment strategies and outcome." *Clinical
Neurology and Neurosurgery* 164 (January 2018), 164–68. doi: https://
doi.org/10.1016/j.clineuro.2017.12.006.

T. Ownsworth, L. C. (2006.) "The association between awareness deficits
and rehabilitation" (vol. 26.) Mt Gravatt Campus, Griffith University,
Australia: *Clinical Psychology Review.*

Tamara Ownsworth, L. C. (2006.) "The association between awareness
deficits and rehabilitation."

Clinical Psychology Review, 783–95.

Tamargo, R. J., and Huang, J. (2012, January.) "Cranial Arteriovenous
Malformations (AVMs) and Cranial Dural Arteriovenous Fistulas
(DAVFs), An Issue of Neurosurgery Clinics." (M. P. Andrew T.
Parsa, and M. M. Paul C. McCormick, eds.) *Clinical Neurology and
Neurosurgery,* 16.

Teasdale TW, E. A. (2001:71.) "Suicide after traumatic brain injury: a
population study." *Journal of Neurology, Neurosurgery & Psychiatry,*
436–40.

Terra C. Holdeman, M. M. (2008.) "Invisible Wounds of War:
Psychological." *RAND Corporation,* 273.

The Gale Group. (2008.) *Encyclopedia Judaica.* "Ancient Jewish History:
The Cult of Moloch." Toronto Brain Vascular Malformation Study
Group. (2018, February.) "Embolization. Treatment for Arteriovenous
Malformations (AVMs) of the Brain and Spinal Cord."

Retrieved from The Toronto Brain Vascular Malformation Study Group: http://brainavm.oci.utoronto.ca/swf/embo.html.

Thomas R. Frieden, M. M. (June 2013.) *Report to Congress on Traumatic Brain Injury in the United States: Understanding the Public Health Problem among Current and Former Military Personnel.* Bethesda, MD: Centers for Disease Control and Prevention.

Tsyben A, G. M. (2018 Jan.) "Spectrum of outcomes following traumatic brain injury—relationship between functional impairment and health-related quality of life. *Acta Neurochirurgica* (January 2018) 160, no. 1, 107–15.

Tsyben, A. G. (2018.) "Spectrum of outcomes following traumatic brain injury—relationship between functional impairment and health-related quality of life." *Acta Neurochir,* 107–15.

Tutino VM, P. K. (2018, January 17.) "Circulating neutrophil transcriptome may reveal intracranial aneurysm signature." *PLoS ONE.* doi:10.1371.

US Department of Health & Human Services. (2018, February 28.) *https://www.cdc.gov/traumaticbraininjury/index.html.* Retrieved from Center for Disease Control: https://www.cdc.gov/traumaticbraininjury/index.html.

US Department of Health and Human Services, Administration for Community Living (n.d.). UNICEF. (2013.) *The State of the World's Children .* UNICEF.

US Government. (2018.) "Historical Background and Development of Social Security." Retrieved 1 12, 2018, from https://www.ssa.gov/history/briefhistory3.html.

US Social Security Administration. (January.) *Disability Evaluation Under Social Security.* Retrieved from 11.18 Traumatic brain injury, characterized by A or B:: https://www.ssa.gov/disability/professionals/bluebook/11.00-Neurological- Adult.htm#11_18.

Ursano, R. J., Stein, M. B., Kessler, R. C., & Heeringa, S. G. (2017.) "Army Study to Assess Risk and Resilience in Servicemembers (STARRS.)" Army. Ann Arbor, MI: Inter-university Consortium for Political and Social Research. doi: https://doi.org/10.3886/ICPSR35197.v1.

Vincent M. Tutino, K. E. (January 17, 2018.) "Circulating neutrophil transcriptome may reveal intracranial aneurysm signature." *PLOS One*. Retrieved from https://doi.org/10.1371/journal.pone.0191407.

Virginia Brain Injury Council. (2016.) "Bylaws of the Virginia Brain Injury Council." Richmond: Virginia Brain Injury Council.

W. Y. Guo, B. K. (1993.) "Even the Smallest Remnant of an AVM Constitutes a Risk." *Acta Neurochir (Wien)*, 121:212–15.

Wilson, S. S. (2001.) *Hurt people hurt people*. Nashville, TN: Thomas Nelson.

Wyburn-Mason, R. (September 1943.) "Arteriovenous aneurysm of midbrain and retina, facial laevi and mental changes." *Brain, 66*, 12. Retrieved from https://academic.oup.com/brain/article-abstract/66/3/163/278076?redirectedFrom=fulltext.

Yang Kwon, M. P. (2000, December.) "Analysis of the causes of treatment failure in gamma knife radiosurgery for intracranial arteriovenous malformations." *Journal of Neurosurgery*: 104–6. Retrieved from http://thejns.org/doi/abs/10.3171/jns.2000.93.supplement%203.0104.

Yang W, P. J.-M. (2018, Feb.) "Treatment decision for occipital arteriovenous malformations (AVMs) to achieve hemorrhagic control while maximizing visual preservation: Our experience and review of literature." *Journal of Clinical Neuroscience*, 50–57. doi:10.1016/j.jocn.2017.10.058.

Yanming Ren, M. J. (2018.) "Risk Factors of Rehemorrhage in Postoperative Patients with Spontaneous Intracerebral Hemorrhage: A Case-Control Study." *Journal Korean Neurosurgical Society*, 35–41.

Yasushi Takagi MD, P. P. (2017.) "Initially Missed or Delayed Diagnosis of Subarachnoid Hemorrhage: A Nationwide Survey of Contributing Factors and Outcomes in Japan." *Journal of Stroke and Cerebrovascular Diseases*, 6 December 2017.

Zhao, Y. J. (January 2018.) "Risk factors for neurological deficits after surgical treatment of brain arteriovenous malformations supplied by deep perforating arteries." *Neurosurgical Review*, 255–65. Retrieved from https://link.springer.com/article/10.1007/s10143-017- 0848-6.

Zoppo, G. J. (2008.) "Virchow's Triad: The Vascular Basis of Cerebral Injury." *Rev Neurol Dis.*, S12–S21.